MISSION TRENDS No. 3

D1264111

Mission Trends No. 3

Third World Theologies

Edited by
Gerald H. Anderson
and
Thomas F. Stransky, C.S.P.

PAULIST PRESS
New York/Ramsey/Toronto
and
WM. B. EERDMANS PUBLISHING CO.
Grand Rapids

The Editors

Gerald H. Anderson, director of the Overseas Ministries Study Center in Ventnor, New Jersey, and secretary-treasurer of the American Society of Missiology, was formerly professor of church history and ecumenics, and academic dean of Union Theological Seminary, Manila, Philippines; and president of Scarritt College for Christian Workers, Nashville, Tennessee.

Thomas F. Stransky, president of the Paulist Fathers—the first missionary society of priests founded in the United States—was a staff member of the Vatican Secretariat for Promoting Christian Unity from 1960 to 1970. He is a member of the United States Catholic Mission Council and a consultant to both the Commission on World Mission and Evangelism of the World Council of Churches and the Vatican Christian Unity Secretariat.

Copyright ©1976 by
Paulist Fathers, Inc.
and Wm. B. Eerdmans Publishing Co.

All rights reserved. No part of this book may be reproduced or transmitted in any form or by any means, electronic or mechanical, including photocopying, recording or by any information storage and retrieval system, without permission in writing from the Publishers.

Library of Congress
Catalog Card Number: 76-24451

Published by
Paulist Press
Editorial Office: 1865 Broadway, N.Y., N.Y. 10023
Business Office: 545 Island Road, Ramsey, N.J. 07446

ISBN: 0-8091-1984-6

and
Wm. B. Eerdmans Publishing Co.
255 Jefferson, S.E., Grand Rapids, Mich. 49502

ISBN: 0-8028-1654-1

Printed and bound in the
United States of America   *Reprinted, May 1983*

Contents

Foreword

A radical theological realignment is taking place in the Church today. The old centers of theological influence in Europe and North America are becoming the new peripheries. The new centers of vitality and importance in theological construction are in Asia, Africa and Latin America—where the majority of Christians will be living in the year 2000.

Ironically, this fact—which in some measure is the fruit of missionary labors over the last one hundred years—is not yet widely recognized or understood in the old centers. There is still a good deal of theological provincialism. Theologians in Asia, Africa and Latin America are not yet well known and widely read in North America and Europe. Dr. John S. Mbiti in the opening essay of this volume says that many Christian scholars in Europe and North America have more meaningful "academic fellowship with heretics long dead than with living brethren of the Church today in the so-called Third World."

To encourage and assist the remedy of this situation we have selected articles that reflect some creative theological currents in these other parts of the world. Among the contributors —representing very varied Church traditions and theological viewpoints—are a Catholic archbishop in Brazil, the President of Zambia, a Filipino Methodist theological educator, an African theologian now serving as director of the Ecumenical Institute near Geneva, a Catholic theologian in Peru, an American Catholic missionary sister working in Kenya, and a joint theological declaration by South Korean clergy who protest the oppressive practices of their authoritarian government.

We use the term "Third World" with some reservation both because it is increasingly ambiguous, and also because there are respected colleagues, such as Raimundo Panikkar, who "detect remnants of unconscious colonialistic attitudes" in the concept.[1] Originally in the 1950s the Third World was seen as a "third force" of non-aligned, non-industrialized, underdeveloped countries of Asia, Africa and Latin America, in contrast to the capitalist forces of the NATO nations (First World) and the communist-aligned nations of the Warsaw Pact (Second World). More recently, the poor and oppressed—especially of racial and ethnic minorities—in the United States and Europe have also been defined as belonging to "Third World peoples."

While Peter Berger and others maintain that this is simply "ideological rhetoric" and that "strictly speaking the 'Third World' as a political, economic or social entity does not exist," they do acknowledge the term as a useful handle or shorthand means for "referring immediately and briefly to a set of societies sharing common characteristics," namely "the less modernized societies of Asia, Africa and Latin America."[2]

For many mission agencies today, however, the Third World is "not so much a geographical concept as it is a definition of an emerging consciousness on the part of deprived and relatively powerless people, wherever they live—an emerging awareness of their condition and a growing conviction that it need not and must not continue." They speak of the Third World "in terms of people, their needs and rights and emerging self-awareness, not in terms of geography or governments or establishments."[3] Feminist theology, for instance, is therefore being identified with Third World liberation theologies because "they are all written out of an experience of oppression in society" (Letty M. Russell). *Mission Trends No. 4* will focus on some of these "Liberation Theologies in North America and Europe."

With this volume we have now reprinted articles in the *Mission Trends* series from 42 journals published in 15 countries on four continents. We thank our consultants, the authors, editors and publishers of these journals—and our own publishers—for making this open-ended venture possible.

Gerald H. Anderson

Thomas F. Stransky, C.S.P.

NOTES

1. Disaffection with the term is by no means universal. President Luis Echeverria Alvarez established a University of the Third World in Mexico City in 1975 which has become a research center on development problems.

2. Peter L. Berger, Brigitte Berger, and Hansfried Kellner, *The Homeless Mind: Modernization and Consciousness* (New York: Random House, 1973), pp. 10-11.

3. From a working paper by the World Development Task Force, Board of Missions, The United Methodist Church, March 31, 1970.

There is also discussion today concerning a Fourth World and a Fifth World. Some evangelical missiologists speak of the Fourth World as "all those people, no matter where they are found, who have yet to commit themselves to Jesus Christ as Savior." C. Peter Wagner, *Stop the World I Want to Get On* (Glendale, California: Regal Books, 1974), p. 7. Economists are defining the Fourth World as the LDCs (less developed countries) such as Peru, Liberia, Jordan, Egypt and Thailand, which are going to need more help and more time than the Third World countries such as Taiwan, Singapore, Mexico and Brazil, to achieve self-sustaining economic growth. The Fifth World is those "catastrophe countries" that are essentially trapped by poverty, with few exploitable resources to sell and seemingly unable to grow enough food to feed themselves—"the globe's true basket cases, perhaps doomed to remain on a permanent dole"—most notably Mali, Chad, Ethiopia, Somalia, Rwanda and Bangladesh. "Poor vs. Rich: A New Global Conflict," *Time,* December 22, 1975, pp. 34-42. Cf. "Focus on the Fourth World," chapter 1 in Overseas Development Council, *The U.S. and World Development—Agenda for Action 1975* (New York: Praeger, 1975).

I: Theology in Context

Theological Impotence and the Universality of the Church

John S. Mbiti

What are the implications for the future of Christian theology that "within our own lifetime the axis of Christendom will shift from the Northern to the Southern regions of the world . . . the new centers of ecclesiastical gravity"? African theologian John S. Mbiti says there has to be "theological mutuality and reciprocity," but thus far "it has all been one-sided. . . . We know you theologically. The question is, do you know us theologically?" Theologians of the younger churches, he says, consider it "utterly scandalous" and are "deeply affronted" that so many Christian scholars in older Christendom know so little about the churches in the Third World. Mbiti asks whether—"as the axis of Christianity tilts southwards"—it may "justify consideration of shifting the World Council of Churches headquarters from Geneva to Kinshasha," and "may force the Roman Catholic Church to elect an African pope . . . and . . . shift his headquarters to a new Vatican at Kampala". Dr. Mbiti—now director of the World Council of Churches' Ecumenical Institute near Geneva—has his doctorate in theology from Cambridge University and was formerly professor of religious studies at Makerere University College in Uganda. His essay is from *Lutheran World* (XXI/3—1974), published quarterly by the Lutheran World Federation in Geneva, Switzerland.

The Church: Kerygmatically Universal but Theologically Provincial

He learned German, Greek, French, Latin, Hebrew, in addition to English, church history, systematics, homiletics, exegesis, and pastoralia, as one part of the requirements for his degree. The other part, the dissertation, he wrote on some obscure theologian of the Middle Ages. Finally, he got what he wanted: a Doctorate in Theology. It took him nine and a half years altogether, from the time he left his home until he passed his orals and set off to return. He was anxious to reach home as soon as possible, so he flew, and he was glad to pay for his excess baggage which, after all, consisted only of the Bible in the various languages he had learned, plus Bultmann, Barth, Bonhoeffer, Brunner, Buber, Cone, Küng, Moltmann, Niebuhr, Tillich, *Christianity Today, Time Magazine* . . .

At home, relatives, neighbors, old friends, dancers, musicians, drums, dogs, cats, all gather to welcome him back. The fatted calves are killed; meat is roasted; girls giggle as they survey him surrounded by his excess baggage; young children have their imaginations rewarded—they had only heard about him but now they see him; he, of course, does not know them by name. He must tell about his experiences overseas, for everyone has come to eat, to rejoice, to listen to their hero who has studied so many northern languages, who has read so many theological books, who is the hope of their small but fast-growing church, the very incarnation of theological learning. People bear with him patiently as he struggles to speak his own language, as occasionally he seeks the help of an interpreter from English. They are used to sitting down and making time; nobody is in a hurry; speech is not a matter of life and death. Dancing, jubilation, eating, feasting—all these go on as if there were nothing else to do, because the man for whom everyone had waited has finally returned.

Suddenly there is a shriek. Someone has fallen to the ground. It is his older sister, now a married woman with six children and still going strong. He rushes to her. People make room for him, and watch him. "Let's take her to the hospital," he calls urgently. They are stunned. He becomes quiet. They all look at him bending over her. Why doesn't someone respond to his advice? Finally a schoolboy says, "Sir, the nearest hospital is 50 miles away, and there are few buses that go there." Someone else says, "She is possessed. Hospitals will not cure her!" The chief says to him, "You have been studying theology overseas for

10 years. Now help your sister. She is troubled by the spirit of her great aunt." He looks around. Slowly he goes to get Bult-mann, looks at the index, finds what he wants, reads again about spirit possession in the New Testament. Of course he gets the an-swer: Bultmann has demythologized it. He insists that his sister is not possessed. The people shout, "Help your sister; she is pos-sessed!" He shouts back, "But Bultmann has demythologized demon possession." (This story is entirely fictional and is not based on the experience of a real person.)

Fantasy? No, for these are the realities of our time. Two of these realities are in sharp contrast, almost contradiction: on the one hand, the Church has become universal in a literal, geo-graphical sense, thanks to the great missionary movement of the last 200 years, and the dedication of men and women from older Christendom plus the assistance of local converts; on the other, theological outreach has not matched this expansion. Con-sequently, half of today's Christendom lies outside the fenced cloisters of traditional theology. This theology is largely ignorant of, and often embarrassingly impotent in the face of, human questions in the churches of Africa, Latin America, parts of Asia, and the South Pacific. Thus the Church has become keryg-matically universal, but is still theologically provincial, in spite of the great giants of theology. This is a serious dilemma, and if we do not resolve it, it will destroy our foundations as the Church in the world.

The Universality of the Church Should Be Affirmed in Theological Concerns

In Christ God dispersed history, salvation history, so that he could gather it up once more in a meaningful whole at the *telos* —the ultimate end—of all things in Christ. The Church exists in this dismantled, disfigured, despised history, a history which is being destroyed in order that newness may arise. If theology has any contribution to make to the Church, and I believe it has, then it should be a healing contribution which accompanies the Church wherever it is in its disfigurement and its martyrdom.

As the Church becomes worldwide, as it affirms the universality for which God's dispersal of history has destined it, let those of us who are its sons and daughters, and who are privileged to be its theologians, also think big, think wide, think far in time and space. Theology should strain its neck to see beyond the horizons of our traditional structures, beyond the comforts of our ready-made methodologies of theologizing; it should be with the Church where it is, rubbing shoulders with human beings whose condition, outlook, concerns, and world views are not those with which we are familiar.

What some of us from new Christendom are saying is that you, our brethren whose forefathers evangelized our forefathers, whose relatives died in bringing the gospel to us across the seas, have no theological interest in us who are the extension of Christ's body to which you belong. We have learned to theologize with you, from you, about your concerns. Now, if you wish, we would like you to theologize with us, and also about our concerns. Only in that way can the universality of the Church be meaningful both evangelistically and theologically.

So a voice says, "Think theologically big, theologically poor, theologically oppressed, theologically hungry, theologically revolutionary, theologically bewitched, theologically spirit possessed." And another voice replies, "But how shall we think theologically big, poor, hungry, etc., when we have all our great theologians, when our libraries are bursting with countless books and periodicals, when we have enough food to eat three times a day, when we can sit down in our library carrels and theologize comfortably?"

It is estimated that in the year 2000—less than a generation away—there will be more Christians in Africa than in the whole of North America, more in Latin America than in Europe. Does this not move us to see that, within our own lifetime, the axis of Christendom will shift from the Northern to the Southern regions of the world, that the centers of the Church's universality may well be no longer Geneva, Rome, Athens, Paris, Berlin, London, and 475 Riverside Drive, New York, but Kinshasa, Buenos Aires, Addis Ababa, and Manila? If a little southward tilting of theology does not come voluntarily, it will be forced upon us by circumstances beyond our control—or else the new centers of ecclesiastical gravity will either be devoid of viable theology or be filled with theology which is largely impotent.

Utilizing Theological Sources of the Place and Time in which the Church Lives

The ultimate purpose of theology is to share, and not just to observe the meaning of God in Christ, God with us. If the Church cannot share this meaning, wherever it may be, then it is failing miserably. This is the challenge which theology must face, as the axis of Christianity tilts southwards towards areas, situations, cultures, concerns, traditions, religions, and problems which are largely different from those which have precipitated or necessitated the theological output of the Church in the West over the last 500 years at least. As an illustration, let us look at what might be considered the dominant or preoccupying words and concerns of Christians in Africa today.

These concerns can be summed up in the word *survival:* national survival, community survival, and personal survival. If the Church cannot theologize around these concerns of survival, it will fail to exercise its universality responsibly.

National Survival. The majority of African peoples have entered the period of independent nationhood only since 1960. Therefore, to make sense of this new era in their history is a major national concern. In most of these countries, Christians have been instrumental in bringing about the spirit of nationhood and actual political independence. They are on the frontlines fighting for independence in African countries still under Portuguese and white minority regimes. What then is the role of the Christian, and of the Church, in the nation?

Liberation, revolution, emancipation—these are the chief concerns of those who are fighting against foreign domination. What is the theology of liberation for these Christians? To what extent do Christians participate in armed liberation movements? And how do African Christians look at the financial grants which the World Council of Churches is giving to freedom fighters through its Program to Combat Racism?

Nation building is a key term in many African countries today. What does it mean? Does the theology of development have any bearing on this, particularly when so much of it comes from theologians who are not indigenous to the countries where the development is taking place and see it only from a distance? The Church is involved in urban work, industrial projects, rural development. How does theology help to bring the meaning of God in Christ into these dimensions of national development?

Then there are the national ideologies: South Africa's apartheid and separate development; African socialism, as it is being tried out in Tanzania and to a lesser extent elsewhere; and dilly-dallying with international ideologies such as communism, neutrality, democracy, and pan-Africanism. What, if anything, has theology to say to these ideologies?

African culture, African personality, African authenticity—for us these are magic terms which cover a multitude of sins. What is the theology of culture, and how can African cultures be employed in the life of the Church? Can the Church afford just to sit by and watch their revival? To what extent can it be instrumental in shaping culture, judging it, redeeming it, transforming it?

Racism, segregation, ethnicism, nepotism, corruption—these are national ills which afflict every country in Africa. The Church in its universality is involved in these ills, and it is not enough for it to hurl condemnations from the pulpit. What is the theology of race, of corruption, of nepotism?

That our countries are poor in relation to many others—this goes almost without saying. Is it not necessary to have a theology of economics, of poverty, of exploitation, a theology of natural resources and their utilization?

Church and state—here is a theme about which older Christendom has already said a great deal. But how does the Church in Africa experience its own relationship with the state? Can we insist on a dichotomy between the two? Can Christians fight for political independence, and once it is achieved, run away and leave the state to the "devil"? How does the Church interpret military coups which are becoming increasingly endemic in Africa? To what extent are our poor nations being exploited by richer countries through the sale of arms? Can the Church assist in drawing up viable national priorities for expenditure? What contribution can it make to raising the gross national product and the annual per capita income, which in many African countries currently averages between $100 and $200?

Community Survival. This is an area of concerns which directly involve the Church. Perhaps first among them is the meaning of the Church as a community of believers, as the giver of fellowship, as a unique unit in society. How is this fellowship realized in an African situation where there are other communities —the tribe, the clan, political parties, age groups, school communities, men's and women's associations—which also demand allegiance? Does a church community fulfil a purpose over and above these other expressions of community life?

Then there are questions of ecumenism and church divisions —both those which have been imported and those many others which have been locally produced. There are, for example, about 650 Anglican, Orthodox, and Protestant mission bodies and church organizations in Africa, in addition to 356 Roman Catholic dioceses (together with all their religious orders and substructures), and in 1972 there were 5,400 African Independent Churches. In addition, we have National Christian Councils and international Christian bodies like the Conferences of Roman Catholic Bishops, the All Africa Conference of Churches, Bible Societies, the YMCA and YWCA, etc. What does a Christian community mean in this context of confusion and diversity? Does the theology of ecumenism take on new forms which make sense of this depressing state of affairs? There are more union discussions going on in Africa today than in any other continent: What bearing do they have on wider ecumenism? And what about the fact that the many churches in Africa created by evangelizing churches in the West may one day outnumber other churches in the World Council of Churches? To what extent will this alter its future history? Does it not justify consideration of shifting WCC headquarters from Geneva to Kinshasa in the not too distant future? Does it not also mean that the rapidly growing number of Christians in Africa may force the Roman Catholic Church to elect an African pope before the close of this century—and what if he should shift his headquarters to a new Vatican in Kampala?

Drought, famine, pestilence, calamities, epidemics; the need for more hospitals and schools, better roads and bridges; other religions, particularly Islam and those which are part of the African religious heritage—these are some other areas with which communities are deeply concerned in their day-to-day life. Is there a theology of rainmaking, of insect pestilence, and of road engineering? Perhaps there has been none in the past, but as the Church expands towards the ultimate reaches of its universality, it will have to formulate a more inclusive theology, for its members are concerned about these issues. And if the Church has nothing to say about them, some other religious system will, and it may edge out the Church in these areas of community concern for survival.

Personal Survival. In relation to these issues, the Christian faith is assimilated and applied more personally than to those on the national and community level. Ultimately, every Christian has to personalize his faith, and as he seeks to do so, theology must not abandon him. Questions of health and healing, of slums and housing, school fees and money for clothes, unemployment, family concerns (especially for children or parents), witchcraft, magic, sorcery, the departed (including those who were not yet Christians and those Christians who anxiously waited for the parousia but died before it came), the spirits and spirit possession, and visions and dreams (together with their interpretation) —these are among the visions which people claim to have had. And if so, what of those innumerably many themes which interest or trouble Christians in their private and family lives? Is a theology of healing irrelevant? Is spirit possession simply to be demythologized in African communities? Do we just dismiss dreams and Churches whose founders or leaders reportedly depend on visions and dreams for their directives from God and communication with him? Dreams and visions are from time to time translated into practical action by both the common man and national figures. A theology of dreams would not, therefore, be an empty exercise. (In passing, I might mention that my own calling to the Christian ministry came originally in the form of a vision, and when, in all seriousness and with profound joy, I confided the experience to trusted American missionaries, they dismissed it with—very hurtful—laughter, saying, "John, you are crazy!" That was in January 1951, and the "crazy" experience completely changed my life.)

New Meanings for New Concerns

We could go on and on asking basic questions about the whole meaning of the Christian revelation, the Church, salvation, Christ, the Holy Spirit, and a host of other fundamental theological themes, as they apply to the Church in Africa today and in the 21st century. For those of us who work there, who belong there, who live with these and other concerns of survival, theology as we have learned it according to Western tradition is very much called in question. If seminaries in Europe and America allow African students, whom we send to them for theological circumcision, to return to us with no idea of the theological meaning of our big words, of our life and death concerns, we will rightly feel betrayed. And the cause of Christ will be gravely imperiled. We send you the sons and daughters of our churches to be truly and realistically equipped for the calling of the gospel in Africa today. Please do not send them back to us as bastards or bearing a watered-down theology. If you educate them in the theology of hope, for example, let them theologize hope in terms of feeding the hungry, eliminating famine, providing employment, being remembered in church after death by one's children—in terms of what is nearby, reachable, desperately necessary. Otherwise the individual and the community will not survive long enough to have their hopes realized. We have a proverb which underlines the theology of hope for African Christians: We say that "Weteele ndakusaa" ("He who is waiting for what has been promised does not die before his hope or expectation is fulfilled")—and every person and community wants to experience the fulfilment of what is hoped for.

Thus we are driven to wider varieties and horizons of theological concerns, which may force us in the so-called younger churches to deviate from a great deal of Western theology, not because we reject the theological heritage which has accumulated in Western Christianity, but simply because we are driven to search for new meanings which are viable for our new concerns. The norm for theology remains the same, since we have the same Lord and the same faith, but the directions for theological outreach need not remain the same for all times and in all places. Indeed, this versatility of theology makes it extremely exciting; without this, it would become stale, while the Church itself is crossing existing frontiers. Theology need not, therefore, be the monopoly of the comfortable, the secure, the highly educated, the rich; it can come also from the songs and hymns of peasants as they till the ground; from the impromptu prayers of Christian parents as they nurse their sick child; from the unorganized sermons of the village catechist; from the charismatic leadership of an illiterate founder of an Independent Church; from the old man who is steeped in traditional religious life, who has been converted, together with his several wives and many children, to the Christian faith, and who is trying to make sense of it. Indeed, there is a great deal of spontaneous theologizing going on in the Church in Africa. It is informal, quiet, unwritten, unpolished theology, but nevertheless theology in its own way, and a theology which must be allowed a place in the Church universal.

Freedom from Theological Inhibitions

The Church cannot exorcise demonic forces in today's world through guesswork. It has to be squarely involved in human concerns, and it must not look back. Theology should assist the Church in this task, and to do so, it must itself be freed from inhibitions handed down from past generations. Christianity has exploded in Africa, and theology too must explode. It can no longer be done only according to St. ABC Seminary in Athens or Rome; it must find its own method, its own direction, its own voice, where the people of God are, so that it may mediate the meaning of God in Christ for them. The African theologian who has experienced the agonies of having a burning appetite but nothing to eat will surely theologize differently on the theme of food from the American theologian who knows the discomfort of having a plate full of steak but no appetite.

Freedom from theological inhibitions also means the freedom to make mistakes. The theologians of the new Christendom must be free to hatch their own heresies and theological errors, for often it is only in response to heresies and errors that sound theological orthodoxy is generated. Too much protectiveness from our mother churches and theologians will only retard our theological output. Indeed, the African Independent Churches are ultimately an expression of theological protest, even if they did not arise out of overt theological controversies with missionary churches. These 5,400 Independent Churches are obviously an ecclesiastical overproduction, and no one would wish to see a matching number of theological offshoots. But inhibitions may drive us even to this, and to schisms and heresies. We must, therefore, aim at striking a meaningful balance between extreme over-reaction to, and blind aping of the theologies and theologians of older Christendom, whom we admire and who have given us theological tools for our task.

There should, however, be mutuality and reciprocity in the theological task facing the universal Church, so that it is carried out by all branches of Christendom in the fellowship of our Lord. But how is this to be accomplished? I do not pretend to know the answers, but I may venture a few daydreams.

Towards Theological Mutuality and Reciprocity

The dichotomy between older and younger Christendom, between Western Christianity and the Christianity of the so-called Third World, is a real one, but it is also a false dichotomy. It is real because it is there; it is false because it ought not to be there. But because it is there when it ought not to be there, it is very agonizing. Can we overcome it? Do we want to overcome it? Are we prepared to overcome it? Is there any advantage in overcoming it, or shall we accept it and make the best of it?

Theologians from the new (or younger) churches have made their pilgrimages to the theological learning of older churches. We had no alternative. We have eaten theology with you; we have drunk theology with you; we have dreamed theology with you. But it has all been one-sided; it has all been, in a sense, your theology (if we can for a moment go back to the agonizing dichotomy which is real and yet false). We know you theologically. The question is, do you know us theologically? Would you like to know us theologically? Can you know us theologically? And how can there be true theological reciprocity and mutuality, if only one side knows the other fairly well, while the other side either does not know or does not want to know the first side? You have become a major subconscious part of our theologizing, and we are privileged to be so involved in you through the fellowship we share in Christ. When will you make us part of your subconscious process of theologizing? How can the rich theological heritage of Europe and America become the heritage of the universal Church on the basis of mutuality and reciprocity? This cannot be accomplished simply by you training our theologians in the northern regions as long as the Church there is largely ignorant of the theological existence of new Christendom. There cannot be theological conversation or dialogue between North and South, East and West, until we can embrace each other's concerns and stretch to each other's horizons. We from the new Christendom believe that we know about most of the constantly changing concerns of older Christendom. Please come to know our concerns of human survival. It is utterly scandalous for so many Christian scholars in older Christendom to know so much about heretical movements in the second and third centuries, when so few of them know anything about Christian movements in areas of the younger churches. We feel deeply affronted and wonder whether it is more meaningful theologically to have academic fellowship with heretics long dead than with the living brethren of the Church today in the so-called Third World.

Would it be practical, for example, to have in the United States one or two seminaries specializing exclusively in the theologies of the younger churches (or Southern churches)? Would it be symbolically meaningful to dismantle the headquarters of the World Council of Churches and set them up in Kinshasa or Brazilia? Would more theological seminaries and faculties in America and Europe accept as full-time visiting professors theologians from the new churches? What revisions would be necessary in the theological curricula to accommodate the theological concerns of the younger churches? Would it be unthinkable for some Ph.D. programs to require the learning of Gujerati, Swahili, or Xhosa, in addition to German, Hebrew, and Greek? And could one recommend that some of you spend a month studying theology in a small cabin where the only light is from a small hurricane lamp? You could try to write dissertations on some of the realities which we face, such as how to present the gospel to a man who is reduced by hunger, disease, and poverty, to the state of a bamboo skeleton; or to a man who was for three years a government minister, with power, privileges, and a chauffeur-driven Mercedes Benz, and then suddenly, after a military coup, was put in prison, where he gets meagre food twice a day on a rusty plate, where he sleeps on his urine, is systematically tortured, tormented, and deprived of his human dignity; or to an African family which has been evicted from the land of its forefathers by a group of recently arrived white settlers who have been received with all possible hospitality by the local chief.

Sometimes one feels theologically paralyzed by the devastating realities of our world. Has our theological weaponry become so blunt and rusty as to be completely impotent in the face of these realities? Or do we cheat ourselves by clinging so tenaciously to this traditional weaponry, while the realities of our times escape beyond our theological outreach?

He returned to his home after nine and a half years of theological training, with a Th.D., and excess baggage in theology, to confront the realities of his people whose hopes he incarnated. At the peak of the celebrations marking his return, his sister fell to the ground, possessed by the spirit of her great aunt—and they looked to him to exorcise the spirit. But all he could do was to demythologize her suffering according to Rudolf Bultmann. Yet the Kingdom of God is a violent kingdom which comes by force and power.

Thy kingdom come on earth as it is in heaven. Amen.

Contextualizing Theology

Shoki Coe

In the developing theologies of the "younger churches" in the Third World, the emphasis has shifted from *indigenization* to *contextualization*. Why? How do they differ? Indigenization, according to Shoki Coe, derives from the idea of "taking root in the soil," and tends to suggest a static response to the Gospel "in terms of traditional culture. Therefore, it is in danger of being past-oriented." The context today, however, "is not that of static culture, but the search for the new, which at the same time has involved the culture itself." Therefore, he says, "in using the word contextualization, we try to convey all that is implied in the familiar term indigenization, yet seek to press beyond for a more dynamic concept which is open to change and which is also future-oriented." He sees dangers in contextuality but he also sees it as "the missiological discernment of the signs of the times, seeing where God is at work and calling us to participate in it." Dr. Coe—formerly principal of Tainan Theological College in Taiwan—is director of the Theological Education Fund, a sponsored agency of the World Council of Churches, administered under the Commission on World Mission and Evangelism, for "the advancement of theological education in the Third World." This article is part of a longer essay that appeared in the summer 1973 issue of *Theological Education,* published in Dayton, Ohio, by the Association of Theological Schools in the United States and Canada.

Indigenization and Contextualization

Throughout the history of the Theological Education Fund there has been a continuing concern for indigenization in theo-

19

logical education—a term and a process which have been debated in mission circles of both older and younger churches for a long time. This is understandable, as indigenization is a missiological necessity when the Gospel moves from one cultural soil to another and has to be retranslated, reinterpreted, and expressed afresh in the new cultural soil. Why, then, do we now use a new word, contextualization, in preference to indigenization?

Indigenous, indigeneity, and indigenization all derive from a nature metaphor, that is, of the soil, or taking root in the soil. It is only right that the younger churches, in search of their own identity, should take seriously their own cultural milieu. However, because of the static nature of the metaphor, indigenization tends to be used in the sense of responding to the Gospel in terms of traditional culture. Therefore, it is in danger of being past-oriented. Furthermore, the impression has been given that it is only applicable to Asia and Africa, for elsewhere it was felt that the danger lay in over-indigenization, an uncritical accommodation such as expressed by the culture faiths, the American Way of Life, etc. But the most important factor, especially since the last war, has been the new phenomenon of radical change. The new context is not that of static culture, but the search for the new, which at the same time has involved the culture itself.

Dr. Kosuke Koyama, a longtime Japanese missionary in Thailand, has put this situation in a graphic way. He says there are two Thailands today: Thailand One, saturated by its nature, the seasons with which the rural community is tied up, symbolized by the leisurely pace of the water buffaloes, and impregnated religiously and culturally by Hinayana Buddhism; Thailand Two, undergoing rapid social change, urbanization, industrialization, modernization, symbolized by the cars crowding the cities and the jet planes coming in from all over the world. He goes on to say that it is as if the Lord of Hosts is conducting the controversy with Thailand One (the unchanging one) through Thailand Two, which is crying out for change. (See Kosuke Koyama, "Thailand: Points of Theological Friction," pp. 65-86 in *Asian Voices in Christian Theology*. Edited by Gerald H. Anderson [Maryknoll, N.Y.: Orbis Books, 1976].—Eds.)

So in using the word *contextualization,* we try to convey all that is implied in the familiar term *indigenization,* yet seek to press beyond for a more dynamic concept which is open to change and which is also future-oriented.

Contextuality and Contextualization

We who are in the Third World are faced with a new historical reality, where many contexts, old and new, are converging, sometimes in coexistence, sometimes in radical conflict. Dr. Koyama mentioned two Thailands. There are many places with even more overlapping contexts, sometimes in a bewildering state of coexistence as in Hongkong, sometimes in a revolutionary ferment, as on the mainland of China seen through its cultural revolution. Either by accident or by providence we have used two words instead of one, *contextuality* and *contextualization.* I believe this to be providential.

To take context seriously does not necessarily mean, it seems to me, taking all contexts equally seriously, because all are not equally strategic for the *Missio Dei* in the working out of His purpose through history. By taking context seriously theological education may have to seek the help of other disciplines, such as sociology, anthropology, etc. But that is not all of the task. Behind it all is the missiological discernment of the signs of the times, required of the People of God.

Dr. Jürgen Moltmann warns of the danger that academic theology may become so contextualized that it becomes fossilized theology, and all the more dangerous because we are not aware of it. But equally there is a danger of contextual theology becoming chameleon theology, changing color according to the contexts. Contextuality, therefore, I believe, is that critical assessment of what makes the context really significant in the light of the *Missio Dei.* It is the missiological discernment of the signs of the times, seeing where God is at work and calling us to participate in it. Thus, contextuality is more than just taking all contexts seriously but indiscriminately. It is the conscientization of the contexts in the particular, historical moment, assessing the peculiarity of the context in the light of the mission of the church as it is called to participate in the *Missio Dei*. Such conscientization can only come through involvement and participation, out of which critical awareness may arise. But it should also engender that capacity to respond and to contextualize. Authentic contextuality leads to contextualization. The two cannot be separated, though they should be distinct. This dialectic between contextuality and contextualization indicates a new way of theologizing. It involves not only words, but actions. Through this, the inherent danger of a dichotomy between theory and practice, action and reflection, the classroom and the street should be overcome. Authentic theological reflection can only take place as the *theologia in loco,* discerning the contextuality within the concrete context. But it must also be aware that such authentic theological reflection is at best, but also at most, *theologia viatorum*; and therefore contextuality must be matched by the contextualization which is an ongoing process, fitting for the pilgrim people, moving from place to place and from time to time, in awareness that there is no abiding place which is not subject also to the changes of time.

Thus, the T.E.F. does not speak about "contextual theology" nor "contextualized theology" but about contextualizing theology.

Incarnation and Contextualization

Contextuality-contextualization are, I believe, a missiological necessity. But are they a theological necessity? Contextualizing theology takes the concrete local context seriously. It is rooted in a concrete, particular situation. Is there, then, a danger of losing the catholicity of the Gospel? To this there is a counter question: Is there such a theology which is not *in loco* and thus *in vacuum?*—a *theologia sub specie aeternitatis,* as it were—a utopian theology? But the concern for the catholicity of the Gospel is a legitimate one, with which contextualizing theology is deeply concerned. And contextualization, I believe, is the authentic way to that catholicity.

Catholicity is both a gift and a task. As a gift, we must see how it was given. This was in a very concrete way, by the Word which became flesh and dwelt among us at a particular time and place. I believe, in fact, that the incarnation is the divine form of contextualization, and if this is so, the way we receive this gift is also through our following His way. That is what I mean by contextualization. As the catholicity of the Gospel is given through the Word becoming flesh, so our task should be through our responsive contextualization, taking our own concrete, local contexts seriously. Furthermore, according to the Philippian passage quoted above, in becoming flesh there was even something more involved, of emptying Himself, becoming a servant, obedient unto death. That gospel which proclaimed the God who cared for all had, at the same time, a cutting edge, precisely in being for the poor, the oppressed, for the prisoners and for the neglected. In that way we see how concrete the incarnation is, and the catholicity which it manifests. The true catholicity is a gift which only becomes ours as we draw our basic power from the gospel of the Incarnate Word. True catholicity could not possibly be a colourless uniformity, but must be a rich fullness of truth and grace, which unfolds and manifests itself as we take the diversified contexts in time and space, where we are set, and respond faithfully as the Incarnate Word did on our behalf, once and for all. The true and authentic catholicity will become fully ours as we not only draw basic power from the same gospel, but as we are committed wholly to serve the same *Missio Dei* in the diversified contexts.

Of course contextuality-contextualization, as our human response, are at most and at best a provisional and fragmentary witness of that divine contextualization of the incarnation. Ours can only be in following in His steps as an ongoing process of the pilgrim people. But in doing so we can accept our relativity with hope and even with joy, as we see in our faithful responses the sign of the divine contextualization unfolding its purpose for the liberation and salvation of mankind.

What Erik Nielsen often said concerning indigenization is even more valid for contextualization. "The crux of the matter is the resurrection." Through the incarnation and the cross there awaits the resurrection. So, for us, authentic contextualization must be open constantly to the painful process of de-contextualization, for the sake of re-contextualization. Only through the pain of the cross is there the glory of the resurrection.

In this way we can welcome with joy the emergence of black theology, and for that matter, yellow theology, and the theology of liberation, for the sake of the true catholicity of the Gospel. There is no colourless theology. But there is all the joy of the multiple colours mobilized for the beauty of the new heaven and the new earth which God has promised. Or to change the metaphor, all the sounds must be mobilized in the great symphony of the Hallelujah Chorus, to be heard not only in heaven but on earth.

The Question of Excellence in Theological Education

Emerito P. Nacpil

"What sort of theological orientation would be most useful to the church at this time in Asia?" asks Philippine theologian Emerito P. Nacpil. "We do not know the answer," he says, "but . . . we are proposing what we call the 'critical Asian principle' as a method in this search. . . . It is a way of saying that we will approach and interpret the Gospel in relation to the needs and issues peculiar to the Asian situation." Together with the "search for a new spirituality," Nacpil says this represents a shift among Asian seminaries in the pursuit of excellence "from the narrower understanding of it as academic excellence to one that is broader and more adequate to the needs of theological education in the region." One goal is to produce "excellence in participation in the struggle for life, be it in the church or elsewhere." Dr. Nacpil—formerly professor of theology and president of Union Theological Seminary in the Philippines—was the only Filipino Protestant observer at the Second Vatican Council. He is now dean of the federated faculty of the South East Asia Graduate School of Theology, executive director of the Association of Theological Schools in South East Asia, and editor of *The South East Asia Journal of Theology* in which this article appeared in 1975 (XVI/1). The journal is published bi-annually in Manila by the Association.

I detect in the current situation of the Association of Theological Schools in South East Asia a shift of emphasis in the pursuit of excellence—from the narrower understanding of it as academic excellence to one that is broader and more adequate to the needs of theological education in the region today. The Association, I would say, is in search of a new kind of excellence in theological education.

What are the reasons for this shift? One set of reasons comes from the measure of success attained in the pursuit of academic excellence. This success produced certain consequences that need to be reckoned with and evaluated for their proper place in a more adequate understanding of excellence in theological education. I shall give only two examples. For one thing, given the secularizing effect of modern knowledge, when theology is taught scientifically—as it should when pursued academically—it inevitably shakes up sooner or later, and rightly so, forms of spirituality which have been reared in pre-secular, and pre-rational cultures. A spirituality whose base is animistic, whose strength is primarily emotional, whose religious content is largely superstitious, whose world-view is predominantly mythological, and whose intellectual appeal is no more than its symbolic and traditional and moralizing value inevitably erodes under the impact of the modern scientific temper. Such a spirituality must indeed go, and it is effectively being eroded more slowly in Asian societies in general, but more quickly in Asian academic circles, and most rapidly in theological seminary campuses, if the confusion and paralysis of the spiritual life in these campuses is any indication.

But some form of spirituality is essential to the life and practice of the Christian faith, and one must be nurtured in it in the process of theological formation. Is there a form of Christian spirituality that goes hand in glove with academic excellence? Must not excellence in theological education be characterized by a living integration of piety and learning? Our problem is that we do not know yet what kind of piety goes well with learning which we know must be pursued academically. And so ATSSEA last April decided to initiate what it calls "a search for a new spirituality" as part of its effort to pursue a more adequate understanding of excellence in theological education.

For another thing, academic excellence pursued in sequestered surroundings and artificially protected from the rough and tumble of mass life in Asia tends to produce, does it not, a type of intellectual elitism and arrogance which often does not want to get its hands dirty, as it were, in the struggle for life in Asia. A touch of this malaise has rubbed upon our own products in the seminaries. This has produced the further consequence of exacerbating the traditional tension between seminary and church, which in our situation in Asia—as in other places in the Third World—is compounded with other factors that I do not need to mention now.

But excellence in theological education must include mutual recognition, acceptance, support and cooperation between seminary and church, does it not? Should it not also include, among its products, excellence in participation in the struggle for life, be it in the church or elsewhere?

III

This leads me to the second set of reasons for this shift of emphasis in the pursuit of excellence which I mentioned earlier. This has to do with the present character of most Southeast Asian societies and the role of the churches in them and, therefore, of the ministry for which we train people in our seminaries. It is now a commonplace to say that societies in Asia—as in the world over—are changing. But there is an understanding of this change that, it seems to me, is significant. It is the view that this change can be initiated and directed, that it can be used as an opportunity for reshaping Asian realities towards a more humanly fulfilling life. As a consequence, almost no sector of Asian life and culture is protected against engineered change. Not only social structures and institutions are being deliberately changed —but more fundamentally—peoples in their persons, roles, values, attitudes, habits, are being changed! The church is fortunate to be in this situation in that it now has an opportunity to spread the leaven of the Gospel as a power for redeeming and creative change, as a power for reshaping realities in the Asian situation.

In this context, is it not fair to ask: what sort of theological knowledge is most helpful to the church in its life and mission? Is it the sort that is pursued in the ivory towers of academe which begins with reflection and ends in contemplation? Is it the sort that is constructed with intellectual rigor and much appreciated for its systematic scope and coherence and architectonic artistry? Or is it the sort whose theoretical substance is validated by its capacity to provide concrete guidance in the management of Asian affairs and in the reshaping of Asian realities? Is theology to be contemplative, reflective, or activistic?

I am sure it is wrong to put the question in these alternative terms, for theology should not have one of these characteristics at the expense of the others. But historically theology does not appear in perfect form, but moves in trends and emphases and orientations; not to say "schools." I can rephrase my original question by asking, what sort of theological orientation would be most useful to the church at this time in Asia? We do not know the answer, but the Association and the Graduate School see themselves as instruments in the search for an answer. To that end, we are proposing what we call the "critical Asian principle" as a method in this search. This principle is designed to operate at various methodological levels. For one thing, it is a way of saying where our area of responsibility and concern is, namely the varieties and dynamics of Asian realities. We are committed to understand this context both sympathetically and critically. For another thing, it is a way of saying that we will approach and interpret the Gospel in relation to the needs and issues peculiar to the Asian situation. It functions therefore partly as a hermeneutical principle. Thirdly, it is a way of saying that a theology worth its salt at this time in Asia must be capable, not only of illuminating Asian realities with the light of the Gospel, but also of helping manage and direct the changes now taking place along lines more consonant with the Gospel and its vision for human life.

Having said so much about the critical Asian principle, I do not wish to give you the impression that we in the Association and the Graduate School are ourselves very clear about it. We are also struggling to discover its range and depth. But we can only do this in the process of engagement. And we are anxious to get on with this engagement.

The Yin-Yang Way of Thinking
A Possible Method for Ecumenical Theology

Jung Young Lee

The either/or way of theological thinking in the West—with its tendency to absolutize and exclude a middle way of both/and—"is responsible for the predicament of Christianity in the world today." That is the premise of Jung Young Lee who proposes that the Chinese concept of change and relativity—expressed in the interplay of *yin* and *yang*—provides a much needed category of thinking that can be helpful "not only for the development of ecumenical theology but for the mutual co-existence of Christianity with other religions in a creative process of becoming." He maintains that *yin-yang* thinking—"a way of both/and thinking which includes the possibility of either/or"—will not only "solve controversial issues in theology but . . . bring to light new meaning and fresh understanding of theological issues." Dr. Lee, a Korean with a Th.D. in systematic theology from Boston University, is associate professor of religious studies and humanities at the University of North Dakota. In his book, *The I: A Christian Concept of Man* (Philosophical Library, 1971), Lee applies the *yin-yang* way of thinking to the Christian understanding of man. This essay appeared originally in the July 1971 issue of the *International Review of Mission*, which is published quarterly in Geneva by the Commission on World Mission and Evangelism of the World Council of Churches.

The Basic Issue and Related Problems

The dominant issue in the history of Christian thought is neither the problem of the divine reality nor that of human belief but the Western way of thinking, that is, thinking in terms of "either/or." This was deeply rooted in the Graeco-Roman view of the world, which became the general framework for theological thinking in the West from the beginning of Christianity. Its origins may go back to the Persian religion, Zoroastrianism, whose basic characteristic is the ultimate dichotomy between the opposing forces of Ormazd, the spirit of good, and Ahriman, the spirit of evil. It was also directly enshrined in Aristotelian logic, which became the foundation of the "Western" way of thinking. Some obvious examples in the West are easily noticeable to Easterners. We in the West think that what is not good must be evil, and what is not evil must be good; what is not wrong must be right, and what is not right must be wrong. But it is also possible that what is wrong may be neither right nor wrong, and what is not right may be both right and wrong at the same time. This Aristotelian conception however excludes the validity of the middle. The axiom of the "excluded middle," which is based on dualistic absolutism, is quite alien to what the Christian faith presupposes and has created some of the serious problems that Christianity has to deal with in our generation.

First of all, the either/or way of theological thinking in the West not only promoted but shaped the absolute dogma of God. The God of dogma is not God at all. The God who is absolutized by human words is less than the God of Christianity. That is why Emil Brunner rightly points out, even though he himself was led into the same mistake, that the formation of the doctrine of the Trinity was an intellectual indulgence of the early Church.[1] The doctrine of the Trinity became the norm to test the validity of the divine nature. Thus the doctrine became the judge of the divine. The Word of God became the servant of human words. The absolutization of human words is very characteristic of the either/or way of thinking, and the Western emphasis on the Absolute Reason, from which even the Divine cannot escape, is primarily derived from it. Thus God has been made an idol of intellectual display.

Secondly, the either/or way of theological thinking is responsible for the predicament of Christianity in the world of today. Christianity seems unable to co-exist with the different religions of the world. Its isolation from other religions in Japan, in India, in China and other countries where major world religions are dominant is chiefly caused by the absolute claim of man-made dogmas, based on the either/or category of thinking. This category does not provide any room for the possibility of reconciliation and compromise with different forms of belief. Accordingly, Christianity has no choice but *either* to accept *or* reject them totally. That is why Christian missions in the past stressed conversion rather than cultivation, and total commitment rather than mutual dialogue. Buddhism, for example, existed very successfully alongside other religions in China, Japan and South-East Asia for many centuries, because of its middle-way approach to other religions. Yet Christianity either dominates others or is isolated from them. The exclusive character of either/or thinking made the inclusive exclusive.

Thirdly, the either/or way of thinking has made scientific technology possible. Thus Christianity is allied with technology to reject the nonrational aspects of human life. It suppressed occult phenomena and devalued the emotional aspects of religious life. Mysticism did not thrive in the life of the Western Church. The Western Church considered the exploration of psychic matters as the works of the devil. Her rejection of them is based on the absolute style of either/or thinking, which allows no room for mysticism. Thus Christianity in the West, and especially Protestantism, failed to meet the needs of the whole man whose nature includes mystic elements, and this failure is responsible for youth turning away from the Church and seeking to satisfy its spiritual needs in Eastern mysticism.

Finally, the either/or style of theological thought has contributed towards the pollution of our environment. It created the dichotomy and conflict between man and nature, between body and spirit. Man must *either* conquer nature *or* nature will conquer him. *Either* the spirit overcomes the body *or* the body will overcome the spirit. In this kind of relationship we can expect nothing but conflict and war. Man gradually overcomes nature through the use of scientific technology but he never conquers it completely. Ultimately neither of them survives. The conquest of nature is ultimately the conquest of himself. Thus, by this way of thinking, the opposites never come together into a harmonious and peaceful co-existence.

The Task before Us

Our task should not be the total elimination of the either/or way of thinking, but the limitation of its function in theological enterprise. Its total elimination might result in the complete renunciation of our theological work. Thus we can summarize our task as two-fold: the limitation of the function of the either/or way of thinking in theology, and the search for the most inclusive category of thinking to complement it.

(a) the limitation of the either/or way of thinking.

The limitation of the either/or way of thinking is essential in theology, because of its tendency to absolutize. The divine nature cannot be absolutized by human thinking. Moreover, the absolute category is no longer compatible with the contemporary understanding of the world. Our way of thinking is relative to our understanding of the world, because we think through the use of world-imagery. The way of thinking in New Testament times, for example, was based on the world viewed as a three-storied structure. The traditional Western view of the world, to which we are still accustomed, is the Euclidean notion of the world, in which both time and space are infinitely extended. Even Newtonian physics did not offer any radically new world view. The absolute categories of space and time were still maintained. However, the contemporary world view which Einsteinian physics describes, is radically different from the traditional Western world view. According to this contemporary view, everything is relative, including time and space. Since everything is relative, the absolute category of either/or thinking is out of harmony with the contemporary world view. Just as Newtonian physics which presupposes the absolute categories of both time and space, functions well in ordinary mechanics, so the either/or style of thinking can deal with ordinary human situations, with penultimate matters. But, just as the former is unable to deal with the wholeness of the universe, theology, which deals with the ultimate concerns of our life, cannot be effectively expressed in either/or categories. Therefore, this must be limited to penultimate matters only and is useful for the method of analysis and discrimination.

(b) the search for an inclusive category of thinking

We have to find the most inclusive category of thinking which can be based on the relativistic world view. And since this relativistic world view, which contemporary physics attempts to describe, has been known to the Eastern people for a long time, it is reasonable to seek the symbol of relativistic thinking in the East. The world view to which Indian people are accustomed is certainly relativistic and inclusive. However, the concept of Maya has been often viewed negatively by Christians since it seems to reject the reality of the world. Thus it may arouse suspicion in some Christians if we take the symbol of thinking from the world view of India. However, the way in which the Chinese people have been thinking for many centuries is not only relativistic but is also compatible with the Christian idea of the world. In other words, the Chinese world view is positive and affirmative, just as the Christian world view is. It is then the Chinese world view which can help us to find the symbol of thinking that is most inclusive.

If Christian theology is to be universal in its orientation, it does not make any difference whether the symbol of thinking is taken from China or from the West as long as it satisfies the frame of reference through which Christian truth is conveyed. Furthermore, the Eastern symbol is much more practical than the Western to establish a point of contact between Christianity and other world religions, which have their origins in the East. Through this point of contact a Christian dialogue with world religions is possible. Thus the use of an Eastern category of thinking can be helpful not only for the development of ecumenical theology but for the mutual co-existence of Christianity with other religions in a creative process of becoming.

(c) the yin-yang symbolism as a possible category of theological thinking

One of the most profound treatments of cosmology in China is found in the Book of Change or the *I Ching,*[2] which is one of the oldest books in China. Since this book was accepted by both Taoism and Confucianism and became the focal point of the intellectual movement in Neo-Confucian philosophy in the later years, the cosmic view of this book is normative for the Chinese people. The Book of Change views the world as the flux of change, which was reaffirmed by Confucius. He stood by a river one day and said, "Like this river, everything is flowing on ceaselessly, day and night" (Analects 9:16). The concept of change then becomes the key to the understanding of the universe. Because of change everything is relative. Time and space are not absolute but relative, for everything including themselves is changing ceaselessly. Time and space are not *a priori* categories of all other forms of existence. Thus the general theory of relativity, which presupposes change, is in conformity with the Chinese view of the world. Since a relativistic world presupposes change, change can become the symbol for the basic categories of all things in the world.

The category of change, according to the Book of Change, is the interplay of *yin* and *yang,* which are the primary categories of all other categories of existence in the world. The idea of *yin-yang* may have a deeper historical root than any other concept in China. It is almost impossible to trace back to the origin of this idea, even though the technical use of these terms may come from sometime during the Han dynasty. The concept of *yin* originally came from the imagery of shadow, while that of *yang* from brightness. *Yin* then came to signify female, receptive, passive, cold, etc., and *yang* male, creative, active, warm, etc. *Yin* represents everything that is not *yang,* and *yang* what is not *yin.* Thus in an ultimate analysis everything, whether spiritual or material and temporal or spatial, can be categorized by the symbol of *yin* and *yang* interplay. The symbol of *yin* and *yang* is then the primordial category of everything that exists in the world. The characteristic nature of this symbol is not the conflict but the complementarity of opposites. It is the category of wholeness rather than of partiality. It is the category of becoming rather than of being. It is the transcendental category of expression, because it transcends the logical and analytical categories of our rational thinking. It is therefore possible to express the divine nature which transcends every dichotomy and conflict of opposites. The characteristic of transcendence is expressed in the complementarity of opposites. *Yin* presupposes the necessity of *yang*, and *yang* cannot exist without *yin*. The one requires the other. Thus *yin-yang* thinking is a way of both/and thinking which includes the possibility of either/or thinking. The latter is effective in dealing with penultimate matters, as the former is with ultimate concerns. Since theology is concerned with the ultimate, theological thinking must be in terms of both/and.

The both/and category of thinking, which is based on the *yin-yang* symbolism, is characteristic not only of the Chinese but also of the Indian way of thinking. As Betty Heinmann pointed out, "The West thinks in *aut-aut*, the disjunctive either-or." India, on the other hand, visualizes a continuous stream of interrelated moments of *sive-sive*, the "this as well as that," in an endless series of changes and transformation.[3] The relativistic world view of India certainly provides this category of both/and thinking which seems to be the general characteristic of Eastern people, and must be adopted by theology.

Scientifically also, the contemporary world view forces the West to think more and more in complementary terms. For example, scientists today do not believe either the wave theory or the quantum theory of light but accept both of them at the same time. In our living the stress of contextualism tends to avoid ethical absolutes. Thus the both/and category of thinking seems to have a universal orientation. If Christian theology also has a universal implication, I believe that it is to be expressed in this universal category of both/and thinking.

There is a growing interest among theologians in the possible use of the *yin-yang* category of thinking in theology. For example, Wilfred Cantwell Smith says, "What I myself see in the *yang-yin* symbol with regard to this matter, if I may be allowed this personal note, is not an image that would reduce Christian truth to a part of some larger whole. Rather, I find it a circle fo'

embracing Christian truth itself. . . . In this, the image says to
me, as in all ultimate matters, truth lies not in an either/or, but
in a both/and."[4] Nels Ferré not only realizes the advantage of
using this complementary category of thinking in theology but
suggests that this is the only possible category. He says, "There
is here no place for paradox, excluded middle, *totum simul* or
Alles auf einmal. What we need is a contrapletal logic."[5] Ferré
recognizes that the idea of contrapletal logic was already used by
Ramanuja in *Vedarthasamgraha,* one of the most profound trea-
tises in Indian literature. He says also, "A prime example has
been the Chinese use of *yin* and *yang*. Two realities like day and
night or light and darkness are contradictory in one dimension
and yet fulfilling of each other within their place in nature and
man's experience."[6] The growing interest in the use of the
both/and category of thinking by Western theologians will have
a profound implication as an impetus for the creation of universal theology.

The Implication of the yin-yang Category for Theological Think-ing

Since the *yin-yang* way of thinking transcends human rea-
soning, its application to theology not only clarifies some paradoxical issues but provides fresh interpretations of divine attributes. It can, for example, illuminate such concepts as the
nature of divine transcendence and immanence, God as personal,
Jesus as the Christ, or the relation of body and spirit.

The West, using either/or categories of thought, finds it difficult to express the divine transcendence and immanence together. For the *yin-yang* way of thinking it is no trouble at all to
think that God is *both* transcendent *and* immanent at the same
time. He cannot be *either* transcendent *or* immanent. The God of
transcendence is *also* the God of immanence.

Similarly, in the West we ask the question, "Is God personal or impersonal?" But God, who transcends all categories
cannot be a personal God *only*. God who is only personal is a
limited God. The God of creation is not only the God of personal
beings but of impersonal beings as well. To make God personal

is to limit him. Thus the use of the *yin-yang* category provides a new understanding of the divine nature.

Further, Jesus as the Christ, as both God and man, cannot really be understood in terms of either/or. How can man also be God? In the West we have to speak in terms of paradox or mystery in order to justify the reality of Christ. However, in *yin-yang* terms, he can be thought of as both God and man at the same time. In him God is not separated from man nor man from God. They are in complementary relationship. He is God because of man: he is man because of God.

Finally, one of the classical dilemmas in theological thinking is the relationship between the spirit and the body (or matter). According to Judaeo-Christian teaching, they are one and inseparable. Our spirit is also our body and our body is also spirit. Nevertheless, because Western thinkers have been pre-occupied with making distinctions, they have thought in terms of dualistic entities, of dichotomy between the spirit and the body. The *yin-yang* way of thinking clarifies the theological meaning of man and reorientates our thinking from a dualistic to a monistic view of the world. It thus renders a great service to the renewed understanding of Christian theology as well as to a universalistic outlook of the Christian message to the world.

Conclusion

The use of this transcendental category of thinking has been shown not only to solve controversial issues in theology but often to bring to light new meaning and fresh understanding of theological issues. The *yin-yang* way of thinking applies to ultimate matters which either/or thinking fails to deal with, just as the latter deals with penultimate matters which the former fails to do. We need both the *yin-yang* and the either/or ways of thinking to carry out successfully the theological task. Christian theology becomes universal only when the either/or category is de-absolutized, and it becomes significant only when the *yin-yang* category allows the creativity of either/or thinking. The effective method of theological thinking is possible when both *yin-yang* and either/or categories complement one another.[7]

NOTES

1. See his *The Christian Doctrine of God:* Dogmatics Vol. 1 (Philadelphia: Westminster Press, 1950), p. 226.

2. For full explanation see my *The Principle of Changes: Understanding the I Ching* (New York: University Books, 1971).

3. Betty Heinmann, *Facets of Indian Thought* (London: George Allen and Unwin, 1964), p. 168.

4. Wilfred Cantwell Smith, *The Faith of Other Men* (New York: The New American Library, 1963), p. 74.

5. Nels F. S. Ferré, *The Universal Word: A Theology for a Universal Faith* (Philadelphia: The Westminster Press, 1969), p. 80.

6. *Ibid.,* p. 100.

7. The *yin-yang* way of thought is applied as a theological method in my book, *The I: A Christian Concept of Man* (New York: Philosophical Library, 1971).

I Cry in the Night From the Torture Chamber
Psalm 129

Ernesto Cardenal

Born in 1925 in Nicaragua, Ernesto Cardenal is a priest, poet, mystic and political activist. For two years, 1957-59, he lived in the Trappist monastery at Gethsemane, Kentucky, where Thomas Merton was his spiritual advisor. Concerned with fighting injustice and developing authentic Christian community—in opposition to the principalities and powers of the world—Cardenal now lives in a cooperative commune which he founded in 1966 at Solentiname, Nicaragua. This poem is reprinted from *Risk,* 1973 (IX/3), which is published quarterly in Geneva by the World Council of Churches. A collection of Cardenal's writings, *The Gospel in Solentiname,* was published by Orbis Books in 1976.

From the depths, I cry to you oh Lord!
I cry in the night from the prison cell
and from the concentration camp
From the torture chamber
in the hour of darkness
hear my voice
     my S.O.S.

If you were to keep a record of sins
Lord, who would be blameless?
But you do pardon sins

you are not implacable as they are in their Investigation!

I trust in the Lord and not in leaders
Nor in slogans
I trust in the Lord and not in their radios!

My soul hopes in the Lord
more than the sentinels of dawn
more than the way one counts the hours of night in a prison cell.

While we are imprisoned
                              they are enjoying themselves!
But the Lord is liberation
the freedom of Israel.

Liberation Theology
and the Captivities of Jesus

Richard J. Neuhaus

Of recent books in missiology, one of the most debated is Gustavo Gutiérrez's *A Theology of Liberation* (Orbis Books, 1973), in which the author—who is professor of theology at the Catholic University of Peru—relates the meaning of the Christian gospel to the revolutionary ferment in Latin America. Richard J. Neuhaus, pastor of St. John the Evangelist Lutheran Church in Brooklyn and Senior Editor of *Worldview*, believes it is a book that must be taken very seriously precisely because Gutiérrez is addressing "the theological consciousness of the universal church" with "the particularities of the Church's struggle in Latin America." But Neuhaus is disturbed and disappointed by what he sees as "a deep and perhaps dangerous abstruseness about what precisely Gutiérrez is advocating." He laments Gutiérrez's nearly "carte blanche legitimation for joining almost any allegedly revolutionary struggle to replace almost any allegedly repressive regime." The resulting impression, Neuhaus says, "is that Gutiérrez's vision is not that of the Church renewed but simply that of the Church switching sides"—and once again "taking Jesus culturally captive." Yet Neuhaus recognizes that "running the risk of cultural captivity is inherent in the Church's mission." His review is reprinted from the June 1973 *Worldview*, published by the Council on Religion and International Affairs in New York City.

Gustavo Gutiérrez is a native of Peru and professor of theology at the Catholic University of Peru. He is also chaplain to the National Union of Catholic University Students and advisor to the Latin American Bishops Conference. Gutiérrez is widely credited with having coined the term "liberation theology," and with the recent publication of his *A Theology of Liberation* (Orbis; 323 pp.; $7.95/4.95) North American readers are challenged by a major systematic effort to articulate the meaning of the Christian gospel in terms attuned to the revolutionary ferment in Latin America.

Advance reviews signal that this is a book to be taken seriously. Jesuit theologian Avery Dulles writes: "Gutiérrez shows in this book that 'liberation theology,' far from being a frivolous or irresponsible movement, arises out of deep compassion and critical reflection on the situation of the poor and oppressed. . . . This new theology builds on, and in part surpasses, the neo-Marxism and the secularization theology of Western Europe." Presbyterian Robert McAfee Brown of Stanford, breathing as he does the heady air of California, declares that with this book "Gutiérrez becomes one of the most important voices on the world theological scene. It may well be the most important book of the year, or of the decade." In a discipline, so to speak, afflicted by faddism, one may hesitate to predict what will catch on this year, to say nothing of what will last for a decade. But if by "important" we understand something other than immediate or popular impact, Brown's estimate may be less euphoric than it at first appears.

The importance one attributes to Gutiérrez's effort is hinged in large part upon where one thinks we (the world generally and Christians particularly) are in this latter part of the twentieth century. If one agrees that relations between poor and rich countries are a, if not the, major challenge of the second half of this century, and if one agrees that what happens in Latin America is central to the hope of rectifying current injustices, and if one agrees that institutional Christianity is critical to social change in Latin America, and if one agrees that theology is the intellectual side of the Church's life and work, both reflecting and shaping the Christian mission, then one must take Gustavo Gutiérrez very seriously indeed. The above proposition admittedly involves many ifs, but I think it fair to say that these are assumptions that inform mainstream theological exchange across denominational lines today. Even if, however, one doubts one or more of these assumptions, Gustavo Gutiérrez must be reckoned with as a theologian of stature, whose stated determination is to address himself to the theological consciousness of the universal church, even as he wants the peculiar form of that address to be determined by the particularities of the Church's struggle in Latin America.

Talk about "liberation theology" is haunted by understandable suspicions. The term liberation, with its socialist and frequently revolutionary content, invites the suspicion that theology is somehow being enlisted to legitimate a specific political option. Certainly recent years have witnessed the enlistment of sociology, political science, history and economics, as well as of theology, in various directions of social change. While we may have no illusions about the absolute "objectivity" that can be sustained in any discipline, we might still want to insist that the integrity of a discipline depends in part upon a serious effort to maintain some critical distance from any form of advocacy. Father Dulles no doubt has in mind the failure of much religious writing about liberation to maintain this distance when he absolves Gutiérrez of promoting "a frivolous or irresponsible movement."

Before examining Gutiérrez's work in greater detail, we should be more specific about the peculiar difficulties that plague theology's effort to maintain critical distance. Anyone who today might write a "theology of imperialism" or a "theology of capitalism" would be considered very marginal indeed; it would be alleged, probably with some justice, that he is impossibly rightist. Yet in other times, and in less intellectually respectable circles today, religious legitimations of the status quo are no occasion for scandal. In Bruce Barton's 1925 best seller, *The Man Nobody Knows,* the "unknown" Jesus is portrayed as the world's greatest business organizer. This Palestinian Babbitt, who was, to paraphrase Sinclair Lewis, "nimble in the calling of selling ideas for more than people could afford to pay," had an enormous appeal for Calvin Coolidge and others who lived by the conviction that Christian America's business is business.

Successive cultural waves have each offered us their new version of Jesus and his gospel: the gospel of wealth, of peace of mind, of therapeutic triumph, of Consciousness III. From Orison Swett Marden (1850-1924) and Andrew Carnegie through Norman Vincent Peale and Charles Reich, Americans have been adept at tailoring the message to fit the mood. Among thoughtful Christians such efforts to take Jesus culturally captive have been generally deplored. They are put off by the prayer-breakfast athlete's description of Jesus as Life's Great Quarterback or the businessman's assurance that He is the Chairman of the Biggest Board of All. Such images appear as outrageous, perhaps blasphemous, cultural constrictions of the Christ figure.

Our protest should, however, be tempered by several considerations. First, many sides can play the game of taking Jesus culturally captive. Second, there is an element of inevitability about playing the game, whereby one distortion can only be countered by another distortion. Finally, running the risk of cultural captivity is inherent in the Church's mission.

On the first score, Peter Berger has recently noted that were he a decade later to rewrite his *The Noise of Solemn Assemblies* (1961), his critique of American religion would be much the same. The difference is that at the end of the 1950's he saw religion captive to the regnant Protestant culture, while at the end of the 1960's it was captive to the minority counterculture. The essential similarity, he contends, is that both situations represent culture religion in bondage to something less than the transcendent dimensions to which Christianity ought to witness. Whether or not one finds Berger's analysis entirely satisfactory, the thrust of his argument can be verified by visiting any moderately radical bookstore selling "Wanted" posters portraying Jesus as a societal dropout and political subversive or, less moderately, as a guerrilla fighter complete with submachine gun. The extent to which the image of Jesus is locked into a particular cluster of political and cultural perceptions may not be qualitatively different from the contraction represented by Bruce Barton's Jesus.

It might be argued—and Gustavo Gutiérrez is among those who make this argument—that the qualitative difference lies not in the formal but in the material aspect of the question. That is, while the image of Jesus might in both cases be formally tied to a particular worldview, the dramatic differences between worldviews makes one image more legitimate than the other. It makes all the difference in the world, for example, whether an image places Jesus with the poor or with the rich, with the oppressed or with the oppressor. The problem, of course, is that terms such as oppressed and oppressor and notions about what might be done to change their relationships are uninteresting abstractions until related to concrete and usually conflictual movements, struggles and political parties. Jesus, knowing the temptations we would face, cautioned his disciples against saying "Lo here!" or "Lo there!" as though we could with absolute certainty identify the presence of the Kingdom in history. Since almost every movement claims to be on behalf of the oppressed, and since even those movements which seem to us to represent the interests of the poor have within them dynamics directed against the rule of God ("sin" is the conventional and still distressingly accurate term for such dynamics), it is not enough to enlist the gospel "on the right side." Serious Christians have been forced again and again, often reluctantly, to respect the gospel's stubborn resistance to being used; it remains unenlistable and unrecruitable.

Yet there is a degree of inevitability in our tendency to take the gospel culturally captive. As Sartre observed that there are no privileged observers, so it might be said that there are no privileged believers. Critics of liberation theology should be pressed as to which adjectives—equally conditioned by culture and political perspective—are appropriate to their own theologies. It is more a boast than a description to say that one is doing simply "theology" or "Christian theology." Such a boast reflects a certain superficiality, a lack of modesty about one's placement within history. To be sure, we aspire toward the universal and catholic, but our grasp falls far short of our reach. Nor is this entirely lamentable, for (and this is the third consideration) running the risk of limitation, of the narrowing represented by cultural captivity, is inherent in the Church's mission.

Running the risk is not the same thing as making a virtue of necessity. Whether the limitations be national, denominational, sexual, racial or ethnic, we ought not to glory in our parochialisms. That way lies the cacophony of competing chauvinisms and the impoverishment of us all. Nonetheless, a religion that affirms the Incarnation and the proposition that the finite can contain the infinite can afford to run some risks. In fact, it has little choice in the matter.

In one of the great prayers in the eucharistic liturgy Jesus is spoken of as "the new man for all men." Over the centuries Jesus has been pictured with the clothing, mannerisms and physical characteristics of Africans, Orientals, Mexicans and others who have appropriated his image. Today in Africa hundreds of burgeoning "independent churches" are bringing together traditional Christian and tribal imagery into something genuinely new under the sun. Historically the Church has had an extraordinarily difficult time drawing the line between creative appropriation and distortive syncretism, but in its healthier moments it has sinned on the side of sympathy with the restatements generated by its missionary impulse. In any case, every cultural appropriation involves some limitation; there is a choice, conscious or not, of accents, a muting or even exclusion of discordant themes. Indeed it is precisely the multiplicity of culturally biased imaginations that has made it possible for countless culturally captive Christians to identify with Jesus as "one of us," and for the more catholic-minded to be gripped by the exploration of the inexhaustible diversity of the Christ figure.

The alternative to running the risk of cultural captivity is to surrender to the theologian's propensity to present the Christ as a cluster of theological propositions. José Comblin describes this failure to culturally enflesh the central figure of Christianity as the "iconization" of Jesus:

> This is a Jesus of hieratic, stereotyped gestures, all representing theological themes. To explain an action of Jesus is to find in it several theological meanings. In this way, the life of Jesus is no longer a human life, submerged in history, but a theological life—an icon. As happens with icons, his actions lose their human context and are stylized, becoming signs of the transcendent and invisible world.

Gutiérrez's protest against the iconization of Jesus and the resulting version of the gospel as revolutionary manifesto will inevitably be compared with efforts to construct a theology of black liberation in this country, efforts associated notably with James Cone of Union Theological Seminary. Cone's main themes are reflected in the statement of the National Committee of Black Churchmen, issued during the height of the debate about the "Black Manifesto," which demanded reparations from white churches:

> Black Theology is a theology of black liberation. It seeks to plumb the black condition in the light of God's revelation in Jesus Christ, so that the black community can see that the gospel is commensurate with the achievement of black humanity. . . . The message of liberation is the revelation of God as revealed in the incarnation of Jesus Christ. Freedom *is* the gospel. Jesus *is* the Liberator!

Like Gutiérrez, Cone has taken care to relate his theology to the larger, more universal, Christian tradition. Again like Gutiérrez, he has been most commonly criticized for reducing the gospel, for repackaging it, so to speak, in order to serve partisan purposes of social change. He has also been criticized from the other side. For example, Gayraud Wilmore (*Black Religion and Black Radicalism*) has suggested it is not necessary to "validate" black theology in the terms of "white Christianity." Indeed the black religious experience, he writes, has its own integrity, which need not be in any exclusive sense related to Christianity at all.

The parallels between Cone and Gutiérrez deserve more careful examination than is possible here. The point is that both are wrestling with the tension between what is indigenous and what is catholic. Both acknowledge the danger of liberation theology becoming captive to a political ideology that is foreign to the believing community within which any significant theological statement must be appropriated and sustained. In Cone one detects a growing respect for the black church as it actually is, and not as the revolutionary vanguard we may want it to be. Similarly, Gutiérrez strives to relate his work not only to world theological discourse but also to papal and episcopal statements in which he seeks warrants for his own arguments, which he clearly views in terms of development rather than repudiation. Although both Cone and Gutiérrez frequently, and carelessly, represent their views as something "entirely new" and as a "complete break with the past," such rhetoric must be discounted in view of their evident consciousness of themselves as members of a continuing community of theological reflection.

Gutiérrez is determined to relate not only to what is contemporarily catholic but also to what is chronologically catholic. That is, the referents from the past are permitted to impinge in an authoritative way upon present reflection. Writing in *Worldview* (September, 1972), Gutiérrez contends, for example, against the view of Jesus as an "apolitical" figure. "A serious reconsideration of this presupposition is necessary." But then he quickly adds: "But it has to be undertaken with a respect for the historical Jesus, not forcing the facts in terms of our current concerns. If we wished to discover in Jesus the least characteristic of a contemporary political militant, we would not only misrepresent his life and witness and demonstrate a lack of understanding of politics in the present world; we would also deprive ourselves of what his life and witness have that is deep and universal and, therefore, valid and concrete for today's man."

The "therefore" in the last sentence is crucial. It contains a host of assumptions about the theological enterprise and about rational discourse in general. The sentence is representative of Gutiérrez's acceptance of the tension between particularity and universality, between indigeneity and catholicity. It is therefore both fair and necessary to hold Gutiérrez to his "therefore" in reading his *A Theology of Liberation*.

Gustavo Gutiérrez clearly belongs to that company commonly described as the theologians of the future. The phrase does not refer to the expectation that they will dominate the theological enterprise in the years ahead, although that may well be the case, but to the key role that the future, under the metaphor of the Kingdom of God, plays in their thinking. The approach is also described as the "theology of hope" or "theology of promise." Its chief luminaries are Wolfhart Pannenberg and Jurgen Moltmann and, on a somewhat lower elevation, Johannes

Metz and another Latin American, Rubem Alves. All draw heavily on the German Marxist philosopher, Ernst Bloch. The extraordinarily rich notes that accompany *A Theology of Liberation* reveal the earnestness with which Gutiérrez has tried to combine these various contributions with his consciousness of contemporary Latin America.

Contrary to Pannenberg and much more relentlessly than Moltmann, Gutiérrez "politicizes" the idea of the Kingdom. He suggests that the significance of any theological statement is in direct proportion to its applicability to the process of liberation. Indeed, theology, we are told at several points, is reflection on the *praxis* of liberation. In this respect he goes beyond Johannes Metz, to whose "new political theology" he is admittedly indebted. Of course, the "process of liberation" in its most expansive sense comprehends the totality of God's purpose in history. More immediately, it might mean the student confrontation with the regime's police in the *plaza de armas* last Thursday afternoon. Unfortunately, Gutiérrez's appeals to the process of liberation are often spectacularly indifferent to the time factor, which leads to no small confusion.

While Gutiérrez does not cite Arend van Leeuwen, the latter's appreciation of Marx as a theologian is consonant with the ways in which Gutiérrez employs Marxist categories in the definition of "the world" that is the object of theological reflection. "Alienation" is perhaps Gutiérrez's dominant metaphor for sin, for example. Rubem Alves has cautioned (see *Worldview,* March, 1972) against the use of Marxism as a "guarantee of faith." That is, he detects a tendency in liberation theology to replace the risk of Christian hope with the certitude of a Marxian "scientific" projection of the future. The tendency could no doubt find support in selected passages from *A Theology of Liberation*, but in general Gutiérrez steers away from the more dogmatic uses of Marxian scenarios and leaves, at least theoretically, wide range for the contingencies of the genuinely new, for divine initiative. This openness to the unexpected is, one must admit, obscured by his frequently uncritical legitimation, in theological terms, of the act of liberation at hand.

Gutiérrez's theologizing about liberation is complementary

to the well-known secular uses of liberation language. Along with most Latin Americans of the Left, Gutiérrez rejects the notion of development. Developmentalism *(desarrollismo)* is implicitly imitative of the oppressor and hopelessly wed to the indefinite projection of capitalist scenarios that can only mean tightening the circle of dependence which enslaves the poor. "In this light, to speak about the process of *liberation* begins to appear more appropriate and richer in human content. Liberation in fact expresses the inescapable moment of radical change which is foreign to the ordinary use of the term development." The terminological ambiguity in this sentence is increased as Gutiérrez continues: "Only in the context of such a process can a policy of development be effectively implemented, have any real meaning, and avoid misleading formulations."

While the particular forms of the future's arrival may be unclear at points, there can be no doubt that theology's business is with history and its future. Drawing directly from Pannenberg's insistence upon "universal history," Gutiérrez's hoped-for liberation assumes that "history is one." There is not a spiritual history that is the proper concern of theology and a temporal history that is left to the world, the devil and the flesh. Repudiated with equal vigor are the dichotomies between "salvation history" and "secular history," or between the realm of redemption and the realm of creation. All history is ultimately, and now in process of becoming, salvation history, and "all of the creation must be included in the order of redemption." There is but one promised Kingdom which is the fulfillment of history in its totality.

Gutiérrez departs from Pannenberg in his greater certainty about what the Kingdom looks like "in process of becoming." The dimension of mystery, which is closely tied to a sense of historical modesty, is frequently absent. Gutiérrez does not exclude as carefully as he might, and apparently intends, a simplistic progressivism of the onward and upward variety. This is the tone that marked much of the American social gospel movement and that provoked Reinhold Niebuhr to his polemic against the belief that "history is the Christ." The liberation struggle is the unfolding of history's script, and "the people" are the motor force of the unfolding and are, therefore, the Christ. Frantz Fanon is quoted favorably: "Everything depends upon the masses . . . there is no such thing as a demiurge . . . the demiurge is the people themselves and the magic hands are finally only the hands of the people."

History, writes Gutiérrez, is a "Christo-finalized" history. The mission of the Church, it is suggested, is not to juxtapose Christ and history, nor merely to help the world perceive the presence of Christ in history, but to see history as the Christ. Among the more attractive features of Gutiérrez's work is the seriousness with which he applies himself to the question of the Church. He shuns both the fashionable mood of anti-institutionalism and the facile Marxist indictment of religion as false consciousness. He wants to affirm and seize upon the religious impulse, turning it toward the task of history and away from the suprahistorical preoccupations that characterize most religious life at present.

The task of history is thus the task of the Church. There can be, then, no question of "mixing" religion and politics; the business of religion is history, including politics. Gutiérrez therefore assaults the notion of the "distinction of planes" whereby it is said that the Church ought to work on the "spiritual plane" and leave the "temporal plane" to others. He notes the irony that in most Latin American countries it used to be assumed that the Church would legitimate the political, economic and social status quo. At that time it was the people who wanted change who promoted the idea of the "distinction of planes." Because the Church's influence tended to place a halo around repressive systems, the progressives demanded that the Church stop mixing in politics. Now that the Church has been stirred, and in part enlisted, by revolutionary forces, "the distinction-of-planes banner has changed hands," and it is the conservatives who are insisting that the Church stay out of politics. In fact, writes Gutiérrez, in our one history "the political options have become radicalized," and for the Church to stand aside from the struggle is to choose against the struggle.

The last proposition has been a perennial problem for the Christian community. At one point Jesus said, "He that is not

with me is against me" (Matt 12:30). Then again he said, "For
he that is not against us is for us" (Mark 9:40). Gutiérrez's Jesus
is clearly the former and, for those who want to be with Jesus,
Gutiérrez seems to have a pretty clear idea of where he is doing
business in the 1970's. While Gutiérrez appears to have an un-
seemly confidence in his locating of the Christic action and tends
to propose the Church as recruitment office for the revolution,
one should also keep in mind that not everywhere have "the political options become radicalized" as they have in many Latin
American countries. Fastidiousness about maintaining the
Church's critical distance from the parties that would capture it
is perhaps a luxury that can be afforded only in societies where
the options are not so restricted as to force to the forefront the
revolutionary alternative. Nonetheless, there is, one hopes, an
approach between fastidiousness and recklessness.

Gutiérrez's approach, it is important to note, seems aimed
more at gaining the attention of the revolutionary than at converting the enemies of the liberation struggle. He recognizes that
many Latin Americans have chosen the revolution despite Christianity—or at least despite the Christianity they were taught in
years past. "If they are not always able to express in appropriate
terms the profound reasons for their commitment, it is because
the theology in which they were formed . . . has not produced
the categories necessary to express this option, which seeks to
respond creatively to the new demands of the Gospel and of the
oppressed and exploited peoples of this continent." Certainly
they were not taught the Christian rationale for the revolutionary
alternative by a church that "is so static and devitalized that it is
not even strong enough to abandon the Gospel. It is the Gospel
which is disowning it." Although Gutiérrez intends to do more
than this, *A Theology of Liberation* is in part an effort to provide for radicals the "appropriate terms" in which to express
"the profound reasons for their commitment." It is one version
of what it means to obey the biblical injunction to "be always
ready to give a reason of the hope that is in you" (I Peter 3:15).

In offering a politicized theology, Gutiérrez recognizes that
religion encompasses much more than what is included in the
conventional definition of politics. He realizes that, if it is to be

relevant to the life of the faithful who actually make up the Church, theology must deal with prayer, the Eucharist, ecclesiastical structures and so forth. Each of these subjects receives careful and even loving attention. His systematic effort is to recast each of these topics and to place it within a greatly expanded idea of politics, in which politics becomes almost synonymous with history. One chapter is devoted, for example, to traditional piety regarding poverty and seeks to demonstrate that the beatitude "Blessed are the poor" is not a statement of resignation or passivity but an assurance that the poor are blessed because they are the revolutionary vanguard. Neither does Gutiérrez neglect the pronouncements of the Church's magisterium. He seeks rather to demonstrate natural developments toward a theology of liberation, arguing, for example, for the continuity between Paul VI's *Populorum Progressio* ("a transitional document") and a commitment to revolutionary change.

Although Gutiérrez does not, then, disdain even the most traditional concerns of religion, it is nonetheless accurate to say that he finally equates the Church's mission with the revolutionary struggle. "The scope and gravity of the process of liberation is such that to ponder its significance is really to examine the meaning of Christianity itself and the mission of the Church in the world."

As we have seen, the phrase "process of liberation" is used in varying ways, with dramatically different degrees of inclusiveness. The goal of liberation's process remains elusive, although one or two summary statements are offered:

> The historical plan, the utopia of liberation as the creation of a new social consciousness and as a social appropriation not only of the means of production, but also of the political process, and, definitively, of freedom, is the proper arena for the cultural revolution. That is to say, it is the arena of the permanent creation of a new man in a different society characterized by solidarity. Therefore, that creation is the place of encounter between political liberation and the communion of all men with God.

The specifically socialist character of the process and its goal is explicit:

> The underdevelopment of the poor countries, as an overall social fact, appears in its true light: as the historical by-product of the development of other countries. The dynamics of the capitalist economy lead to the establishment of a center and a periphery, simultaneously generating progress and growing wealth for the few and social imbalances, political tensions and poverty for the many.

The conclusion is clear: "autonomous Latin American development is not viable within the framework of the international capitalist system." The socialism he envisions is not, Gutiérrez writes, monolithic nor slavishly imitative of the socialist constructions of others. It will be a distinctively Latin American construction.

"Socialism" is presented more as a conceptual model than as a political or economic blueprint. There seems to be greater clarity regarding the role of nationalism in the liberation process, although nationalism is in this context really Latin American continentalism. "It is becoming more obvious that the revolutionary process ought to embrace the whole continent. There is little chance of success for attempts limited to a national scope." As the late Marxist theoretician György Lukacs noted (see "The Failure of Marxist Theory," *Worldview*, May, 1972), much Third World socialist language disguises an essentially nationalist impulse that is far removed from Marxist understandings of the revolutionary struggle. There is more than a hint in *A Theology of Liberation* that the nationalist impulse toward the Greater Latin America could result, as has happened elsewhere, in some kind of capitalist corporate state that would be quite capable of overcoming alienation through social solidarity. Thus it is possible that Gutiérrez's "Marxism" is more a matter of utilizing the language available among those who view themselves as engaged in the liberation struggle, and ought not, therefore, be interpreted in a literalistic fashion. If "the hope that is in" those whom he is addressing is framed in Marxist categories, then the "reason" for that hope must be similarly framed.

A passion for social solidarity can take many forms. In the utopia (not a pejorative term in Gutiérrez's vocabulary) toward which he presses the "social appropriation of freedom" is, as we have seen, "definitive" for Gutiérrez. When anyone projects a "new order" it is always well to look carefully at what he says about freedom. There is, of course, the individualistic idea of freedom which is the bad joke of laissez-faire exploitation. That is the well-known freedom that both rich and poor have the right to sleep under bridges. There is the equally well-known "socialist freedom" of totalitarian states. This is the freedom of those enslaved to official and "scientific" definitions of the historical process. Rejecting both those perverse notions of freedom, one looks for the clear analysis and affirmation of freedom that nourishes the dialectic between individual and community, between the existent and the possible, between present and future. In *A Theology of Liberation* such clarity is distressingly absent. All the more distressing because one would suppose that in a theology of *liberation* the idea of freedom, or liberty, would receive particularly careful attention.

Gutiérrez, to be sure, frequently alludes to freedom, and the language of liberation marks almost every sentence. He cites Hegel to the effect that "world history is the progression of the awareness of freedom." The process of liberation, he says, is indebted to Marx, who advanced beyond Hegel in pointing the way "from awareness of freedom to real freedom." This real freedom is gained "through the dialectical process [by which] man constructs himself and attains a real awareness of his own being; he liberates himself in the acquisition of genuine freedom which through work transforms the world and educates man." The "man" in question seems always to be collective man. "The gradual conquest of true freedom leads to the creation of a new man and a qualitatively different society." Even Bonhoeffer, whose resistance to totalist pretensions about establishing "new orders" needs no comment, is quoted to the effect that "Being free means being free for the other, because the other has bound me to him. Only in relationship with the other am I free." When dramatically different statements on freedom are cited, Gutiérrez is not provoked to examine the contradictions; freedom is invoked rather than defined. Gutiérrez inveighs against older "political theologies" which sought to restore a "Christian State." Such ideas, he writes, are "repressive and authoritarian." He seems curiously indifferent to the repressive and authoritarian potentialities within other forms of the state which assert, with an authority of religious intensity, the establishment of "new orders."

Thus *A Theology of Liberation* comes close to providing carte blanche legitimation for joining almost any allegedly revolutionary struggle to replace almost any allegedly repressive regime. The absence of conceptual clarity in the statement of the goal is matched by a deep obscurity about the means by which the goal is to be achieved. As of this writing, rumblings are traveling north from Latin American prelates who are accusing Gutiérrez and other "liberation theologians" of advocating violent revolution. No doubt Gutiérrez has opponents in high places who are profoundly conservative and understandably fearful of what he represents. Yet it is not possible, on the basis of *A Theology of Liberation*, to dismiss their criticisms as being motivated merely by conservative fear. There is in fact a deep and perhaps dangerous abstruseness about what precisely Gutiérrez is advocating.

There is no effort in *A Theology of Liberation* to weigh means and ends in the revolutionary struggle or to develop criteria by which the justice of a cause might be judged. I hold no ultimate brief for the "just war" criteria (see my "The Thorough Revolutionary" in *Movement and Revolution*), which no doubt have their limitations, but one does expect a theologian to at least suggest an alternative apparatus for critical ethical reflection. As it is, almost any struggle that fashions itself a liberation struggle is reinforced by Gutiérrez with all the moral warrants appropriate to Christ's work in the world.

The dialectic in Gutiérrez's argument might be strengthened by a stronger emphasis on the negative. Barrington Moore *(Reflections on the Causes of Human Misery)* writes on "the unity of misery and the diversity of happiness." He understands, in a way one misses in Gutiérrez, that radical efforts at social change are best directed toward the elimination of readily agreed upon miseries than toward the establishment of a much more elusive happiness. Projections of "a new man in a new society" are always deserving of the greatest suspicion. Relating this insight specifically to the Church's mission in the world, Dom Helder Camara of Brazil has suggested that the Church, in addressing itself to the social situation, must always say No. That is, the Church must protest evil and be sophisticated in its analysis of the roots of evil, but never offer a blueprint for the new order, nor open-ended moral legitimation for those who might propose such a blueprint.

In this way the Christian community is captive neither to the prevailing order nor to those who would overthrow it. It neither keeps silent about injustice nor does it apotheosize particular manifestations of the revolutionary struggle. This is not to be confused with a course of neutrality or of standing above the battle. It is not a refusal to choose. It is clear choice against clear evil. It is courageous refusal, in view of the modesty appropriate to our placement in history, to absolutize any alternative to the Kingdom, anything short of the Kingdom. *A Theology of Liberation*, on the other hand, comes very close to being an indiscriminate apotheosis of diverse revolutionary struggles, at least in Latin America.

It must be said, in fairness to Gutiérrez, that he seems to sense this danger, and his writing reflects a certain uneasiness about being misunderstood. On one page he makes statements of absolutist rigidity, but then, a few pages on or perhaps in a footnote, he urges the reader to keep in mind the variety of ways in which God may be working today in history. Ringing "Lo heres" in the text are frequently tempered by "maybes" in the footnotes. At times the struggle for the control of the means of production is unequivocally equated with faithfulness to Christ, but then we are cautioned that the new society cannot yet be defined and, at one point, that the just society is not, in any case, the same thing as the Kingdom.

There seem almost to be two Gutiérrezes. The one quotes Fanon and Che Guevara almost as scripture, proclaiming we are on the edge of a "revolutionary anthropophany" in which historically inexorable forces are creating "the new man in the new society" (the slogan appears with distressing regularity). The second Gutiérrez comes out of the closet in the notes, carefully positioning his arguments in relation to the larger theological and political discourse both of the past and of the international community. He cautions the reader against understanding what he has just said as what he has just said.

In criticizing another thinker, Gutiérrez says at one point: "We believe that the danger is not averted simply by noting its presence." It is an astute observation, and one that is applicable to Gutiérrez's own writing. Gutiérrez's qualifications of his own pronunciamentos are reassuring in that they anticipate the reader's objections to some of his more sweeping generalizations, but adding qualifications is not enough. It reveals the author's intelligent ambivalence about simple assertions on complex topics, but it does not result in the systematic achievement that the author intended and others have claimed to find in *A Theology of Liberation*.

Such a systematic treatment requires a much more searching examination of the presuppositions in current, usually Marxist, languages of liberation. The reason for Gutiérrez's frequent failure to undertake such an examination is perhaps to be discovered in what might be called his pastoral intention in *A Theology of Liberation*. He clearly believes the revolutionaries hold the cards that will shape the Latin American future, and he may well be right. He is admittedly unhappy that many leaders of the liberation struggle are alienated from Christianity. He wants to offer them an explicitly Christian theoretical framework within which their revolutionary commitment might be understood, strengthened and communicated. Theology, we are told again and again, is reflection on the *praxis* of the liberation process. Perhaps it is his pastoral desire to identify with that process that gets in the way of his offering a theology that exercises critical resources for evaluating and redirecting that *praxis*. The necessary tension between Christ and that part of culture that is the liberation struggle is relaxed, and sometimes completely collapsed.

When the pastoral intention leads to a collapse of tension,

the result is the chaplaincy syndrome. Criticism is suspended in order better to "minister." The search for rapport distorts the perception of reality. The comfort/challenge dialectic of the Christian message can be diffused also when one is comforting the challengers. The chaplaincy syndrome, in its more advanced stage, is a late prelate ministering to U.S. troops in Vietnam, assuring them they are the "soldiers of Christ." It is the professional ethicist ministering to the medical researchers, offering situational legitimations for most anything they can get a financial grant to do. To be sure, the Church has usually provided chaplains to comfort the comfortable. That *A Theology of Liberation* might help right the imbalance is no little merit. But the real need is to break out of the chaplaincy syndrome.

The chaplain to the National Union of Catholic University Students does not intend by this book simply to call more Christians to chaplaincy on the other side of the barricades. He calls rather for the Church as such to position itself in the lines of the liberation struggle. Obviously, any call to radical commitment will be divisive, disturbing the suprahistorical tranquility that many look for in the life of the Church. A healthy Christian community is one in which different and often conflicting views and commitments are not only openly admitted but celebrated. Within the sure bond of Christ a restless community interacts around disparate and always provisional sightings of the Kingdom's coming. This is the lively interaction that too many churchmen fear and try to mute in the name of Christian unity.

Yet Gutiérrez too seems to fear the radical disparity within Christian perceptions of God's purposes in history. The tensions are collapsed, the conflicts resolved, by calling the Church to choose one side. Gutiérrez, too, appeals to Christian unity. Real unity, he writes, requires division; it means pressing the class struggle in order to "build a socialist society, more just, free, and human, and not a society of superficial and false reconciliation and equality." Is there not, however, something "superficial" and "false" about a reconciliation that is merely a reconciliation among radicals? Of course a merely formal unity that seeks to contain conflicting elements can be profoundly dishonest. But there is nothing superficial or false about Paul's vision of the

Church, where in Christ Jesus "There is neither Jew nor Greek, there is neither slave nor free, there is neither male nor female," and, we might add, there is neither bourgeoisie nor proletariat (Galatians 3:28). To welcome and celebrate the particularity of each member, and yet to affirm that that particularity does not define or restrict one's status in the community—that is the challenge to be the Church and the answer to "superficial and false reconciliation."

Gutiérrez, on the other hand, suggests that the Church can no longer be a meeting place where understanding can be sought, ideas shared and communion celebrated among those on opposite sides of the barricades. The Church must decide, it must make an unambiguously partisan commitment. "The Gospel announces the love of God for all people and calls us to love as he loves. But to accept class struggle means to decide for some people and against others." (It is not much help when "the second Gutiérrez" adds: "This is a challenge that leads the Christian to deepen his faith and to mature in his love for others.") One's impression is that Gutiérrez's vision is not that of the Church renewed but simply that of the Church switching sides.

A Theology of Liberation is an important book. It will no doubt be a major point of reference in the further development of liberation theologies, not only in Latin America, but also in other Third World countries and in the United States. We can, unfortunately, expect that Gutiérrez's work will be put down by two apparently conflicting but symbiotic forms of condescension. The first is the arrogant condescension of North Americans and Western Europeans who applaud the new boy in the class who surprises everybody with his familiarity with the literature and very scholarly critical apparatus. The second is the romantic condescension of those who have made a faith commitment to the proposition that "salvation comes from the Third World" and therefore accept as the new gospel any militant echoes of their own vocal disillusionment with themselves and their culture. It would be as easy as it would be false to import theologies of liberation as adrenalin to stimulate the North American theological enterprise in this its period of pervasive boredom. Neither condescension can respond adequately to Gustavo Gutiérrez and his search for theological restatement in a time of high confusion.

Speaking at the opening of the Thomas Merton Life Center in New York City, Daniel Berrigan recently remarked that, unlike many who see themselves as radicals, he has no taste for nurturing or exporting anti-Americanism. "In my sympathy with liberation struggles elsewhere, I never forget that I am an American and a Christian. I want to be as indigenous to my culture as they are to theirs." It is an exercise in false consciousness for North American Christians to parrot liberation theologies that are born, through much suffering, from situations dramatically different from our own. Our task, inspired by thinkers such as Gustavo Gutiérrez, is to apply ourselves to the North American experience, trying to reshape it in a way that might result in a more fulfilling society here and a society that is less oppressive, if not liberating, for our brothers and sisters to the south. Reshaping the North American experience means breathing new life into culturally formative metaphors such as accountability to the poor, covenant responsibility, and an empathy that makes us vulnerable to the yearning of the oppressed. When the radically empathic Jesus of the rich encounters the revolutionary Jesus of the poor we may all be liberated from his cultural captivity--and ours.

II: Latin American Perspectives

The Hope of Liberation

Gustavo Gutiérrez

Continuing the discussion—and responding to some criticism—of his book *A Theology of Liberation* (Orbis Books, 1973), Gustavo Gutiérrez calls for new ways of thinking theologically, for making "a qualitative leap—the radical challenging of a social order and its ideology and the breaking with old ways of knowing." Gutiérrez distinguishes "the theology of liberation from theologies such as those of development, revolution and violence, to which it is at times connected and even erroneously reduced." The context of liberation, he says, "changes our way of doing theology. We do not stand before new fields of application for old theological notions; rather we stand before the challenge and need to live out and think through faith in different sociocultural categories. . . . This context obliges us to rethink radically our being Christian and our being Church." Fr. Gutiérrez is professor of theology at the Catholic University of Peru in Lima, and was the Henry Luce Visiting Professor at Union Theological Seminary, New York, in 1976-77. His essay is from the June 1974 issue of *Worldview*, published in New York City by the Council on Religion and International Affairs.

The resistance of those who persist in maintaining old ways of thinking theologically and their accusations that the faith is being distorted are reminiscent of the opposition to the use of Aristotelian philosophy in theology. Notwithstanding the unfounded alarms and episodic condemnations these protests might provoke in the present, they, like their predecessors, have no future.

The future is in the hands of a faith which has no fear of the advances in thought and no fear of the social practice of man, a faith which allows itself to be interrogated by these phenomena, but also challenges them, a faith which is enriched but does not submit acritically.

Such a task is complex and must have recourse to multiple specialties, to a serious knowledge of the different facets—both philosophical and scientific—of contemporary thought. It is a task of understanding the faith which can be undertaken only from within historical praxis, from within the place where people struggle to be able to live like human beings. It is a task inspired by hope in Him who, by revealing himself, reveals man in all the fullness within him, a task inspired by hope in the Lord of history, in whom all things were and by whom all things were saved.

Commitment to the process of liberation introduces Christians into a world quite unfamiliar to them and forces them to make what we have called a qualitative leap—the radical challenging of a social order and of its ideology and the breaking with old ways of knowing ("epistemological rupture"). For this reason theological reflections carried out in another cultural context say very little to them. Such reflections transmit the consciousness which preceding Christian generations had of their faith. Their expressions are a reference point for these committed Christians; they do not, however, rescue them from their theological orphanhood, because such expressions do not speak to them in the strong, clear and incisive language which corresponds to the human and Christian experience which they are living.

But, simultaneously, the buds of a new type of understanding of the faith are emerging within these same experiences. In them we have learned how to link knowing and transforming, theory and practice. A rereading of the Gospel forces itself upon us. And in this rereading we will discover something traditional, authentically traditional—and perhaps therefore forgotten by more recent "traditions": The Gospel truth is done! We must work the truth, John tells us, and that truth is love. To live love is to affirm God. To believe in God is not to limit ourselves to affirming his existence; to believe in God is to commit our lives to Him and to all people. To have faith is to go out of ourselves and to give ourselves to God and others. Faith works through charity, as Paul makes clear.

Faith thus appears to us ever more as a liberating praxis. Faith—the acceptance of, and the response to, the love of the Father—goes to the deepest root of social injustice, namely, sin, the sundering of friendship with God and of fellowship among human beings. But it will not reach this depth by sidestepping historical mediations, by avoiding the sociopolitical analyses of these historical realities. Sin occurs in the negation of man as a brother, in oppressive structures created for the benefit of the few and for the exploitation of peoples, races and social classes. Sin is fundamental alienation which, because it is such, cannot be reached in itself; it occurs only in concrete, historical situations, in particular alienations.

Sin requires a radical liberation, but this necessarily includes a liberation of a political nature. Only by participating militantly and effectively in the historical process of liberation will it be possible for us to discern the fundamental alienation present in every partial alienation. This radical liberation is the gift which Christ brings. By his death and resurrection he redeems us from sin and from all its consequences. As the Latin American bishops assembled at Medellin said:

> It is the same God who, in the fulness of time, sends his son so that, made flesh, he might come to liberate all men from *all* the enslavements to which sin has subjected them —ignorance, misery, hunger and oppression, in a word, injustice and hatred, which have their origin in human selfishness.

To have faith is to accept the gratuitous gift of divine sonship. The mystery hidden from all time and revealed now is the love of the Father which makes us sons in his Son. The Son was made man and thereby transforms men into brothers. Sonship and brotherhood require each other. By working to make brothers of all men we accept, not in word, but in work, the gift of sonship. To struggle against all injustice, despoliation and exploitation, to commit ourselves to the creation of a more brotherly and human society, is, in a single act, both to live the love of the Father and to witness to it.

But, as we have already noted, political action has its own demands and its own laws. To recall the profound meaning which this action has for a Christian is something very different from taking a leap backward toward stages in which man was unable to understand the internal mechanisms of an oppressive society and political action had not yet come of age. To accept the gift of divine sonship by working to make all men brothers will be no more than a phrase, useless except to satisfy ourselves with the nobility of our ideal, unless we live this sonship daily (and amid conflict) in history, unless we translate it into a real identification with the interests of people who suffer oppression by other people and with the struggles of the exploited classes, unless we make use of the instruments offered us by the social sciences for understanding those social realities which deny the justice and brotherhood which we seek.

In this context, theology will be a critical reflection in and on historical praxis in confrontation with the word of the Lord lived and accepted in faith. It will be a reflection in and on faith as liberating praxis. It will be an understanding of a faith which has as its starting point a commitment to create a just and human society, a faith which should enable this commitment to become more radical and fuller. It will be an understanding of a faith which is made truth, is verified, in a real and fruitful insertion into the process of liberation. To reflect on faith as liberating praxis is to reflect on a truth which is done and is not only affirmed. In the last instance our exegesis of the word, to which theology hopes to contribute, occurs in deed. The creation of fellowship among human beings is the acceptance of the gratuitous gift of sonship. It is to live in and through Christ and his Spirit.

The context of liberation changes our way of doing theology. We do not stand before new fields of application for old theological notions; rather we stand before the challenge and need to live out and think through faith in different sociocultural categories. Such a challenge has occurred before in the history of the Christian community. It always has given rise to fear and anxiety. But in the quest we are driven by the urgent need to say the word of the Lord in our everyday words.

This approach distinguishes the theology of liberation from theologies such as those of development, revolution and violence, to which it is at times connected and even erroneously reduced. With regard to these theologies, the theology of liberation is characterized not only by its different analyses of reality and its more comprehensive and radical political options, but above all by its differences in the theological task itself. The theology of liberation does not try to justify in a Christian way postures already taken; it does not yearn to be a revolutionary Christian ideology. Rather it seeks to think through the faith from the starting point of the way it is lived within the commitment to liberation. Therefore its themes are the great themes of all true theology, but the focus, the way of approaching them, is different. Its relationship to historical praxis is different. To say that the theology of liberation does not hope to be a revolutionary Christian ideology is not to assert that it is unrelated to the revolutionary process. On the contrary, its starting point is precisely its insertion into this process, and it tries to assist this process in becoming more radical and more comprehensive. This will be done by situating the political commitment to liberation within the perspective of the gratuitous gift of Christ's total liberation.

Christ's liberation is not reduced to political liberation, but it occurs in liberating historical events. It is not possible to bypass these mediations. On the other hand, political liberation is not a religious messianism; it has its autonomy and its own laws. It supposes social analyses and well-determined political options. But to see human history as a history in which Christ's liberation is at work enlarges our perspective and gives to what is involved in political commitment its full depth and its true meaning. We are not speaking of facile and impoverishing equations or of simplistic and distorting reductions of one liberation to the other, but rather of an illumination and of reciprocal and fruitful demands.

The theology of liberation is a theology of salvation in the concrete historical and political circumstances of today. These present-day historical and political mediations, evaluated by this theology itself, change the experience of, and the reflection on, the mystery hidden from all times and now revealed, that is, the Father's love and human fellowship—salvation. This change is what the term *liberation* hopes to make "present."

A theological reflection in the context of liberation starts from the perception that this context obliges us to rethink radically our being Christian and our being Church. In this reflection we will have recourse to the different expressions of contemporary human reason, to the human sciences, and not to philosophy alone. But above all we will refer to historical praxis in a new way. This historical praxis is a liberating praxis. It is an identification with persons, specifically, the interests and conflicts of those social classes which suffer misery and exploitation. It is an insertion into the political process of liberation, in order to live and to announce Christ's liberating love from within that process. And his love goes to the very root of all exploitation and injustice—the sundering of friendship with God and among human beings.

But we definitely will not have an authentic theology of liberation until the oppressed themselves can freely and creatively express themselves in society and among the poeple of God, until they are the artisans of their own liberation, until they account with their own values for that hope of total liberation which they bear within them.

Evangelization and Cultural Liberation

Segundo Galilea

Defining the missionary as "one who leaves his culture in order to proclaim the Gospel in a different culture," Father Segundo Galilea, a pastoral theologian, maintains that the missionary must reject "both cultural domination and blind cultural assimilation." "Authentic mission," he says, "implies a *cultural exchange,* a giving and a receiving." In Latin America this calls for helping "to devise a radically Latin American way of development and liberation," together with evangelization, "in the way proposed by Christ." Fr. Galilea until recently was director of pastoral studies at the Pastoral Institute of CELAM (Latin America Episcopal Conference) in Medellín. He is now doing pastoral work in his native Chile. This article is part of a longer essay that first appeared in English in *Teaching All Nations* (1975/1 & 2), which is published in Manila, Philippines, by the East Asian Pastoral Institute.

For the Third World, and particularly for Latin America (which belongs to the Western cultural family), one of the most disastrous consequences of the economic and eventually social and political dependence is cultural dependence and alienation. Unfortunately, the Medellín Conference (August 1968) did not pay enough attention to this matter. Such an oversight is reflected in subsequent currents of theological thinking and in the Christian concern vis-à-vis liberation and commitment. Moreover this lacuna was strongly influenced by political ideologies, especially Marxist, which neglect or even sacrifice the cultural dimension in favor of the socio-political or economic concern.

The growing cultural alienation in Latin America is obvious. Its most alarming symptoms seem to be the following:

1. The adoption of development patterns which are alien or

unsuited to the social cultural reality of our peoples. Mainly through the mass media, such models are imposed by the "developed" countries for the benefit of their economic imperialism. Such an imposition fosters pseudo-values, foreign to the local culture, and activates frustrating and alienating aspirations. This pseudo-development increases our dependence and does not foster growth in the proper cultural line. Instead it fosters growth along the lines of the capitalistic-bourgeois ideology in most cases. In the case of Cuba, it fostered growth along the lines of Marxist-Leninist ideology.

2. In other words, there is an ideological-cultural imposition accompanying the imposed model of development. Even in institutions which consider themselves popular, the peculiar way of the people is not being sufficiently discerned. By this we are criticizing the Latin-American Left and singling out an intrinsic cause for their failures. This also implies a negative criticism of strategic plans—such as armed subversion—and of certain serious neglect of "popular" ideologies. Popular religiosity is a case in point.

3. All this forces the Latin American people to life-styles which are both inconsistent and alienating. Their authentic values are not appreciated, become obsolete and the end-result is a loss of cultural and national identity.

4. In extreme cases—like that of indigenous tribes and other marginal minority races—this form of dependence is leading to a cultural genocide.

Confronted with this serious situation, it is necessary to devise a radically Latin American way of development and liberation. This imperative appears today all the more obvious because of the historical developments of the recent past in which there is a tendency to re-evaluate the cultural dimension. At the same time, politics, or rather political parties and their prestige are in real crisis. This is a fact almost without exception in the Latin American continent. There is also a "dead point" in the true participation in power by the people. Even in governments of a socialist orientation, the power of the state—increasingly more centralized—would at best be "at the service" of the people but without the people's decisively sharing in the power.

This political diagnosis applies both to the capitalistic and socialist systems—to the point of surprising convergence. In a more or less overt or subtle form, there is a tendency to form a dominant state which relies on the so-called "military-industrial complex," and at times also on a one-party system. The problem of power and the "idolatry of power" is a grave one in Latin America today both as a cultural question and as a requirement for liberation. From the point of view of this general trend, Brazil and Cuba—at the opposite extremes of the ideological spectrum—are astonishingly similar.

Faced with such a situation, the model of a just society in the continent is still to be devised. And for this task, the free expression and the appreciation of cultural values at all levels of society, especially those of the most oppressed and voiceless, appear as indispensable.

The quiet and native genius of these oppressed and silent peoples has already created a folklore, a popular religiosity. They have also been able to defend, no matter what, their own life-styles. They will, we can be sure, use the same genius to create —within the context of their cultural liberation—new and viable social and political expressions towards a better and more equitable society.

This cultural liberation is perhaps all the more difficult, because it has to do with an "ethos" and with a change of mentality. There is nothing more sensitive about a culture than its growth through its own values, by self-criticism and self-transformation. There is nothing as difficult as liberating a mentality. This involves the whole problem of conscientization, which is often being caricatured or used as ideological politicization. Political imposition and cultural oppression remain permanent dangers threatening an authentic conscientization. This consists in passing from a mentality which is uncritical, conformist and characterized by a complex of cultural infidelity, to a creative attitude which is in contact with its own identity, conscious and critical of every subtle form of cultural or politico-ideological alienation.

Christianity—the Church—through the values which it transmits by evangelizing, possesses the ethical ingredient for genuine conscientization, and thus, for a true cultural liberation. This is the attitude of a people who take up their own changes and their historical vocation as their own task and project, using their own values as the *point of departure*. These values, and that vocation to liberate the creativity of a culture—the dream of a people—are stimulated by the Gospel. As the Gospel is not tied to any particular cultural form or ideology, it is capable of accompanying from within the liberation of a culture, unifying it without alienation ("Gaudium et Spes" 58).

This is evangelization at its ideal. For that, Catholicism itself must exercise a permanent self-critique in its historical context and in the concrete effects of its message, since there is a permanent temptation for it to identify itself with the dominant cultures and the existing ideologies. When this happens, decadent forms of Christianity are transmitted and enter into subtle complicity with those cultures or ideologies, slowing down liberation instead of stimulating it. This evokes the whole problem of liberating evangelization. The Latin American Church is today only too conscious of this task.

Such an authentic evangelization, by its very nature, will lend a special dynamism to people as free agents of their own Christian vocation along the lines of a given culture. Christianity communicates the ultimate and profound sense of the dignity and value of peoples and cultures by revealing the presence of Christ in each person and of the "seeds of the Word" in each culture. Further, in proclaiming that the salvation of individuals—and of cultures—takes place in history, it communicates to the peoples the fundamental reason for their historic responsibility, bringing them to a dynamism of growth and commitment. By criticizing the prevailing ideologies and cultures—to the extent that Christianity itself has managed to liberate itself from them— by criticizing power as well as the models and strategies of a materialistic and de-humanizing development, Christianity overcomes the radical obstacles. It thus paves the way for the cultural liberation of human beings.

Missionaries and Culture

The task of accompanying the growth of a culture with a purifying prophetic attitude both liberating and transforming, is a very delicate enterprise. In fact, the history of the Christian mission shows us that the encounter of the Gospel with new cultures always resulted in something as paradoxical as it was astonishing. On the one hand evangelization assumed and respected—to a very relative degree according to the case—the new cultures.

In Latin America, the formation of an Indo-American popular Catholicism is proof of this. But on the other hand, evangelization both baffled and unsettled the cultures. Surprisingly one could bring apparently contradictory accusations against the missionary activity. It has excessively acculturized Christianity (popular folkloric or syncretistic forms of the Indo-American Catholicism) and/or has demolished or dominated local culture (the various indigenous groups of the Caribbean).

That is why we are dealing with a delicate problem inasmuch as both results take place simultaneously and dialectically. A balanced approach to it must be sought in what we have already called the liberation of a culture "from within." This makes the problem all the more serious for the "evangelizers" who come from other cultures—as happens in the Third World countries. Today the cultural problem is the most acute for a missionary. We could even say that the very concept of missionary has changed: from the concept of someone who went to the pagans to that of one who leaves his culture in order to proclaim the Gospel in a different culture. This new view is overcoming—at least in the West—the old distinction between "mission territories" and "Christian countries." We can today speak about "mission among the workers," "mission in Catholic countries"— as it is in Latin America, "mission in the Andes" (even though all the indigenous people there may be Christians).

In the missionary who goes from one culture to another, the whole problematic of the Church vis-à-vis cultural liberation takes flesh in a concrete person. The abstract temptations of evangelization in any culture become in him personal temptations. The danger of his communicating his own ideals and his own cultural values as necessarily linked with Christianity, demands of him a form of conversion and of "kenosis." Such a conversion and "emptying" go far beyond his good-will and imply a special charism and a pastoral and cultural training. The tragedy of the missionary is that his action may well be a two-edged sword: he can do much good or much evil, depending on his attitude towards the local churches and cultures.

There is also the opposite temptation. That is, the missionary may completely abandon the values of his own culture and understand evangelization as an acculturation so radical, that he may end up assuming "the sins" (the defects) of the culture to which he is sent. And he may do this without bringing any prophetic and questioning element. In other words, the danger is that his cultural incarnation may eliminate the ultimate reason for his missionary presence. This is why I feel that the missionary-culture relationship is infinitely complex. What we as "cultures to be evangelized" reject in the name of the very nature of the Gospel is *cultural domination.* Very often such cultures are politically and sociologically weaker than those of the missionary. A typical example is the evangelization of America by Charles V's Spain. Cultural domination means that Christian forms that alienate an identity and hinder its liberation are imposed on a people. Further impositions in the form of ideologies of "development"—tending to become "ideological" Christianity—in the name and for the sake of human promotion may ensue. This amounts to a dominating and forced integration—which takes little account of the prevailing culture which may reject such a foreign transplant.

Authentic mission implies a *cultural exchange,* a giving and a receiving. Neither the culture of the missionary nor that of the "missionized" is perfect. Both have their values. Both are limited. Certainly both have complementary and mutually enriching aspects. The same must be said of the way in which Christianity is lived. Therefore, we can affirm with the assurance that the centuries-old missionary experience of the Church gives us, that there is no such thing as culturally pure local churches whose Christianity would be the result of their "locality" alone without any external influences. And we believe that this is positive and enriching both in the cultural as well as in the Christian level. Thus today, the Spanish Church is not "pure Spanish" but all the way from its conversion to Christianity it has undergone varied influence from the Gauls, Africans, the Nordics, Romans, and later Americans. The Church of Rome is not "Rome" but the result of Byzantine, Gaelic, Mozarabic and other influences. The same has happened with the Latin American Church. The only difference is that in the Third World this interchange and mutually beneficial enrichment has been radically ambiguous since the process historically took place within a colonial context of cultural domination, which we are still trying to correct.

A typical case of this ambiguous interchange-domination is the phenomenon of the *evangelization of the Latin American*

popular religiosity. In the foreign missionary we can detect two
attitudes which have been very prominent especially in the
pastoral context of the last 25 years. The first attitude—reinforced by many local people who have studied in Europe—is
one of radical critique. He questions and discounts a form of
Catholicism which is ritualistic, devotional, baroque, and without
a sufficient social and temporal dimension (at least apparently).
This is a religion, he feels, which alienates and encourages
escapism from the task of development and liberation; a form
of "religion of poverty." Pastorally speaking, he feels one should
not bother with such a religiosity; it should be left to die a
natural death, since, anyway, development and social revolution
will do away with it. In contrast with such an attitude there is
a consensus today among the evangelizers who are most lucid
and who are truly one with the people in criticism of the previous
position for its cultural Western and European bias and its
"bourgeois Christian" point of departure. They see this as
another form of cultural imposition and of domination by a
European type of Christianity. Their own efforts, in the name of
popular culture and of its autochthonous genius which has created
that form of Catholicism as its own, are made to re-appreciate
it—though critically—as the expression of a deeply respectable
cultural identity. This understanding from within, elaborated
in non-Western cultural categories, leads them to re-interpret
many attitudes which at first glance seemed to be alienating and
far from the movement of liberation. Thus, an evaluation of
popular religiosity is emerging which does not proceed from
"our" cultural categories or Christian expressions, but from
"their" culture, meanings and scale of values.

Thus humanization and liberation of human beings in the
way proposed by Christ become the criterion of such an evaluation, as it is the criterion of evangelization.

The Force of Right,
or the Right of Force?

Dom Helder Camara

Upon the occasion of receiving an honorary Doctor of Laws degree from Harvard University in June 1974—for his defense of human rights—Dom Helder Camara, the Archbishop of Olinda and Recife in Brazil, suggested that a pessimist today would point to "the mockery of a doctorate in Law . . . in a world increasingly dominated by force, by violence, by fraud, by injustice, by avarice—in a word, by egoism." The Archbishop, however, affirmed his "faith in the force of right," and urged universities such as Harvard to encourage students and staff to work "for a world where justice and love open the way for an authentic and lasting peace," and to change "the structures that oppress more than two-thirds of humanity." He warned those "who decide to defend the Law" of the problems they will face, but concluded with the "conviction that one day the force of Right will conquer the pretended right of force." His address was published in *Christianity and Crisis* (New York) for August 5, 1974, and is reprinted by permission.

Within us dwell together an optimist and a pessimist. When the pessimist who lives in me—and who nearly always remains hidden, asleep or silent for want of courage—learned that your university, numbered among the greatest of your country and of the world, would bestow on me the Honorary Doctor of Law degree, he laughed.

He questioned me, asking if I had not yet discovered the

farce, the mockery of a doctorate in Law, when Law is ever more a hollow word, resonant but empty, in a world increasingly dominated by force, by violence, by fraud, by injustice, by avarice—in a word, by egoism.

It seemed to me that the best way to thank you for your kindness would be to listen courageously to the tirades that the pessimist poured forth against the Law, so that in the end the 300 of Gideon—the Abrahamic Minorities scattered by the Spirit of God throughout the world—will be strengthened still more in the decision to spend their lives in such a way that the force of Right might conquer the pretended right of force.

This, in synthesis, is what the pessimist stated regarding the conclusive defeat and banishment of Law in today's world. Amid sardonic laughter, these were the questions he asked:

—Is the doctorate in Constitutional Law? Does your blindness prevent your seeing the multiplying of constitutions that are torn up or used for scratch paper? Who is not aware of existing governments that proclaim themselves above and beyond the Law—omniscient, omnipotent, infallible, divine?

—Is the doctorate in Civil Law? But who does not know that the statute books are used to defend the privileges both of minorities in rich countries who exploit racism and create areas of poverty and of wealthy groups in destitute countries? And who doesn't know that the statute books are permitting the progressive and rapid increase of oppressed people who continue being swept towards ghettos, without work, without health, without instruction, without diversion and, not rarely, without God?

—Is Penal Law the area of your doctorate? Penal Law that establishes or restores the death penalty as if men were masters of life? Penal Law that at the dawn of the 21st century maintains prisons, veritable cages in which sons and daughters of God are detained like tigers or panthers, thus confessing the failure of psychology and of pedagogy? Penal Law at whose margin, throughout the world, persists terrorism in response to terrorism —or to what it pleases to call terrorism? Penal Law that neither disappears, nor hides, nor commits suicide upon seeing that tortures persist throughout the world—tortures comparable to the most abject practices of the worst inquisitions?

—Would the doctorate be in International Law? Poor International Law, which didn't know how to prevent the injustices of international trade politics from bringing our century to its terrible balance—with more than two-thirds of humanity in situations of misery, of hunger, of subhuman life? Sad International Law, which recognizes its impotence before the most skillful manipulations of the multinational macrocorporations—seemingly destined to be the empires of tomorrow—and of the ideological systems and the actual superpowers of the right and the left?

The pessimist who resides in me—and, as I said, who nearly always remains hidden or silent or sleeping—hearing of my doctorate in Law, did not cease his ironic, malicious, perverse questioning.

—Is it in Agrarian Law or, indeed, already in Spacial Law? While man, even now, is uprooting himself from the earth and heading for the stars, the world balance in the situation of agrarian reform remains shameful: Today's powerful rural landowners continue to live at the cost of misery for unhappy pariahs. Where modern technology achieves marvels from the earth with an ever-reduced number of rural workers, those not needed in the fields live sublives in depressing slums on the outskirts of nearly all the large cities.

As for Spacial Law, which might begin passionately, it is incredible—judging in the heights—that it initiates the same greed, the same divisions, the same conflicts that rendered the earth inhuman.

The most cruel laughter, the strongest mockery, came when the pessimist asked if my doctorate would be in Human Rights. He challenged me to indicate even one of the human rights that is not stepped on, not demoralized, not ridiculed.

On written texts there can be found the four fundamental freedoms presented by your President Roosevelt in his message of January 6, 1941 to the Congress of the United States: freedom of speech and of expression; freedom for all human persons to pray to God in a manner that suits them; freedom from want; freedom from fear.

The four fundamental freedoms—portrayed so brilliantly on

paper—soar like mockery, like jeers for the absolute majority of humanity. If we select any one of the particular rights, we will encounter the same sadness as that caused by the beautiful and most human right: the right to work. In countries that produce raw materials, the phantasm is that of subwork leading to sublife. In industrialized countries, the specter of unemployment begins to thrive—fruit of the egoistic application of automation or of the greed of multinationals that export entire factories to paradises of investment where salaries are low and dispute impossible.

The pessimist exposes the naivete of revising the 30 fundamental rights or of joining to them new rights unless the United Nations decide—which they would never do—to transform the mere Universal "Declaration" of Human Rights to a "Commandment" of Rights, accompanied by adequate sanctions for transgressors.

And the pessimist concludes: If Law always ends up having to appeal to force, why not close at once the schools of law and open schools of war.

In spite of the fact that there exists truth in all of the pessimist's questions, permit me to record the principal reasons that justify our act of faith in the force of Right. I believe in a Creator and Father, who desired man as co-Creator and who gave man intelligence and a creative imagination to dominate the universe and to complete the Creation. The Creator, in order to help man, desired that his own Son be made man; and he constantly sends his Spirit to make the human mind fruitful, even as he made the waters fertile at the beginning of Creation.

Permit me to propose here a suggestion for study that—who knows—might be caught up, accepted by some university or some institute in the West or the East, in the North or the South. Researches multiply constantly. Many are of indisputable scientific value; but many are bizarre.

Is it not true that within all countries—of all races, of all religions and of all human groups—there are minorities who, with the greatest sincerity and even at great sacrifice, if necessary, desire to construct a world that is more breathable, more just, more human? If Harvard University, with all scientific rigor, examined its various rosters—of students, of professors, of researchers, of technicians—it would have the surprise of verifying that there is not one of these lists without such minorities determined to fight in a peaceful, but resolute and valid, manner for a world where justice and love open the way for an authentic and lasting peace. And if Harvard continued its study in other universities or in any institutions or human groups, I do not hesitate to affirm that the study would give a scientific base to what we see, we hear, we touch in our travels throughout the world.

Harvard, if it wished, might also substantiate that which is known empirically: Determined minorities can catalyse a good part of those people of good will who conform through a desire to avoid complications but who are capable of awakening to a personal critical conscience that egoism manages to divert but not destroy.

What I am looking for among youth is a new type of leadership for tomorrow, capable of uniting—while in no way unifying —these minorities. I come searching for youth who will discover the secret of joining the diverse minorities around primary goals, with all groups sharing the common denominator of desiring— without violence, but with determination—the change of the structures that oppress more than two-thirds of humanity.

The minorities will keep their own names, their own leaders, their own specific objectives. They will not be transformed into new political parties or new religious sects. But they will be impetuous waters, stirred by the breath of God's Spirit.

It is a sad sign of the times that we are obliged to remember that the right to engage in research such as this may not exist for universities that—self-destructively—stoop to the baseness of using results of research for purges, as unhappily occurs not only under dictatorships of the right or left but also in pseudodemocracies turned shortsighted by obsessions such as anti-Communism.

Some Warnings

There are important warnings for the minorities who decide

to defend the Law. Let us remember some of the more urgent and current.

—Beware of allegations of "internal problems" that cannot be discussed abroad—under penalty of accusations of betrayal or of distorting the image of the country.

Let us clarify that there are no longer problems that can be contained within the limits of a country. Radio and television bring to the entire world all important happenings—even in the farthest island or in the least developed country.

And how can one speak of "internal problems" in an era of multinational macrocorporations? Let us also note the pharisaism existing in this regard. When Solzhenitsyn denounces injustices and atrocities committed by Russia, he is rightly hailed a hero in the Occident. But woe to Solzhenitsyn had he been born on this side and had the audacity to denounce the injustices of our regimes—in no way minor to those committed by Russia and by China, but only more sophisticated.

—Beware of the distorted allegations of "national security." Clearly, it is the right and duty of the government to guarantee national security. But in some countries in the name of national security are committed arbitrary acts and atrocities worthy of the worst days of Hitler and Stalin.

—Beware of the makers of arms and the makers of wars. Wars become ever more cowardly and absurd. After the monstrous mistake of the war in Viet Nam, how much longer will we subject our best youth to the tremendous dilemma of killing or of dying—with the hypothesis of return in utter demolition or of retreat to drugs?

For how long will we abstain from choosing the clear alternative of contributing towards the abolition of misery from the entire earth—as the decisive point of departure for an authentic human promotion—and continue to watch an arms race that can lead to the annihilation of life upon the face of the earth?

Why do we still wait to recognize—officially—misery as the bloodiest of wars when statistics prove that misery deforms and kills more people than nuclear or biochemical war?

—Beware of those who urge immediate, total, political decolonization of the world without courage to recognize, openly and clearly, that without economic independence, mere political independence means almost nothing.

—Beware of escape mechanisms, conscious or not, such as that of demographic explosion. Some, with the best of intentions, start from a real evil—like the dizzying population growth in certain areas—but end by reducing to this item the responsibility for underdevelopment and misery. Let us not permit the demographic explosion to lead us to forget the tremendous injustices in international trade policies—the root of an evil that consciously or not many try to forget or to leave in the background.

—Beware, especially, of a very serious sign—and here I think, above all, of the admirable youth of today's world: the danger that after the enthusiasm, the dedication without limits, the commitment during university days, they will reach the phase of installation in life, of conformism, of bourgeoisieism, of the death of ideals.

Gestures such as this one of your university commit me more and more to the peaceful fight for justice, to the courageous defense of human rights.

The doctorate with which you honor me brings me to ask of God that at this point of life, I do not betray the confidence of youth, and that I spend myself to the end in the service of humanity—as the most secure means of giving glory to our Lord.

God permit that the symbol of my life be a candle that burns itself, that spends itself, that consumes itself while there is still wax to burn; when nothing more remains to be consumed, that my flame, yet an instant, dare to remain alive and afoot, to rumble after, happy in the conviction that one day the force of Right will conquer the pretended right of force.

That The World May Believe

Mortimer Arias

Confessing "with shame that evangelism has been the Cinderella of the World Council of Churches," Bishop Mortimer Arias challenged the Fifth Assembly of the Council—meeting at Nairobi, Kenya in November 1975—to a renewed recognition of evangelism as "an essential priority." While recognizing that "everything the Church does has an evangelistic dimension," Arias observed that "often the evangelistic dimension is not translated into evangelistic intention; . . . the implicit does not become explicit." As a criterion he suggested that "all action that claims to be evangelistic will have to name 'the Name that is above all names,' attempt the crossing of the frontier between faith and non-faith and communicate the Good News in some way or other and to some degree." Such evangelism, he said, should be holistic and contextual; it will be costly and vulnerable; it must be both local and universal. Renewal for the task, he argued, "does not come *before* mission but *in* mission." Since the Assembly, Arias—an Uruguayan by birth—has resigned from the episcopacy of the Evangelical Methodist Church in Bolivia and asked for a pastorate in the Altiplano mining town of Oruro, where he hopes to do evangelistic work among the oppressed miners whom he discusses in his address. First published in the *International Review of Mission* for January 1976, it is reprinted with permission of the Commission on World Mission and Evangelism of the World Council of Churches.

That they may all be one . . . so that the world may believe . . . (John 17:21).

Its purpose is to assist the Christian community in the proclamation of the Gospel of Jesus Christ, by word and deed, to the whole world to the end *that all may believe in him* and be saved. (Aims of CWME.)

On the occasion of the Twenty-fifth Anniversary of the World Council of Churches the magazine *Risk* asked Dr. W. A. Visser 't Hooft the question: "What motivated the ecumenical idea in the thirties?" His reply came without hesitation: "It's quite clear that it was born first in the missionary movement."[1]

Unity—for What?

The present general secretary, Philip Potter, addressing the Synod of Bishops in Rome last year, was quite clear on this subject:

The ecumenical movement finds its origin, among other things, in the requirements of evangelization that call for unity among Christians. . . . The conviction of the World Council of Churches has been that evangelization is the ecumenical theme *par excellence*. . . . Evangelization . . . can only be conceived and carried out in an ecumenical perspective and fellowship.[2]

This means that from the perspective of the Church's mission, unity is not merely an eschatological hope, a spiritual reality or an inter-ecclesiastical aim; it is an actual prerequisite of mission. We are not seeking unity *per se*, but rather, as in the prayer of Jesus, *"that the world may believe."*

The initial purpose behind the creation of the World Council of Churches was "to support the churches in their task of evangelism," on the basis of the conviction held at that time that "today more than ever before evangelism is the supreme task of the churches." The Amsterdam Assembly in 1948, after reviewing the situation of the world and the Church, declared: "The evident demand of God in this situation is that the whole Church

set itself to the total task of winning the whole world for Christ."
And the Central Committee in 1951 reminded the churches that
the word *ecumenical* "is properly used to describe everything
that relates to the whole task of the whole Church to bring the
Gospel to the whole world."

Similarly, the vision that lay behind the decision to fuse the
International Missionary Council with the World Council of
Churches in New Delhi, 1961, was also that of giving a structural
content to the theme: "The whole Church with one Gospel for
the whole world." And it sought to ensure that mission did not
remain a specialized task for a few missionary organizations but
became the responsibility of the whole Church and all the
churches.[3]

It should be clear to us, then, that the intention of the
World Council "to stay together," is secondary to the indispensable task of the Church of Christ: the evangelization of the
world. Hence Potter's dramatic conclusion of his message to the
Synod of Rome: "Evangelization is the test of our ecumenical
vocation." It will also be the test of this Fifth Assembly, called
together to make the most daring missionary and evangelistic affirmation that can be made in the world today: "Jesus Christ
Frees and Unites."

Evangelism: An Essential Priority

The Spirit seems to be calling the churches of the whole
world to take up once again their essential and primary responsibility: witness the International Congress on World Evangelization in Lausanne, the Synod of Bishops in Rome, and many national and regional meetings. In June 1974, representatives of
Orthodox churches in Europe, America and Asia met in Bucharest for a consultation on the subject: "Confessing Christ
Today." They declared:

We do not have the option of keeping the Good News to
ourselves (Romans 10:1). The uncommunicated Gospel
(Good News) is a patent contradiction.[4]

The Evangelical Methodist Church in Bolivia, to which I belong, is so small that it can only be an associate member of the World Council of Churches. But after a long history of service and commitment to the Bolivian people through its many programs and ministries, the church felt that the moment had come to define its understanding of the evangelistic task in the light of the whole Gospel which it claimed to represent. Last year, after much reflection on its experience as well as that of the Universal Church, it drew up 27 theses on "Evangelism in Latin America Today." We would like to share this ecumenical harvest with you, as an offering in gratitude for all we have received from the Universal Church.

Evangelism is *essential* for the Church; it is its *primary* task. Evangelism springs from God's election of "a special people of his own"; it is based on the continued mission of the Son of God among men; it originates in the Great Commission which Jesus left to his Church and it is sustained by the promise of the Spirit for this saving community. The fruit of evangelism is the building up of the Body of Christ on earth; the very survival of the Church depends on it. Gen. 12:1-2; Ex. 19:5; Matt. 10:28; Mark 16:15; John 15:16; 17:18; 20:21; Acts 1:8; I Peter 2:9-10. *(Thesis 7)*

Evangelism is a *permanent* task: "in season out of season." No situation absolves us from "announcing the great works of him who has called us from darkness into light." Neither secularism, nor the existence of other religions and ideologies, nor the population explosion, nor the demands of other urgent tasks which Christians must fulfil, can relieve the Church of this responsibility which no other human institution can fulfil in its place. Evangelism must be carried on in a capitalist or in a socialist society or in any other which may emerge in history. Only the coming of God's kingdom in its fulness will relieve us from the task of evangelizing. Acts 4:12; Gal. 1:18; II Cor. 11:4; I Tim. 2:5-7; II Tim. 4:1-5; I Peter 2:9. *(Thesis 10)*[5]

My purpose in quoting these declarations of assemblies, consultations and churches within the diverse fellowship of the WCC is not to appease our own consciences or to reflect an attitude of triumphalism, but rather to confess before God that:

We have not always been faithful to our recognized calling;
We have not always given priority to what ought to be our priorities;
We have not always been worthy of our predecessors from Edinburgh 1910 to Mexico 1963;
And we have not always fulfilled the hopes which gave rise to the WCC and its merging with the IMC.

The reaffirmation of these purposes does not, on the other hand, mean that we accept as the faithful fulfilment of our mission all that is done in our churches under the label of evangelism, nor that we believe that we must go on repeating "the same old story in the same old way" as if nothing had changed. Neither does it mean that we renounce everything that we have been trying to do through the ecumenical movement to respond to the needs and challenges of our world during the past twenty-five years.

An Affirmation

On the contrary, I believe the moment has come to acclaim the missionary and evangelistic potential of all that the WCC has been doing through us and in our name. I take the liberty of suggesting that we acclaim and affirm:

— Thirty years of programmes on behalf of migrants and refugees who have been pushed to the margins of history by our wars and dehumanizing societies ("the most impressive expression of the whole of the Church's ministry in our time," as Newbigin has said);
— The persistent protests against social injustice, violence, racism, oppression and repression of peoples in various parts of the world;

— The constant search for justice and reconciliation through CICARWS, CCIA, PCR, CCPD, CMC[6] and other bodies and programmes;
— The attempt to find creative and courageous responses to the overwhelming problems of urbanization through Urban Industrial Mission(s);
— The unceasing call for union and renewal of the churches;
— The expansion of lay, youth and biblical renewal movements in Europe;
— The denouncing of imperialism which is implicit, explicit or latent in the Western missionary undertaking; the participation of the young churches of the Third World; the recognition of cultural identity in the receiving and propagation of the Christian faith; and the openness to new relationships of maturity and co-participation in mission;
— The repudiation of proselytism as a corruption of witness;
— The sensitive efforts to detect the "signs of the times" and to respond to the demands of the "world agenda";
— The sharing of human and financial resources through imaginative programmes of theological education (TEF) and the development of Christian literature (CLD) in the Third World;
— The agonizing search for the meaning of "Salvation Today" and the affirmation that the sufferings and struggles of the people for humanization and liberation are not foreign to God's purpose for his world and the total process of salvation in history;
— The thinking of our theologians concerning "Giving Account of the Hope that Is Within Us";
— The constant efforts to relate church and society, and to deepen our understanding of the implications of new developments in science and technology for the life of mankind on earth;
— The concern to respond to the terrible and apocalyptic spectre of hunger which hangs over most of our planet;

ALL THIS IS MISSION, AND IT CAN BE AN INTEGRAL PART OF TRUE EVANGELISM IN THE WORLD TODAY.

Confession and Repentance

Yet we must also admit that the WCC has not always been able to convey and make available to the churches the evangelistic potential of the impressive series of studies, priorities and projects, any more than our churches, organizations and councils have succeeded in putting to practical use the wealth of ecumenical experience. We must acknowledge that sometimes we have done theology in a vacuum, without reference to the contemporary practice of the churches or to actual ecumenical programmes. At other times too we have allowed ourselves to be impelled by an activism that owes more to fashionable slogans than to adequate biblical and theological reflection. And above all we must admit with shame that evangelism has been the Cinderella of the WCC, at least to judge by the extent to which it appears in its structure, where it figures as nothing more than one office with a single occupant, in a sub-structure which is itself merely part of a unit, and with no more than a monthly letter by which to communicate with the churches of the whole world.

Everything the Church does has an evangelical dimension, it was said at Evanston and reiterated at Bangkok. Yet we have to admit that often the evangelistic dimension is not translated into evangelistic intention; that evangelistic potential is not actually realized; that the implicit does not become explicit. Let us say at once that all action that claims to be evangelistic will have to name "the Name that is above all names," attempt the crossing of the frontier between faith and non-faith and communicate the Good News in some way or other and to some degree. The New Testament proclamation unites sign and word. Some people announce the Word and forget the Sign; perhaps our sin of omission is to have multiplied signs in the world and forgotten to speak the Word.

At all events the sincerity of these affirmations and confessions will have to be shown by "works of repentance" and by plans for the next seven years, such as, for example, the following: 1) to strengthen the line already begun of correlating strategies, methods of approach and structures inside the WCC; 2) to make more visible and functional the influence of mission and evangelism within the movement as a whole; 3) to give evangelistic and missionary meaning and content to the new programme of theological education; 4) to stimulate the emergence of a new contextual missiology, particularly in the Third World, but with the participation of the Universal Church; finally 5) to risk a rationalization based on priorities, of the human, economic and academic resources of the One Church, going much further than the timid beginnings of ESP (ecumenical sharing of personnel—moratoria as redeployment).

A Holistic Approach

What I have said so far derives its meaning from what has been called the "holistic or integral approach" to evangelism. The Evangelical Methodist Church in Bolivia has put it in these words:

> True evangelism is holistic; the whole Gospel for the whole man and the whole of mankind. Evangelism addresses man in the totality of his being: individual and social, physical and spiritual, historical and eternal. We reject, therefore, all dichotomies, ancient and modern, which reduce the Gospel to one dimension or fragment man who was created in the image and likeness of God. We do not accept the idea that evangelism means only "saving souls" and seeking exclusively "a change in the eternal status of the individual"; these concepts are biblically insufficient. We reject also the reduction of the Gospel to a programme for service or social development or to a mere instrument of socio-political programmes. Matt. 9:35-38; Luke 4:18-19; Acts 16:31; I Tim. 4:6-10; II Tim. 1:10. *(Thesis 2)*

Consequently there seems to be good reason for Patriarch Pimen of Moscow to have called attention to the fact that the Bangkok Letter to the Churches says nothing of the ultimate goal of salvation, namely, eternal life in God. This reminder is similar to that of evangelical colleagues who ask us to make clear that declarations on "the total man" include eternal salvation through faith in Jesus Christ.

It may be useful here to recall the comments of Emilio Castro, Director of the Commission on World Mission and Evangelism, concerning the Bangkok Conference's emphasis on historical salvation: "We surely cannot understand our participation in the history of mankind, in the search for social justice, as a manifestation of that salvation which God has promised us, without relating it to the eternal life which is promised to us and that neither life nor death can take away from us. . . . Social justice, personal salvation, cultural affirmation, church growth, are all seen as integral parts of God's saving acts."[7]

But evangelism is not only integral in content; it is also integral in form, in the inseparable union of "word and action."

> True evangelism is *incarnate*: proclamation in words and deeds in a concrete situation. The Gospel is eternal but not atemporal or ahistorical. It addresses itself to the whole man in his context. This does not mean that concrete historical situations are a part of the content of the Gospel. Evangelism must be inserted in this world and in the total experience of man, who must respond out of the depth of his historical existence. . . . Evangelism cannot, therefore, be reduced to a formula which can be applied indiscriminately to any situation or to the mere verbalism of evangelical propaganda. Luke 7:22; John 1:14; Phil. 2:5-11; II Cor. 3:2-3; James 1:22. *(Thesis 5)*

To say that evangelism must be incarnate does not mean that it must be silent. There are times and places when we must hold our tongues and let our witness speak through our presence and action, but such an extreme situation must not be considered normal or normative. There comes a moment when we must name the Name and proclaim the Word.

Because it concerns a whole message, evangelism includes announcement, prophetic denouncement, personal and community witness, the call to repentance, to conversion and to incorporation in the Christian Church, and participation in the struggle for a more just and human life, inspired in the purpose of God (Theses 3, 4, 12, 18-20). The Orthodox Consultation in Bucharest referred to earlier stated that while "the final aim of evangelistic witness is conversion and baptism," there are also "intermediary aims," such as love and dialogue between Christians and non-Christians, "the penetration of the structures of society" and a "prophetic challenge to society's values."

Contextual Evangelism

Evangelism must also be contextual.

In Bolivia we decided recently to put our theses to the test of experience. We formed a national interdisciplinary team complemented by people from three local churches in areas near the towns of Oruro and Cochabamba. We launched an experiment in "evangelistic immersion" which lasted for some weeks.

First we tried to *incarnate the Gospel* which we were to announce within our own group. We devoted entire mornings to study, meditation, sharing, evaluation and planning. Messages were prepared in groups, on the basis of each day's experience. If we were to proclaim reconciliation, we had to make it a reality within the dynamics of our group, and then try to extend it to the local church and community.

Second, we tried to get *to know the people and their context* really well. Through study, analysis of surveys, visits to the area, contacts with neighbours and the local authorities, we tried to get to know the people to whom we intended to proclaim the Gospel and to understand their community and family problems.

Third, we aimed at *an integrated presentation of the Gospel* through word and action. We invited people to come to evening meetings to share the problems of the community, to hear the Gospel and discuss the message, to reflect together on its meaning and to spend some time in friendship and community. The message was presented through hymns reflecting present-day situations and sung to national music, through social drama, preaching, teaching, and dialogue. It was also presented through practical action with the people and community. Our prayers were related to the problems of light, water, sickness, violence on the streets, and so on, which the people themselves suggested.

We discovered several things. 1) It is not necessary to leave aside social action in order to evangelize, nor to use it as a bait to attract the people. People are ready to receive a whole Gospel which is related to the total context of their lives. 2) One of the most gratifying experiences was to see how the Christian message arose spontaneously in response to the specific situations which came up as we went along. The people themselves and daily events provided the theme and the illustrations. The Gospel sounded natural, authentic and relevant in a familiar context. 3) We saw changes in people's attitudes, despite the brevity of our experiment: there was a clear movement from discouragement and isolation to hope and joint action. We saw how the liberating power of the risen Christ can work through people and groups.

We also discovered that we had much to learn and much to receive. The most memorable—and educational—experience was our visit to the tin mines, where Bolivian miners work in incredibly inhuman conditions—an eight-hour day spent below the ground, several kilometers inside the mountain, amid dust, explosive gases and the water coming from their drills. Their daily ration consists of a loaf of bread. Sometimes they do not even have that—only a bottle of watery tea and a few coca leaves to chew. Miners have a life expectancy of only 32 years, with some eight or ten years of active work before tuberculosis and silicosis eat away their lungs. We stayed for only five hours in the tunnels, talking to the miners, listening to their informed and critical comments on the problems of the country, of Portugal, of the United States or China.

Later in the day we attended the union meeting, where we met some of the men we had seen in the mine. After that long day, beginning at five in the morning, they now came to discuss democratically a request for support from the country's university students. It was a real school of politics! And when later we were able to talk with the leaders, we were amazed at the clarity of their aims, their feelings of solidarity, and their willingness to work for Bolivia's future, although they knew very well that change would only come slowly and perhaps they would not be there to see the fruits of their work. Hope indeed flourishes in the "tunnels of death."

We who had been proclaiming the new man—open, critical and committed—found these traits among these people, who spent their day digging like moles below the mountains of Bolivia and who did not consider themselves members of the Church. All that was missing was the naming of the Name. And we had to recognize that perhaps these people had more of Christ in them than we who spoke in his name. The same thing happened to us as happened to Peter, who learned new dimensions of the Gospel in his experience with Cornelius the Gentile (Acts 10). Thus we discovered the true meaning of evangelistic dialogue.

> The Church must be aware that Christ *precedes* us in evangelism. God has not left himself without a witness. The light of the Word illuminates every man that comes into this world. The Spirit of God "is no respecter of persons". The grace of God is not confined to the Church. Just as there is a solidarity in sin, there is also a solidarity in Christ which originates in the Incarnation, the Cross and the Resurrection. To evangelize is to help men to discover the Christ hidden in them and revealed in the Gospel. All men and all human values are destined to be recapitulated in Christ. John 1:1-18; Acts 10; 17:16-34; Rom. 5:12-21. *(Thesis 17)*

Priorities and Anticipations

In context, too, we understand that there are "priorities and anticipations," as Bangkok said, in the access to the process of salvation. In the United States, many Christians have read the book *Jonathan Livingstone Seagull,* about a philosopher seagull. In Bolivia a book was published last year about a condor called *Mallko.*[8] Both books reflect the nature of our respective societies and the philosophy which prevails in them. The seagull begins by despising the "breakfast flock" which flies in crowds around the fishing boats. "What is important is not eating but flying," says the seagull. The young condor, in his cave high up in the Andes, is orphaned early in life when his parents are caught by the peasants and taken to a zoo. For the young bird, wracked by hunger, the priority is to eat and later, if he can, to fly. What does this tell us about the priorities and methods of evangelism? Can we present the Gospel in the same way to the overfed and bored who seek escape from the rut through drugs or suicide, as we present it to the hungry, desperate for survival? Can it be presented in the same way to the members of an English country club, the young people of New York's "Village" and the dying in the streets of Calcutta? To whom must we say "Man does not live by bread alone," and with whom must we pray—and struggle for —saying "Give us this day our daily bread"? Can we continue to treat men as "Souls with ears"? Or as stomachs without souls? Can we announce the Gospel in the same way to the oppressor and to the oppressed, to the torturer and to the tortured? In other words, how can evangelism be authentic unless it is faithful both to the Scriptures and to real people in real contexts?

Some say that we must return to the sixteenth century and concern ourselves solely with "justification by faith" as Luther formulated it. We ought to remember that that fundamental Protestant doctrine did not contain the whole of Christian truth, but was a key to open a door and gain access to the Gospel in an age when an absolutist system came between God and man. More than a definitive system of theology, justification by faith, for Luther, meant a firm place to take his stand. But it seems to us that to be faithful to that same gospel of justification, to God's great Yes to humanity, we must take our stand side by side with the person who is struggling, suffering and hoping, usually "without God and without hope in the world." The *humanization* of people, properly understood, not as negation of transcendence, but as affirmation of God's loving plan for every person, is not a heresy, but perhaps the very heart of our Christian testimony, anchored in the turning point of the ages—the Incarnation. Our Yes to the person of today is simply a pale reflection of the Yes of the "God for us." Humanization is simply a translation of what Barth called "the humanity of God."

Or of Bonhoeffer's moving expression in his *Letters from Prison*, when he describes for us the "worldliness" of the Christian as throwing oneself into the arms of God and sharing in his suffering and keeping watch with Christ in Gethsemane.

Costly and Vulnerable Evangelism

To stand side by side with human beings is costly and vulnerable. We have said that true evangelism is free. To paraphrase Bonhoeffer's essay on grace, we should add that *it is free, but not cheap. True evangelism is costly.*

> Authentic evangelism will not be achieved without paying a *high price*. . . . What price did Jesus pay for evangelizing? What price did the Apostles pay? Do we believe that we shall pay a lower price today thanks to a convenient, efficient and cheap circulation of the Gospel? Evangelical evangelism will require that we pay in sacrifice, painful change and radical options. In particular, an option in favour of the oppressed, rejecting the temptation of false neutrality or open alliance with oppressive powers. *There is no evangelism without a cross.* Matt. 10; Mark 8:31-38; John 15-16:4. *(Thesis 15)*

It is not a matter of money and modern, costly equipment but rather of placing the life of the witness behind his witness. The great majority of the 2,700 millions who do not know Christ live under global (or closed) ideological or religious systems. In the "developed" countries people live in an ever-present atmosphere of secularism. In many countries of the Third World people live under repressive regimes which do not respect human rights and take as subversive any contextual or prophetic proclamation of the Gospel—and sometimes even the most aseptic biblical affirmations! What will evangelism cost in these places? Ask those involved in urban industrial ministries standing side by side with the poor in our big cities around the world.

And precisely because it is personal, local and contextual, *evangelism is irremediably vulnerable.*

Both the witness and the witnessing community are also a part of the *world,* and therefore subject to God's judgement and mercy. The Church is confronted by the same Word with which it intends to confront the world. And like the world, it also needs the divine teaching which works through history. It must therefore be alert to the "signs of the times" and open to dialogue with the world through its evangelistic work. The witness must renounce any claim to a holiness which he does not possess, and he must fully accept his vulnerability. (Jonah) *(Thesis 16)*

This is what D. T. Niles meant when he defined evangelism as "a beggar telling another beggar where *both* could find something to eat." This is vulnerable evangelism.

The Gospel is like manna—it cannot be kept. If we do not share it, we lose it. If we do not use it, it goes stale. It has been given to us, like bread, for our daily use.

We need to make this a reality in our congregations around the world so that they may be freed from their present paralysis. Their apparent humility and reticence to communicate the Gospel may be merely unfaithfulness. "The crisis we are going through today is not so much a crisis of faith as a crisis of faithfulness." (Potter)

We all know that the most difficult place in which to evangelize is our own home. Because at home they know us as we really are, inside and out. We must begin by accepting our vulnerability, for in any case it is obvious to everyone else!

Many churches have lost the impetus to evangelize. They seem to be dominated by a guilt complex. They are aware, or partly aware, of their weaknesses, of the image they project with their buildings, their social composition, their programmes. They do not feel worthy to communicate the Gospel, and they go on searching by all possible means for a "renewal" which never comes. There is only one biblical response to the guilt complex: "Remember then from what you have failed, repent and do the works you did at first. If not, I will come to you and remove your lampstand from its place, unless you repent." (Rev. 2:5)

We should already know that renewal does not come *before* mission but *in* mission. It will not come through study and reflection alone, but through practical action which includes reflection in action and prayer. We must not give in to the temptation of perfectionism: we must take risks, we must commit ourselves to the Gospel. A strikingly successful missionary in the New Testament was the woman of Samaria, who certainly had little training and less prestige. But she brought a whole people to hear Jesus, simply through a question, after she herself had been disturbed by a brief conversation with the Lord.

Evangelism Is Local

In the past few years, I have reached two conclusions concerning evangelism. 1) There is only *one medium* for the communication of the Gospel: the Christian and the Christian community. All other so-called "media" can only be instruments which are superfluous or of doubtful usefulness. 2) True evangelism is *free:* it goes from person to person, from community to community.

The word *communicate* means to share, to exchange, to relate, to live together, to participate, to converse, to have something in common. From the same root come communion, commune, community. And it is interesting to discover that it has the same meanings as *koinonia* in the New Testament, which refers both to communion with Christ—to the point of sharing in his passion and death—and communion with each other, both in spiritual and in material gifts. In other words, *koinonia, communication,* is the whole life of the Christian community, both internal and external. How can the Gospel be communicated, then, except through the congregation which lives out the Gospel? Jesus did not only leave a message to be published, but a community with a message to be shared. Hence New Testament evangelism is a true *communication* of a *community* which calls to *communion* (RSV = fellowship):

That which we have seen and heard we proclaim also to you, *so that you may have fellowship with us;* and our fellowship is with the Father, and with his Son Jesus Christ. (I John 1:3)

The congregation is the strategic base for the evangelism of the world, the transmitting center of the communication of the Gospel, through worship, through preaching, through teaching, community life or life of service to the world which surrounds it. The Orthodox tradition gives us an example, throughout its history, not only of the power of irradiation of the Christian community, but also of the power of attraction of the liturgical community.

Philip Potter has said: "Evangelization is not a strategy which can be worked out by a Synod of Bishops, or by the World Council of Churches, or by a world fellowship of evangelicals. It takes place in a given place and with particular persons or groups. Therefore, the base of evangelization is the local church, the whole people of God in the community as they worship, live and work in a dialogue of solidarity." And Emilio Castro adds: "We need to recover this world dimension of the local engagement as a way of incorporating the faithfulness and experiences of the local congregation into the total missionary outreach. ... It is the necessary foundation, the real test of our missionary vocation."[9]

This being so, one is tempted to reverse the famous phrase of John Wesley, "the world is my parish," and say that *"my parish is the world."* And so it is, in more than one sense, especially in what we call today the "global village." And if we go deeper into this phrase we will reach a true philosophy of mission and world evangelism. We will find the criterion to measure any church or parachurch organization or programme: Does it help or hinder the local witness of the Christian congregation?

What a tremendous challenge to our congregations! It is a challenge to conversion, renewal, authenticity, quantitative and qualitative growth. It brings us back to the Bangkok theme: "the churches renewed in mission." There we were reminded that the local congregation is God's "audio-visual medium" for mission, but that it can also constitute a "saboteur" of God's mission.

Donald McGavran holds a similar position: "Many churches find it difficult if not impossible to communicate the faith to those with whom they are in daily contact. Or to put it the other way around, many populations of non-Christians steadfastly refuse to receive the Gospel from Christians in their locali-

ties." To overcome this situation, some churches opt to "remove
the bars and locks by emphasizing solidarity with non-Christian
neighbours, quiet Christian presence, and cooperative working at
common humane goals." Where there is no alternative this is
quite correct, according to the Director of the Pasadena Institute
of Church Growth, but at the same time it reveals the need to
send missionaries from other neighborhoods and cultures.[10]

If we read the New Testament carefully, we will see that
this exchange of persons and groups was part of Paul's missionary strategy, a natural expression of the *koinonia* between
the churches. There are some animals which reproduce by au-
togenesis or self-fertilization. Perhaps we need some process of
"cross fertilization" between congregations which have become
sterile. Are we ready to devote personnel and resources to mutual ministry between congregations, just as we do to large service or research projects? This is another challenge to our
churches, boards, councils and the CWME itself.

And What about Universality?

All this may sound very personal and local, too modest for
the global objective, "that the world may believe." It seems so
little, in face of the 2,700 millions who know nothing of Christ.
And so it is.

There is no doubt that the Gospel belongs to the whole
world—it is not an article to be consumed exclusively by any
particular religious community. "And I have *other* sheep, that
are not of this fold," says Jesus, "I must bring them also." (John
10:16) And the evangelist, commenting on Caiaphas' ambiguous
declaration, gives the key to Christ's universal mission: "He
prophesied that Jesus should die for the nation; and not for the
nation only, but to *gather into one the children of God who are
scattered abroad*." (John 11:52-3) And Jesus declared to his disciples when some Greeks came to speak to him: "And I, when I
am lifted up from the earth, will draw all men to myself." (John
12:32)

The Last Commission is equally categorical, in all its forms, in relation to the universal intention of the Gospel: "to all nations," "unto all the world," "to every creature," "to the ends of the earth" (Matt. 28:20; Mark 16:15; John 20:21; Acts 1:8).

On the other hand, "God has his time which is not our time" (E. Castro). And God has chosen his own means of bringing in the universal perspective through the particular. His purpose to "bless all nations" takes a humble form in the call to an old man and his family to leave Ur of the Chaldeans. And then the call to a nation of slaves. Later, to a "remnant" within that nation. And "in the fullness of time" he concentrated his action in a vulnerable child born in a stable, in the humblest village of a people submitted to the greatest empire of history. The mystery of the Incarnation is the mystery of the local: "And the word became flesh and dwelt among us." (John 1:14)

Mission is centrifugal, and begins in a given place: "You will be my witnesses in Jerusalem and in all Judea and Samaria and to the end of the earth." But it took fifteen centuries after our Lord came, great ships and fearless sailors, before they discovered the part of the world known as America and the people who lived there. Today masses of human beings are inaccessible to the missionary work of the rest of the world, or the local church, and God only knows how long they will depend exclusively on the small seeds of Christianity which have remained in China, for instance, and what other ways God will use.

We must not fall into either guilty resignation or frantic activism. We must trust in God, and act with hope.

We only know that we have been given a command and that the Gospel must be shared. That "the love of Christ obliges us," that "it is required of us absolutely," and that "we cannot cease to tell what we have seen and heard," even though "we have this treasure in earthen vessels."

Many of us today hear the heart-rending cry of those whose human rights are violated. Is it not a basic right of every human being to know God's purpose for his life which was revealed in Jesus Christ? It is not written in any charter of Human Rights, but it is in the Scriptures and in the heart of God, "who desires all men to be saved and to come to the knowledge of the truth." (I Tim. 2:4)

. . . every woman or man, every child who is born becomes our creditor and we are his debtor. The Gospel is not a possession; it is a stewardship. Nobody can deprive us of this privilege or relieve us from this responsibility. Hence the urgency of evangelism. *(Thesis 9)*

And in this task we are sustained not only by the horror of a world without Christ, or by our feeling of gratitude and obligation, but above all by the assurance of the all-powerful intercession of him who still prays, "That they may all be one, that the world may believe."

NOTES

1. *Risk*, Vol. 9, No. 4, 1973, p. 11.

2. Philip Potter, "Evangelization in the Modern World," *Monthly Letter about Evangelism*, WCC (CWME) January 1975, p. 2; also in *Mission Trends No. 2*, pp. 164-65.

3. Lesslie Newbigin, *One Body, One Gospel, One World* (London: IMC, 1966).

4. *International Review of Mission*, Vol. LXIV, No. 253, January 1975, p. 87; also in *Mission Trends No. 2*, p. 269.

5. "Tesis Boliviana de Evangelización en América Latina Hoy", IEMB, La Paz, June 1975. Translations in English, French and German were published in *Monthly Letter about Evangelism*, WCC (CWME), February 1975.

6. Commission on Inter-Church Aid, Refugee and World Service; Commission of the Churches on International Affairs; Programme to Combat Racism; Commission on the Churches' Participation in Development; Christian Medical Commission.

7. Emilio Castro: "Director's Report," Figueira da Foz, WCC (CWME), February 1975, Document No. 3, p. 5.

8. Richard Bach, *Jonathan Livingstone Seagull* (New York, 1973); Gaston Suarez, *Mallko* (La Paz, 1974).

9. Emilio Castro, "Evangelism in the World," paper read to foreign missions representatives, London, 1975, p. 3.

10. Donald McGavran, "Barred Populations and Missionaries," *International Review of Mission*, Vol. LXIV, No. 253, January 1975, pp. 56-61.

The Search For Freedom, Justice, and Fulfillment

Samuel Escobar

At the International Congress on World Evangelization in Lausanne, Switzerland in July 1974, there was a strong emphasis—especially among "young evangelicals" and Third World participants—on the need to relate the Gospel to issues of social justice, and to see the inter-connection in Scripture between evangelization and the prophetic ministry of the Church. In his address to the Congress, Samuel Escobar said, "Jesus takes seriously the problems of property and power relationships. . . . He identified with the oppressed." Speaking from his Latin American experience to the 2,700 participants at Lausanne, Escobar argued: "The heart which has been made free with the freedom of Christ cannot be indifferent to the human longings for deliverance from economic, political, or social oppression." There is a continuing need, he said, for missionaries "ready to pioneer in areas of social justice and evangelism." Mr. Escobar—Peruvian by birth and now based in Cordoba, Argentina—is associate general secretary at large of the International Fellowship of Evangelical Students, and president of the Latin American Theological Fraternity. This excerpt from his address first appeared in *engage/social action* for November 1974, published by the United Methodist Board of Church and Society in Washington, D.C. The full text is in *Let the Earth Hear His Voice,* the official reference volume for the Lausanne Congress, edited by J. D. Douglas and published in 1975 by World Wide Publications, Minneapolis, Minnesota.

The first and most powerful answer to the social and political needs of human beings—to the search for freedom, justice, and fulfillment—is given by Jesus in his own work and in the church. Jesus takes seriously the problems of property and power relationships, which are essentially the problems that cause social and political maladjustment and injustice.

Jesus creates a new people, a new community, where social problems are dealt with under the Lordship of Christ. This is the community, *distinct from the rest of society,* that we find around Jesus first, then growing in Jerusalem, and then expanding into the world.

In this community there is a new attitude to money and property (Luke 6:29-31, 35; Acts 2:43-45; 4:34; 20:35; James 2: 14-16; I John 3:16-17). In this community there is a new attitude to power and its exercise (Luke 22:23-27 and parallels in Matthew and Mark; 2 Corinthians 10:8; 12:10-15; 1 Peter 5:1-3). It is a community where human barriers and prejudices have been overcome under Christ's rule (Galatians 3:28; Colossians 3:11; Philemon 15-17). It is a community ready to suffer for justice and good (Matthew 5:10-12; Acts 7:51-60; Acts 16:16-24; 1 Peter 3:13-18),

The biblical model of evangelism includes the radically different community that calls people to faith in the crucified and resurrected Christ that has transformed their lives, and the new life in the Spirit that enables them to follow the example of Christ. Such a community has a revolutionary effect in changing a society.

Let us take a specific example. It is false, as some have written, that Paul did not do anything about the evil of slavery. He did at least three things.

First, he announced the gospel equally to masters and slaves. His own lifestyle and training added credibility to his message for both social classes.

Second, as part of his message he taught basic truths about the nature of man (Acts 17:26, a common origin for all persons) and the new type of relationship that human beings had under Christ (Galatians 3:28). These truths were contrary to the basic tenets of the then prevalent philosophy, in which slavery was based.

Third, he asked specifically for an application of his teaching in the context of the Christian community (Philemon). It has been demonstrated that by addressing himself to the slaves as moral agents (Col. 3:22-25; Eph. 6:5-8), Paul was doing something completely new in his day, treating them as responsible persons, not as things or animals, which was the way in those days. Moreover, Paul asked from masters in the same passage what not even the most advanced moralists or philosophers would have asked at that point.

Thus Paul, in his teaching and practice in the primitive church, was attacking slavery at its very base. The example and influence of the church in the first century, and later the active involvement of Christians in civil life, brought eventually the abolition of the system.

Later Christians and Slavery

When the south of Africa was discovered by the Portuguese in the fifteenth century, slavery soon appeared again, and in a matter of decades Christendom had accepted it. However, in 1774, in the wake of a spiritual revival, a great evangelist, John Wesley, published his short treatise, *Thoughts Upon Slavery.*

For Wesley, development without social justice was unacceptable. I pray that God will raise evangelists like Wesley, who also care about social evils enough to do research and write about them and throw the weight of their moral and spiritual authority on the side of the correction of injustices. Wesley, however, did more than write. He encouraged the political action that eventually was going to abolish slavery in England. Six days before his death, Wesley wrote to the famous evangelical politician William Wilberforce, encouraging him in the name of God to fight against slavery.

More than sixty years ago, a group called Peniel Hall Society bought some land in Bolivia, in order to help Aymara peasants with a school and a hospital. As it was a practice until recent date in Latin America, the land was sold to them with 250 Aymara serfs who belonged to the estate. After a long period of failures and hesitations, the project in 1920 was handed to the

Canadian Baptist Mission Board, which eventually brought an agricultural missionary. After the fruitless efforts of several years, it finally dawned on the missionaries that their position as land owners and serf masters was overriding every benevolent attempt to uplift the people.

Finally, in 1942, economic serfdom was abolished, the land was parceled and the Indians were given title of property to their plots. Norman Dabbs, the missionary martyr, comments: "Both missionaries and peons felt that a crushing weight had been lifted from their lives."

When ten years later a nationalist revolutionary government passed the desperately needed law of land reform, the pioneer experiment of the Baptists in Huatajata was recognized as a valid antecedent. The amazing fact is that the freedom of Indians and the distribution of land was immediately followed by church growth in the area; and also after the revolution of 1952 a wave of church growth started in Bolivia.

These examples are illustrations of how Christians can be obedient to God's word. We need a revival of life in our churches around the world, so that they again will be communities "distinct from the rest of society." We need evangelists who are also prophets like John Wesley. Where possible, we need Christian politicians like Wilberforce. We need imaginative missionaries, ready to pioneer in areas of social justice and evangelism.

Liberation is not Gospel Freedom

Please notice that the simple liberation from human masters is not the freedom of which the gospel speaks. Freedom in Christian terms means subjection to Jesus Christ as Lord, deliverance from bondage to sin and Satan (John 8:31-38), and consequently the beginning of new life under the law of Christ (1 Cor. 9:19), life in the family of the faith where the old human master becomes also the new brother in Christ.

However, the heart which has been made free with the freedom of Christ cannot be indifferent to the human longings for deliverance from economic, political, or social oppression. And that is what many expect from the one who evangelizes. Not that he says: "I come to announce to you a spiritual freedom and because of that I do not care about your social, economic, or political oppression." But rather that he says: "I care for your oppression. I am with you in your search for a way out, and I can show you a deeper and most decisive deliverance that may help you also to find a better way out of your social and political oppression."

That is what Christ did. He identified with the oppressed. For instance, he became poor both by taking upon himself human limitations and by the social strata in which he chose to live when he came. When Jesus, who made himself poor, tells me "You always have the poor with you," I listen to him. He added to that, let us remember, "and whenever you will, you can do good to them" (Mark 14:7). But when a rich man tells me the same thing, I have the suspicion that he really means "You always have the rich with you . . . and that should not change."

Do We Stand with Rich or Poor?

What is the image that our missionary and evangelistic work projects? Do we stand with the rich or with the poor? Do we stand usually with oppressors or with the oppressed? What a contradiction it would be, says James, if not being rich, we would forget the poor and favour the rich (James 2:5-9). In my opinion the tough question is not "Are you rich?" The question is "Where do you stand when you preach the gospel?" "Where did your master stand?"

A dramatic example of this dilemma was recently presented to me by a missionary friend among a tribe in Latin America. He was torn apart by the dilemma of standing with his poor unknown tribe of "savages" or with the oil company that wanted to use him to move the Indians out of the area, getting them away in order to continue with exploration, thus eliminating "the Indian problem." Such hard decisions may increase in number, especially for those willing to reach parts of the so-called "fourth world," remote areas where the desperate search for raw materials and oil is going to center now. If these situations are not taken seriously by evangelists, in both their style and their message, the credibility of the gospel is at stake.

I do not think we can measure the effects that were registered in the conscience of evangelicals and of the hearers of the gospel by the firm stand that evangelist Billy Graham took on racial issues from the very beginning of his career. His refusal to preach to segregated audiences closed some doors and provoked disaffections. I think that it stems from his biblical convictions about the nature of man and God's design for him. I praise the Lord for it! He did not downgrade the demands of the gospel in order to have access to more numbers of hearers or in order to have the blessing of racists that consider themselves "fundamental Christians." A stance like this is already communicating something about the nature of the gospel that gives credibility to the gospel itself when it is announced. This is especially so for those who are the victims of injustice and are conscious of it.

Don't Reduce the Gospel!

In some societies and nations, there is desperate need for healing in the area of interracial relationships. In those cases, the Christian church might be the only place where the miracle of encounter, acceptance, and coexistence can happen because the redemptive power of Christ acts. To perpetuate segregation for the sake of numerical growth, arguing that segregated churches grow faster, is yielding to the sinfulness of society, refusing to show a new and unique way of life. It is an example of reducing the gospel to make it more palatable. Such "numerical growth" might not be the numerical growth of the church of Jesus Christ.

I wonder sometimes if taking into account the demonic forces at work behind racism, prejudice, oppression, corruption, and exploitation of the weak and the poor everywhere, and taking also into account evangelistic and missionary efforts that are totally unaware of those facts, the Lord would not tell us: "Woe to you zealous evangelists, hypocrites, for you traverse sea and land to make a single proselyte, and when he becomes a prosely-

te, you make him twice as much a child of hell as yourselves"
(Matthew 23:15).

It has been said that there is the danger that, if we concen-
trate on working out the social implications of the gospel, we will
forget evangelism, and that history proves this fact. I do not
believe that statement. I think that the Social Gospel, for instance, deteriorated because of poor theology. The sad thing is
that those who have the right theology have not applied it to
social issues. The practical answer must be seen in a different
area. We have to rediscover the ministry of teaching in the
church, the close link between evangelism and church life, and
the role of the layman in the world.

In the life of our Lord, and in the life of the Apostles, there
was no separation or gap between preaching and teaching. Both
were very important and essential to their ministry. I think that
the idea that you can "evangelize" and leave teaching for ten
years later is antibiblical. Teaching is an indispensable part of the
life of the body and, if it is not provided, a group called church
can degenerate into nothing but a social club or a sect.

Part of the teaching is *how to live in the world as a Christian:* the ethics of the Kingdom. Laypersons then penetrate society by a *way of life* that is new in family relations, business, citi-
zenship, and every area of daily life. Consequently, to mobilize
laypersons is not only to teach them short summaries of the gospel, mini-sermons, and to send them to repeat these to their
neighbors. It is also to teach them how to apply the teaching and
example of Christ in their family life, in their business activities,
in their social relationships, in their studies, and so forth.

Those who teach need to be solidly rooted in the word of
God but also very aware of the world around them, so that they
can help in the application. In societies that are increasingly hostile to Christianity, this task is more crucial and necessary, because you cannot take for granted that the value system and the
social uses are "Christian." We desperately need this ministry in
the Third World! We desperately need this ministry in the Western nations!

Néstor Paz:
Mystic, Christian, Guerrilla

Néstor Paz, member of a small band of guerrillas engaged in armed resistance, died of starvation at the age of 25 in the Bolivian jungle near Teoponte in October 1970. His body, wrapped in a plastic covering, slipped from his friends' hands as they were crossing a river and was swept downstream without being recovered, just seven days before the survivors in his group surrendered to government forces. Poet, mystic, former Catholic seminarian and medical student, Paz understood his guerrilla commitment as an evangelical imperative of fidelity to Jesus Christ in resisting oppression and striving for the liberation of his exploited people. His "campaign journal" is less a record of combat action than a meditation of continuing conversation with God, and with his young wife Cecilia Avila ("Cecy"). Cecilia was subsequently killed by Bolivian troopers during the repression of students and tin miners under the Banzer regime in Cochabamba on March 23, 1972. Néstor and Cecilia, influenced by the examples of Camilo Torres and Che Guevara, tried to synthesize their Christianity with Marxist thought, through prayerful study of the Psalms, the New Testament, and the writings of Che Guevara. Néstor was devoted to St. Francis of Assisi, and took the name "Francisco" as a sign of his love for the poor when he joined the guerrillas. Bishop Mortimer Arias of the Methodist Church in Bolivia called attention to the death of Paz and published several of his letters (*The Christian Century,* Jan. 6, 1971); James and Margaret Goff and Jordan Bishop translated and circulated some of the letters in North America in 1971; a selection of the letters was published in *IDOC-International,* North American Edition, No. 23, April 10, 1971; and in 1975 Orbis Books, Maryknoll, New York, published the complete journal: *My Life For My Friends—The Guerrilla Journal of Néstor Paz, Christian,* translated and edited by Ed Garcia and John Eagleson.

Message of Néstor Paz
on Leaving to Join the Guerrillas
in Teoponte, July 17, 1970

> "Every sincere revolutionary must realize
> that armed struggle is the only way that
> remains" (Camilo Torres, January 7, 1966)

Following the glorious example of the Peruvian highland
guerrillas and of the continental heroes, Bolívar and Sucre, and
the heroic stance of Ernesto Guevara, the Peredo brothers,
Darío, and many other guerrillas who lead the march for the liberation of the people, we take our place in the long guerrilla file,
rifle in hand, to combat the symbol and instrument of oppression
—the gorilla army.

As long as blood flows in our veins we will make the la-
cerating cry of the exploited be heard. Our lives do not matter if
we can make Latin America, *la patria grande,* a free territory of
free people who are masters of their own destiny.

I realize that my decision and that of many of my companions will produce a flood of accusations, from the paternalistic "poor misguided person," to the open charge of "demagogic
criminal." But Yahweh our God, the Christ of the Gospel, has
announced the "good news of the liberation of humanity," and
acted in accordance. We cannot sit down to spend a long time
reading the Gospel with cardinals, bishops, and pastors, all of
whom are doing quite well where they are, while the situation of
the flock is one of hunger and solitude. This state of affairs is
called "non-violence," peace, Gospel. These persons sadly to say,
are the Pharisees of today.

People no longer listen to the "Good News." They are being
betrayed by their "brothers and sisters."

"Peace" does not happen by chance; it is the product of
equality among people, as Isaiah says in his chapter 58. Peace is
the result of love among people, the result of an end to exploitation.

"Peace" is not attained by dressing up in silk and living in a
medieval palace, or by robbing the people in order to have a

millionaire's salary, or by playing on people's religious superstition in order to live at their expense.

"Greater love has no man than this, that a man lay down his life for his friends." This is the commandment which sums up the "Law."

For this reason we have taken up arms: to defend the illiterate and undernourished majority from exploitation by a minority, and to win back dignity for a dehumanized people.

We know that violence is painful, because we feel in our own flesh the violent repression of the established disorder. But we are determined to liberate our people because we consider them as brothers and sisters. We are the people in arms. This is the only road which remains open. "The sabbath was made for man," not the reverse.

They say that violence is not evangelical; let them remember Yahweh slaying the first-born of the Egyptians to free his people from exploitation.

They say that they believe in "non-violence." Then let them stand clearly with the people. Then the wealthy and the "gorillas" will demand their lives, just as they demanded Christ's. Let them take courage and try it; we'll see if they are consistent enough to face a Good Friday. But all that is demagoguery, isn't it, you canons, generals, and *cursillistas,* you priests of the established disorder, of the peace enforced by violence, of the massacre of San Juan, of the complicity of silence, of the 200-peso salaries, of the widespread tuberculosis, and of pie in the sky when you die?

The Gospel is not mechanical moralism. It is a shell hiding a "life" which must be discovered if we are not to fall into pharisaism. The Gospel is "Jesus among us."

We have chosen this method because it is the only one open to us, painful though it may be.

Fortunately, there are some, more numerous every day, who recognize the authenticity of our position and who either help us or have joined our ranks. I think of what the "gorilla" Government of Brazil does with a Church which commits itself. Father Pereira Neto was assassinated in a most cruel and inhuman manner. I think of Father Ildefonso, a Tupamaro, assassinated in Uruguay. I think of Father Camilo Torres, silenced by the Government and the servile Church. With his blood he ratified what he had said about Christianity:

> In Catholicism what is essential is love for one's neighbor. "He who loves his neighbor has fulfilled the law." For this love to be genuine it must seek to be effective. If works of beneficence, almsgiving, a few tuition-free schools, a few housing developments—everything which goes by the name of charity—does not succeed in feeding the majority of the hungry, nor in clothing the majority of the naked, nor in teaching the majority of the ignorant, then we must seek effective means for achieving the well-being of the majorities. . . . Therefore the Revolution is not only permitted but is obligatory for Christians who see it as the only effective and complete way to make love for all people a reality.

I believe that the only effective way of protecting the poor against their present exploitation is by taking up arms. I believe that the struggle for liberation is rooted in the prophetic line of Salvation History. Enough of the languid faces of the over-pious! The oft-betrayed whip of justice will fall on the exploiter, those false Christians who forget that the force of their love ought to drive them to liberate their neighbors from sin, that is to say, from every lack of love.

We believe in a "New Man," made free by the blood and resurrection of Jesus. We believe in a New Earth, where love will be the fundamental law. This will come about, however, only by breaking the old patterns based on selfishness. We don't want patches. New cloth can't be used to mend old garments, neither can new wine be put into old wineskins. Conversion implies an inner violence which is then followed by violence against the exploiter. May both people and the Lord judge the rightness of our decision. At least no one can imply that we search for profit or comfort. Those are precisely the things which we don't find in this struggle; they are what we leave behind.

The Lord said, "He who loves father or mother more than

me is not worthy of me" (Matthew), and "He who does not hate even his own life cannot be my disciple" (Luke). We believe that this refers to the person tied to his "own little world" and his "own little problems." The "other person" is out there beyond "our own comfort."

There are those who defend themselves with lyrical discourses about the "revolution," yet in the moment of truth, because of their cowardice, take the side of the oppressor. The sin of "omission" is the fault of our Church, just as it was of the "lukewarm" members (Rev. 3:14-22) and of those who do not want "to get their hands dirty." We don't want to bequeath to our children a vision of life based upon competition as a means to possession, or on possessions as a measure of a person's worth.

We believe that people have value for what they *are* and not for what they *have*. We believe in a completely liberated people who will be able to live and build friendly structures through which love may be expressed. My certainty that we can achieve this goal is based on the statement that the Lord "is able to do far more abundantly than all that we ask or think" (Ephesians 3:20). The duty of every Christian is to be a revolutionary. The duty of every revolutionary is to bring about the revolution.

Victory or Death!

Francisco

*From the Campaign Journal
of Néstor Paz ("Francisco")*

A Letter to God, Dated September 12, 1970

Dear Lord:

It has been a long time since I wrote to you. Today I feel a real need for you and your presence, perhaps because of the nearness of death or the relative failure of the struggle. You know that I have tried to be faithful to you—always and by all means—consistent with my whole being. That is why I am here. I understand love as the urgency of helping to solve the problems of the "other person"—in whom you are present.

I left what I had and came here. Perhaps today is my Holy Thursday and tonight my Good Friday. Because I love you I surrender everything I am into your hands, without limit. What hurts me is the thought of leaving those I most love—Cecy and my family—and perhaps not being here to participate in the triumph of the people—their liberation.

We are a group filled with authentic, "Christian" humanity, and I think we will change the course of history. The thought of this encourages me. I love you and I give to you all that I am and all that we are, completely—because you are my Father. No one's death is meaningless if his life has been filled with meaning; and I believe this has been true of us, here.

Chau, Lord! Perhaps until we meet in your heaven, that new world we yearn for so much!

Two Letters to His Wife

My dearest:

Just a few lines for you. I don't have the energy for any more. I have been tremendously happy with you, through every fiber of my being. It hurts me deeply to leave you alone, but if it is necessary, I'll have to do it. I am in this to the end, and that means "Victory or Death." I love you. I give you all that I am, all that I can, with all the strength I have. We will see each other soon—either here or over there. I kiss you with all my heart and protect you with my arms.

(Francisco's last entry)

My dearest princess:

It has been a long time since I wrote to you; I have had no strength to do so. Yesterday I was thinking a lot about everything that is OURS.

We are going through extremely hard and difficult times. My body is exhausted, but my spirit strives to remain intact. I want to give myself to you, to love you with all my strength, as much as I am able, because you incarnate my life, my struggle, and my hopes. We probably won't be able to be together on the 9th; perhaps it will be the 29th; (Dates of his birthday and wedding anniversary) or Christmas. But I am confident that we'll see each other.

We are a small group. Fortunately, I am with friends and relatives and this makes it easier. It is difficult at this stage not to despair. Confidence in the Lord Jesus gives me strength to go forward. We have definitely lost the battle, at least this one. We have to recoup our forces and plan the future with a clear and realistic criterion. We'll see what happens.

I only hope that we'll see each other on this side of death, even though after death our reunion will be complete and full of happiness. I believe in this and it comforts me. I hope to be with you soon, to have long talks with you. We'll look into each other's eyes. We'll bring a little Paz boy or girl into the world who will fill our days with joy. We'll go forward together.

I am frightened at the thought of some misfortune happening to you, but I hope you will be all right. I will leave you now. As always, I have difficulty expressing myself on paper. I am thinking about my parents, about my brothers and sisters. Some day we will embrace each other. More than anything else I want to eat, eat, eat for a few days. We haven't had anything for a month except for an occasional bit of food we have found along the trail. I love you, and of that you may be sure. I love you more than anything; I love you completely.

VIOLENCE:
A THEOLOGICAL
REFLECTION

José Miguez Bonino

"Whether Christians or not, we are always actively involved in violence," charges José Miguez Bonino, and theological reflection tests "our willingness to become aware of our participation . . . to submit it to the critical verdict of the Word of God, and to accept it as part of our obedience in faith." The question, therefore, is not whether Christians should participate in violence, but—"of the kinds, forms and limits of violence present in a conflict involving oppression and liberation"—whether "my violence is . . . obedience to or betrayal of Jesus Christ." The criteria for deciding or answering that question constitute the central concern of the author in this essay. He argues that God's announcement-commandment in Scripture "almost always takes the form of a call to create a new situation, to transform and correct present conditions—a summons to conversion and justice," and that "the call to exercise or renounce violence always seems to lead to an 'opening up' in which human beings can exist on the earth and be what corresponds to their particular humanity." It also leads to "a breaking down of the restrictions which leave a person, a group or a people in a state of weakness and inferiority." Dr. Miguez Bonino concludes with a warning against the idolatry of ideology—"which Christians must fight in every revolutionary process." The Rev. José Miguez Bonino, a Methodist, is dean of graduate studies at

Union Theological Seminary in Buenos Aires, Argentina, and is a president of the World Council of Churches. The only Latin American Protestant observer at the Second Vatican Council, his recent books in English include *Christians and Marxists: The Mutual Challenge to Revolution* (Eerdmans, 1976), and *Doing Theology in a Revolutionary Situation* (Fortress, 1975). First published in *Cristianismo y Sociedad* in 1971 (IX, 28), the English translation of this article is reprinted from *The Ecumenical Review* for October, 1973, with permission of the World Council of Churches.

Critical reflection on our use of violence

Theological discussion on the theme of violence often gives the impression of being conceived as an abstract discussion on the basis of which the Christian will decide whether or not to accept violence and whether or not to take part in it. The fallacy of such a starting point is apparent to the most superficial observer. What is this neutral standpoint, detached from the interplay of different kinds of violence, from which such discussion could begin? Both the biblical idea of man (which always regards him as involved in "the world") and daily experience show us clearly that such a standpoint does not exist. Whether Christians or not, we are always actively involved in violence—repressive, subversive, systemic, insurrectional, open, or hidden. I say actively involved because our militancy or lack of it, our daily use of the machinery of the society in which we live, our ethical decisions or our refusal to make decisions make us actors in this drama.

What then is the significance of theological reflection? Simply put, it is our willingness to become aware of our participation in the process, to submit it to the critical verdict of the Word of God and to accept it as part of our obedience in faith. To put it in very simple terms, there is no ethical decision, no personal or collective human plan, which does not involve the Christian in a choice between obedience to the divine will and purpose, or infidelity. Consequently we never start from a neutral standpoint, but always from some definite event—in this case the interplay of different kinds of violence—which we submit to critical scrutiny. Normally we do so through "discernment," which includes drawing on our memory of biblical teaching and tradition, seeking the sense of what is of Christ, which the New Testament attributes to the work of the Spirit, and using all the human means—technical and ideological—at our disposal. The function of the theologian is to make explicit the elements of this discernment, not to substitute his own judgment for it or prescribe the decision.

It should scarcely be necessary to point out that in a continent where thousands die every day as victims of various forms of violence, no neutral standpoint exists. *My* violence is direct or indirect, institutional or revolutionary, conscious or unconscious. But it is violence. Accordingly, the discussion of the theme is not, for the Christian, a luxury or a fashionable fad. It is a test of the authenticity of one's faith. My violence is either obedience to or betrayal of Jesus Christ.

Two starting points

I have the impression that theological talk about violence at the present time starts from two general perspectives of the Christian concept of man and the world and the ethical thinking that results. One is built on the principle of the rationality of the universe, the conviction that a universal order pervades everything. Heaven and earth, nature and society, moral and spiritual life, seek the balance that corresponds to their rational place in the order of things. The preservation of this order is the supreme good. What disturbs it is, as the tango says, "an offence against reason." In its crudest form this belief amounts simply and solely to a defence of the status quo, which is identified with cosmic reason. Violence is then conceived in relation to that order, and because it disturbs it, is regarded as irrational and bad. Therefore it must be stopped by a rational use of force. This false logic appears frequently in "Christian" right-wing rhetoric. The will of God is identified with order, which in turn is identified with the prevailing, though threatened, order of things. To resist the threat is to obey God.

The argument is not however restricted to its false forms. It is possible to link it with a more usual view which does not identify the rational order with the existing social structure, and which therefore leaves room for the possibility of change and even of a rational use of force in the service of change. This kind of violence may in fact be "subversive" of the existing order, but it is systemic or repressive in relation to what is regarded as the rational order. The problem here is to discern what is the rational order. Perhaps the most complete expression of this view has been the idea of natural law put forward in Aristotelian-Thomist ethics, and which has been subsequently refurbished in various ways. It is impossible to pursue the discussion of this problem here. But it is necessary to point out how easily such views become prisoners of a past historical model or of an ideological conception which sacralizes itself as a rational and eternal order.

The other perspective sees man as a process for liberation in the constant struggle against existing limitations in nature, history, society and religion. Man is creative, and creation in any medium is violence exercised over things as they are, the affirmation of the new against "what exists," an eruption which can only succeed by destroying the existing systems of integration. In this schema, violence plays a creative role; it acts as a midwife (although I do not think Marx's famous phrase can be interpreted entirely in this sense). This view can also be taken to its extreme by presenting violence as the ultimate creative principle, intrinsically valid because it destroys every existing limitation. Only by the destruction of what limits me—nature, social order, divinity, ethical norm—do I find my freedom, that is to say, my humanity. The exaltation of creative irrationality is a well-known phenomenon in human history. But it is not necessary to follow this argument in its extreme form; history may be conceived as a dialectic in which the overthrowing of the old to make possible the new ways involves a certain amount of violence.

As theological positions, both perspectives are based on biblical and ecclesiastical tradition. Frequently they are identified with the priestly and prophetic traditions respectively. It would not be difficult to trace both currents in the history of Christian theology. Although both represent significant aspects of Christian thought, I am convinced that neither of them corresponds to the starting point of biblical thought, either in approach or content.

As regards approach, both rationality and liberty are abstract concepts—speculative constructions very remote from the specific modes of thought and situations in which the biblical message comes to us. As regards content, it seems obvious to me that the biblical conception does not regard man in terms of reason or liberty but in terms of the actual historical relationships in which the man-objects-God equation is always defined. The word of scripture is always an announcement-commandment referring to a particular human situation that needs to be corrected and transformed in accordance with the word.

If we ask for the criteria by which these transformations are to be carried through, we encounter a curious situation. On the one hand, notions like justice (*tsedaqa, mishpat*, etc.), mercy, fidelity, truth (*hesed, emunah*) and peace (*shalom*) are presented as characteristic of the way Yahweh works, and at the same time as requisites of human life (material, social, religious). If, however, we seek to define the content of these terms, we find only specific narratives or commands; the definitions are contained in the action announced by God or called for from His people in this or that situation. This does not mean that the notions in question are empty labels covering any number of hetero-geneous or capricious actions. It does mean, however, and this seems very important, that the ethical criteria are not defined in a non-temporal or abstract form but in relation to the actual conditions of people's lives in a given historical situation. These facts taken together constitute the direction, the Kingdom of God, which enables us to speak of conditions or actions as "worthy" or "unworthy" of the Kingdom. But this direction cannot be translated into a universal principle—reason, order, liberty— or into an anthropological statement; it always has to be linked with the concrete "words" of God.

Against this background, violence appears repeatedly in the Bible, not as a general form of human conduct that ought to be accepted or rejected, but as an element of the announcement-commandment of God, as concrete acts that have to be executed or avoided in view of a result, a relationship, or a project in-dicated in the announcement-commandment. Thus the Law proscribes certain forms of violence towards persons and things, and authorizes and even orders others. Some wars are commanded—even against Israel—while others are forbidden even in favor of Israel. If one tries to find a pattern in these events, a first and very simple interpretation is that the call to exercise or renounce violence always seems to lead to an "opening up" in which human beings (stranger, widow, orphan, nation, family) can exist on the earth and be what corresponds to their particular humanity. A more precise definition would involve us in a detailed study which is beyond the scope of these reflections. In general terms, however, the Bible shows us a breaking down of the restrictions (slavery, revenge, whim, absence of defence or protection, usurpation, etc.) which leave a person, a group or a people in a state of weakness and inferiority. They are freed to be and to act as responsible (the typical instance being "as a partner in a pact") before God, other persons and things.

Since this is the general direction of the biblical announcement-commandment, it is not surprising that, in simple terms, peace is preferable to hostility, generosity to revenge, preservation of life to its destruction, production to destruction, trust and tranquility to threats and fear. This is where the idea of order and rationality has its subordinate but meaningful place in a Christian ethics. At the same time, given the conditions in which, according to the same biblical testimony, human life is lived, it is not surprising that God's announcement-commandment almost always takes the form of a call to create a new situation, to transform and correct present conditions—a summons to conversion and justice. This is the undoubted truth of the interpretation of the action of God in terms of "liberation." Liberation and order are not, however, key concepts for a philosophy of history; they are elements which guide our reflection on the Word of God in a given situation. Nor are we dealing with two symmetrical elements. The biblical vision—centered in the person and work of Jesus Christ and its eschatological axis—always includes the dimension of order, rationality and conservation within the dynamic of transformation, not vice versa. Consequently, the actual human reality which we have pointed to as the locus of Christian ethics is not simply man as he exists in his immediate circumstances, but man in the dynamics of the new being, the new humanity given in Christ as part of the announcement-mandate. In other words, neither the prophetic nor the priestly interpretations are general principles; they are modes of action relative to man in his concrete reality. And as such they are not balanced in a static equilibrium, or swinging like a pendulum; the priority belongs to the prophetic, with a full integration of the priestly task.

Consequences

If the picture suggested by a critical reflection on our practice of violence is acceptable in principle, it seems to me that we should continue in certain directions.

1. It can only be a reflection on the violence and violent conditions of our actual situation in Latin America. It has to do with who practises and suffers from violence here today, and for what purpose and how the various forms of violence are used (or not!). We must avoid the substantialization of violence, so frequent in recent discussions, or dissertations on the nature of violence as such. The discussion of violence can only be adjectival—incidental to something else.

2. Incidental to what? We would have to expound a whole standpoint in regard to present-day Latin American reality, a standpoint conceived as a discernment of the Word of God, as concrete obedience, for that is the substance to which violence can be added as an adjective. The growing consensus in Christian interpretation indicates liberation as the content of this announce-commandment for us today. It is important to make it clear at this point that I am not thinking of reintroducing a principle of liberation except into the political, economic, cultural and religious situations of Latin American society that deprive people of human space and are therefore so clearly contrary to the biblical announcement-commandment that no complicated exegesis or hermeneutics are necessary to perceive it. The context in which we must discuss violence is the one defined by the search for liberation.

3. This choice, which seems to me incontestable for the Christian in Latin America today, does not exclude but must incorporate the dimensions of order, rationality, conservation—which might also be expressed as strategy, planning, technology,

theory—and respect for objective reality, natural and human. This analysis prevents any enthusiasm for violence that would sacralize it or directly identify it with liberation.

4. Following from this, there is another restriction on the relation between liberation and violence, which emerges from consideration of human values, both personal and communal. This restriction has to do with very important aspects of a revolutionary process: the human cost of the revolution, and regard for the enemy. There is surely no place here for the shallow sentimentality which passes for Christian ethics in these matters, hiding reactionary attitudes under basic theological categories like reconciliation, forgiveness or peace, which in the long run are most costly in human lives and suffering and less respectful of the human person. But this fact must not hide the real problem for which the Christian has a particular responsibility, namely, the loss of feeling for what is human, the elevation of hatred and reprisal into an ultimate ethical category, the non-dialectical annihilation of the enemy—all of which repeatedly occur in liberation processes, and the risk of which increases the more violence has to be used.

5. Seen in this perspective, the question of nonviolence (so much discussed by many Christians) assumes a different meaning. It ceases to be a question of "personal purity." Strictly speaking, it is not a question of nonviolence but of the kinds, forms and limits of violence present in a conflict involving oppression and liberation. The Christian legitimately asks how it may be possible to humanize this struggle as much as possible. Here again, Christian participation should avoid absolutizing abstract principles (liberation, revolution, order, etc.) which tend first to subordinate and then to sacrifice the concrete human condition, ideologizing the struggle for liberation so that it is transformed into a dialectic of terms rather than the liberation of humanity.

These observations will certainly prompt some to ask whether we have not given the struggle for liberation too relative a character. Isn't a firmer ideological perspective needed to give meaning to the struggle? This is a theme that merits discussion with our non-Christian companions in the fight for liberation. In principle, as subject for discussion, I would dare to say that the eschatological perspective of the Gospel—the confidence in the Kingdom that God brings and which comes "at its hour" permits the Christian to take part in the present struggle (and even in specific activities directed by a particular ideology) without absolutizing an ideology and submitting to it as a prescriptive code. Ultimately one might say that the substantialization of ideology is the temptation to idolatry which Christians must fight in every revolutionary process. Idols always destroy people. Perhaps that is the most important insight that the Christian has to offer—especially as self-criticism—in regard to violence.

III: *African Perspectives*

I Am An African

Gabriel M. Setiloane

What appeals most in the life and witness of Jesus Christ to an African today? "It is when He is on the cross . . . stripped naked like us . . . sweating water and blood in the heat of the sun . . . that we cannot resist Him. How like us He is, this Jesus of Nazareth." South African theologian and poet, Gabriel M. Setiloane, at the University of Botswana, Lesotho and Swaziland in Gaborone, Botswana, is a vice president of the World Methodist Council and was formerly youth secretary of the All Africa Conference of Churches. "I am an African" is reprinted from *Risk* for 1973 (IX/3) with permission of the World Council of Churches.

They call me African:
African indeed am I:
Rugged son of the soil of Africa,
Black as my father, and his before him;
As my mother and sisters and brothers, living and gone from
this world.

They ask me what I believe . . . my faith.
Some even think I have none
But live like the beasts of the field.

"What of God, the Creator
Revealed to mankind through the Jews of old,
the YAHWEH: I AM

Who has been and ever shall be?
Do you acknowledge Him?"

My fathers and theirs, many generations before, knew Him.
They bowed the knee to Him
By many names they knew Him,
And yet 'tis He the One and only God
They called Him:
UVELINGQAKI:
 The First One
  Who came ere ever anything appeared:
UNKULUNKULU:
 The BIG BIG ONE,
  so big indeed that no space could ever contain Him.
MODIMO:
 Because His abode is far up in the sky.
They also knew Him as MODIRI:
 For He has made all;
and LESA:
 The spirit without which the breath of man cannot be.

But, my fathers, from the mouths of their fathers, say
That this God of old shone
With a brightness so bright
It blinded them . . . Therefore . . .
He died himself, UVELINGQAKI,
That none should reach His presence . . .
Unless they die (for pity flowed in His heart).
Only the fathers who are dead come into His presence.

Little gods bearing up the prayers and supplications
Of their children to the GREAT GOD . . .
"Tell us further you African:
 What of Jesus, the Christ,
Born in Bethlehem:
 Son of Man and Son of God
Do you believe in Him?"

For ages He eluded us, this Jesus of Bethlehem, Son of Man:
Going first to Asia and to Europe, and the western sphere,
Some say He tried to come to us,
Sending His messengers of old . . . But . . .
They were cut off by the desert and the great mountains of
                                      Ethiopia!

Wanderers from behind those mountains have told
Strange tales to our fathers,
And they in turn to others.

Tales of the Man of Bethlehem
     Who went about doing good!
The theme of His truths is now lost in the mouths of women
As they sissed their little children and themselves to sleep.

Later on, He came, this Son of Man:
Like a child delayed He came to us.
The White Man brought Him.
He was pale, and not the Sunburnt Son of the Desert.
As a child He came.

A wee little babe wrapped in swaddling clothes.
Ah, if only He had been like little Moses, lying
Sun-scorched on the banks of the River of God
We would have recognized Him.
He eludes us still this Jesus, Son of Man.

His words. Ah, they taste so good
As sweet and refreshing as the sap of the palm
     raised and nourished on African soil
The Truths of His words are for all men, for all time.

And yet for us it is when He is on the cross,
This Jesus of Nazareth, with holed hands
     and open side, like a beast at a sacrifice:
When He is stripped naked like us,
Browned and sweating water and blood in the heat of the sun,
Yet silent,
That we cannot resist Him.

How like us He is, this Jesus of Nazareth,
Beaten, tortured, imprisoned, spat upon, truncheoned,
Denied by His own, and chased like a thief in the night.
Despised, and rejected like a dog that has fleas,
for NO REASON.

No reason, but that He was Son of his Father,
OR . . . Was there a reason?
There was indeed . . .
As in that sheep or goat we offer in sacrifice,
Quiet and uncomplaining.
Its blood falling to the ground to cleanse it, as us:
And making peace between us and our fathers long passed away.
He is that LAMB!
His blood cleanses,
    not only us,
    not only the clan,
    not only the tribe,
    But all, all MANKIND:
    Black and White and Brown and Red,
    All Mankind!

HO! . . . Jesus, Lord, Son of Man and Son of God,
Make peace with your blood and sweat and suffering,
With God, UVELINGQAKI, UNKULUNKULU,
For the sins of Mankind, our fathers and us,
That standing in the same Sonship with all mankind and you,
Together with you, we can pray to Him above:
FATHER FORGIVE.

The Confession of Alexandria

All Africa Conference of Churches

What are the concerns of Christians confessing the faith in Africa today? Meeting at Alexandria, Egypt in February 1976, the General Committee of the All Africa Conference of Churches—representing 114 member churches in 33 African countries—issued a "Confession" which affirms that God, through the continuing work of Christ, "is charting His Highway of Freedom from Alexandria to the Cape of Good Hope." The document—first read before 2,000 members of the Coptic Church of Egypt at St. Mark's in Alexandria—calls for a more comprehensive understanding of liberation, and asks for God's forgiveness of African Christians who have sinned in speaking against evil when convenient and in siding with oppressive forces in their own societies. The "Confession" first appeared in the *AACC Newsletter,* for March 1976 (II, 3), published in Nairobi, Kenya.

We African Christians gathered from all parts of the continent in the General Committee of the All Africa Conference of Churches, praise God for having brought us together in Alexandria, the holy city in which tradition places the martyrdom of St. Mark, the Evangelist.

Therefore God calls us to repentance
He grants us forgiveness,
He leads us to confess our faith with joy,
in the great fellowship of the saints
throughout the ages:

132

The Christian Community in Africa gives praise to God for His revelation through Jesus Christ, His Son and His constant presence among His people through the Holy Spirit.

As members of Christ's Church in Africa today, we have become conscious of the fact that we are inheritors of a rich tradition.

Our current concern with issues related to:

— economic justice
— the total liberation of men and women from every form of oppression and exploitation, and
— peace in Africa

as well as our contemporary search for authentic responses to Christ as Lord over the whole of our lives have led us to a deeper understanding of the heritage delivered to us by the Fathers of the Early Church in North Africa.

Our commitment to the struggle for human liberation is one of the ways we confess our faith in an Incarnate God, who loved us so much that He came among us in our own human form, suffered, was crucified for our redemption and was raised for our justification. Such undeserved grace evokes a response of love and joy that we are seeking to express and to share in language, modes of spirituality, liturgical forms, patterns of mission and structures of organization that belong uniquely to our own cultural context.

This is what the Fathers of the Early Church in North Africa did with the Gospel brought to them by St. Mark. As a result they were able to develop a Christianity that was orthodox and catholic both in its outreach and in its cultural authenticity—and a Church which throughout the ages has endured persecution and martyrdom, and still survives, with renewed strength, until our day.

It is this heritage which inspires us to confess that it is the same Incarnate Christ who is calling us to respond to Him in terms that are authentic, faithful and relevant to the men and women in Africa today. His call is our present and our future.

As this future breaks into the present, Christians in Africa have every reason to be joyful. Through the continuing work of Christ, God is charting His Highway of Freedom (Isaiah 40:3-5) from Alexandria to the Cape of Good Hope. By witnessing to the victorious power of the Cross (Romans 8) we Christians in Africa are encouraged to be co-workers with all those who are called by God to participate in His work.

The storms of history have sometimes led us astray. We have been too willing to rush off this Highway into dead-end paths. We have not always kept close round Christ. We have spoken against evil when it was convenient. We have often avoided suffering for the sake of others, thus refusing to follow His example (I Peter 2:21). We have preferred religiosity to listening to what the Holy Spirit might be whispering to us. We have struggled against colonialism and many other evils, and yet have built up again those things which we had torn down (Gal. 2:18). We confess that we have often been too paternalistic toward others. We have often condoned exploitation and oppression by foreigners. When we have condemned these evils we have condoned the same things by our people. We have turned a blind eye to the structures of injustice in our societies, concentrating on the survival of our churches as institutions. We have been a stumbling block for too many. For these and many other sins, we are sorry and ask God to forgive us.

A full understanding of this forgiveness leaves us no choice but to continue the struggle for the full liberation of all men and women, and of their societies.

We accept that political liberation in Africa, and the Middle East, is part of this liberation. But the enslaving forces and the abuse of human rights in independent Africa point to the need for a more comprehensive understanding of Liberation. Liberation is therefore a CONTINUING STRUGGLE (Lusaka '74).

> Now to Him who is able to do immeasurably
> more than all we can ask or conceive,
> by the power which is at work among us,
> to Him be glory in the Church and in
> Christ Jesus from generation to generation
> evermore! (Ephesians 3:20-21).

The Quest for African Christian Theologies

E. W. Fashole-Luke

There has been more progress in the last fifteen years toward developing African Christian theology than in the previous century. Dr. E. W. Fashole-Luke at the University of Sierre Leone, West Africa—in reviewing what has been achieved thus far—says that "the nature of the quest for African Christian theologies is to translate the one Faith of Jesus Christ to suit the tongue, style, genius, character and culture of African peoples." While an important beginning has been made, the future agenda, he says, "is gargantuan." Among the tasks to be tackled are: "the interpretation of the Bible in the African context"—but there are few African biblical scholars; the relation of Christian faith to African traditional religion—"conversion to Christianity must be coupled with cultural continuity"; and Christology—"there are no signs that Christological ideas are being wrestled with by African theologians." Who should participate in the quest for African Christian theologies? Fashole-Luke says it "should be looked upon as a medium by which Africans and non-Africans can think together about the fundamental articles of the Christian faith in Africa. The quest must be ecumenical and all inclusive." This is a shortened version of a paper presented at the consultation on African and Black Theology, Accra, December 1974, and is reprinted from *The Ecumenical Review* for July 1975, by permission of the World Council of Churches, Geneva.

In 1965, Prof. Bolaji Idowu of the University of Ibadan, who is currently the President of the Methodist Church in Nigeria and the doyen of West African theologians, lamented the fact that West African Christians, after almost two hundred years of Christian experience in the region, have neglected the fundamental task of relating the Gospel message to the political, social and cultural milieux of West African peoples. Idowu unsparingly and relentlessly attacked African theologians and ministers for failing to produce relevant and meaningful theologies which unmistakably bear the hallmarks of the mature thinking and reflection of Africans. Africans must, Idowu claimed, produce indigenous theologies, which will satisfy the deepest emotional and spiritual needs of Africans. When he wrote in 1965,[1] expressions like "African theology," "African Christian theology," *Theologia Africana,* were hardly, if ever, used. It is fair to add, however, that since the beginning of the 20th century, here and there, attempts had been made to relate Christianity to the diverse social, cultural and political situations in West Africa. But no systematic attempts were made to produce African Christian theologies. Worthy of special mention was the attempt to tackle the relation between Christianity and African culture, made in Ghana (then Gold Coast) in 1955 and published in a pamphlet entitled *Christianity and African Culture.* Meanwhile, in the political sphere violent winds of change were blowing throughout the continent; the rapid growth of Independent churches was an indication that some African Christians were, at least, dissatisfied with the imported Church structures, patterns of ministry, liturgical forms, hymnody and architectural buildings which had been introduced into Africa by western Christian missionaries.

Henry Venn, of the Church Missionary Society, had attempted to produce self-supporting, self-governing and self-expanding churches in West Africa, and his policies were brought to fruition with the consecration of Samuel Ajayi Crowther as the first black bishop of the Anglican Church. Unfortunately, Crowther's appointment was not supported by the white CMS missionary agents in West Africa, and several attempts were made by them to frustrate and limit the effectiveness of

Crowther's episcopate. His career ended in a cloud of recriminations and accusations that he was too lenient with his clergy and lay agents; several attempts were made both to discredit his work and to undervalue his achievements. The whole atmosphere of Crowther's last years was unpleasant in the extreme, but fortunately it coincided with the nascent development of West African nationalism. James Johnson and Edward Blyden were in the vanguard of the development of African nationalism and resisted attempts to impose western cultural values upon African Christians.[2] It is fair to add that the Bible was translated into the vernacular languages of West Africa and this inevitably led to the forging of links between West African culture and the Christian faith.[3]

Where are meaningful theologies for African settings?

I have digressed a little to underline the point that the creation of indigenous African churches does not necessarily result in the production of local theologies, liturgies or church structures. What, then, is the basic reason for the failure of West African churches to produce relevant and meaningful theologies for our peoples, in spite of the phenomenal growth of Christianity in our continent? John Mbiti has, I believe, given us a major reason: "The Church in Africa is a Church without a theology and a Church without theological concern."[4] Furthermore, the churches in West Africa have made little or no attempt to train theologians, and even the few who have been trained have received this instruction in western cultural situations, so that on their return home some have moved to the sphere of African traditional religion, where they cannot tread on the toes of church leaders who believe that criticisms of western missionary policies and methods of evangelism are tantamount to ingratitude. Others continue to mouth the theological platitudes they have picked up in universities, theological seminaries or colleges abroad or parade their erudition by quoting the latest theological ideas in Europe and North America. "Barth says," "Tillich thinks," "Eliade suggests," "Bultmann argues," "Robinson believes," "McQuarrie comments," are typical phrases which spice the lectures, seminars and tutorials of professors and theological teachers in university departments, theological colleges or seminaries and Bible schools in West Africa.

Another basic reason for the failure to create relevant and meaningful theologies is the fact that western missionaries came from theological backgrounds where aspects of discontinuity between Christianity and every culture were stressed to the exclusion of the aspects of continuity with local cultures. Conversion to Christianity was thus interpreted in terms of a radical breaking away from the past and being set in a new pattern of life, even if one still continued to live close to one's cultural and social situation.[5]

With the growth of political independence in Africa and the mushrooming of African Independent churches, the tempo of the quest for relevant Church structures, liturgies, hymns, theologies and vestments was quickened. Let me here pay tribute to Prof. Bolaji Idowu for stimulating and giving fresh impetus to the quest for an African Christian theology in West Africa. Three other figures who have influenced this quest in this area are Christian Baeta of Ghana, Harry Sawyerr of Sierra Leone and S. G. Williamson. By their teaching and writing, they have stimulated the younger theologians to take seriously the task of relating the Gospel message to the various West African situations in which they live and work.[6]

In this paper, I shall discuss the nature of the quest for African Christian theologies, paying special attention to West Africa, and I shall finally give an assessment of the fundamental tasks in the quest that still need to be tackled. But there are a few preliminary issues which must be considered. First, should we speak of "African theology," *Theologia Africana,* "African Christian theology" or "African theologies"? Some scholars hold the view that African theology, strictly defined, is the systematic presentation of the religious beliefs, ideas and practices of African traditional religions; we should therefore distinguish between African theology and African Christian theology.[7] Other scholars believe that this is a pedantic distinction, but then go on to confuse the issue further by labelling it *Theologia Africana.* The Latin phrase may well be useful, and has a respectable ancestry, in view of the immense contribution of North African theologians—notably Tertullian, Cyprian, Augustine and Donatus—to the development of early Latin theology, which forms the basis of modern western theology.

There is also the problem of defining the term "African," which involves another question: Who should participate in the quest for African Christian theologies? These matters are of primary importance, particularly in the Republic of South Africa where whites oppress blacks, racial discrimination is enshrined in legislation, and African theology is identified with black theology;[8] non-blacks in this situation are excluded from participating in the creation of black theology, perhaps because black theology is defined as "a theology of the oppressed, by the oppressed, for the liberation of the oppressed."[9] But Harry Sawyerr, in defining the term "African" when applied to African Christian theologies as "a mythological term, expressive of love for a continent or commitment to an ideal,"[10] produces a genuine insight.

The nature of the quest: to "translate" the one Faith

What, then, is the nature of the quest for African Christian theologies? This question can be quickly answered by stating the ideas of four witnesses. First Pope Paul, in his address to African bishops in Uganda in 1969, declared: "The expression, that is the language and mode of manifesting the one Faith, may be manifold; hence it may be original, suited to the tongue, the style, the character, the genius and the culture of the one who professes this one Faith. From this point of view, a certain pluralism is not only legitimate but desirable. An adaptation of the Christian life in the fields of pastoral, ritual, didactic and spiritual activities is not only possible, it is even favored by the Church. The liturgical renewal is a living example of this. And in this sense you may and you must have an African Christianity."[11]

With these challenging words, we turn to our next witness, Trevor Beetham, formerly Africa Secretary of the Methodist Missionary Society in London. He claims that there is only "one eternal Word of God, unchangeable," so "there can only be one theology." However, "the Word becomes incarnate for each generation and if it is in every generation to be 'touched and handled' so as to be universally recognized, it must be incarnate in the life of every people. In this sense, there is need for an African liturgy and an African theology."[12]

My third witness will be Harry Sawyerr, my former teacher and colleague, and I would like to quote two extracts from his perceptive essay: "What is African theology?" In the first extract Sawyerr declares: "A *Theologia Africana* based on sound philosophical discussion need therefore not be a 'native' product, but a searching investigation into the content of traditional religious thought-forms with a view to erecting bridgeheads by which the Christian Gospel could be effectively transmitted to the African peoples. One area which is perhaps most promising in this regard is the community. The African sees himself as part of a cultic community—a community which is incomplete without the supernatural world."[13] Sawyerr then sums up the situation thus: "There is a strong case for a *Theologia Africana* which will seek to interpret Christ to the African in such a way that he feels at home in the new faith. . . . Care must be taken to avoid syncretistic tendencies as well as a hollow theology for Africa. . . . The answer lies in the rigorous pursuit of systematic theology, based on a philosophical appraisal of the thought-forms of the African peoples."[14]

The fourth witness is the Consultation of African theologians held at Ibadan in 1965, which stated that: "We believe that the God and Father of our Lord Jesus Christ, Creator of heaven and earth, Lord of history, has been dealing with mankind at all times and in all parts of the world. It is with this conviction that we study the rich heritage of our African peoples, and we have evidence that they know of him and worship him. We recognize the radical quality of God's self-revelation in Jesus Christ; and yet it is because of this revelation we can discern what is truly of God in our pre-Christian heritage: this knowledge of God is not totally discontinuous with our people's previous traditional knowledge of him."[15]

From the above, then, we can see that in essence the nature

of the quest for African Christian theologies is to translate the one Faith of Jesus Christ to suit the tongue, style, genius, character and culture of African peoples. While noting that there are aspects of discontinuity between the Gospel and African life, practices and culture, we must not neglect the aspects of continuity, as the Ibadan Consultation so rightly stressed. On the other hand, we must take seriously the words of H. W. Turner, who has studied an African Independent church with thoroughness and sympathy, when he says that he is not convinced that "the limitations of a culture-bound white western theology are best corrected by the development of other cultural theologies, black, brown or yellow."[16]

The sources for developing African Christian theologies

Now it is universally accepted by all engaged in this quest that the Bible is the primary and basic source for the development of African Christian theologies. The subject of dispute is the role of the Old Testament witness and the interpretation and use made of Scripture in the process of theologizing in Africa. For the vast majority of Africans, an uncritical approach to Scripture is the norm. Having the Bible in their own native tongue, they can hear God speaking directly to their hearts and their lives, convicting them of sin, giving them assurance of salvation and victory over evil and the powers of evil, as well as entrusting them with the firm belief of life with Christ in heaven. There has been a tendency to ridicule these "biblical fundamentalists," but they underline a basic feature of the Christian faith which cannot be neglected: the uniqueness and finality of Christ's revelation and the judgment of every other revelation, religion or culture by that criterion.[17]

The second line of approach is to recognize the unique revelation of Jesus Christ, and to maintain that this is not found in a book but in a living relationship with the risen Christ. This implies that the Old Testament witness can be dispensed with, and in its place we can substitute the ideas and philosophies of African traditional religions. On the foundation of these, together with the New Testament revelation, under the guidance of the Holy Spirit, and in the fellowship of the Church, we can develop African Christian theologies. The question which arises is: Can we genuinely understand the unique revelation of Christ, who became incarnate in the person of a first century Jew, without the Old Testament witness? And there is another basic question which flows from the first one: Can Christians both affirm the uniqueness of Christ's revelation and at the same time assign some value to the indigenous religions? Here we are in the twilight zones, and African scholars have not yet begun to wrestle with these problems. However, as in twilight zones, immense care and caution should be exercised, in order to avoid statements like that of Dr Samuel Kibichu of Kenya, who claims that Africans had the full revelation of God before the arrival of Christianity.[18]

The third approach is to regard Scripture as both the Word of God and words of men. This approach enables us to make full use of the findings of biblical scholarship, and to employ the critical tools that have been used to study the Bible throughout the universal Church. Two points will emerge from this approach. First it will become clear, despite the sloganeering about progressive revelation, that to dispense with the Old Testament is to destroy the authority of the Bible. Furthermore, it will also be fairly clear that we cannot simply use the African traditional religions as the stocks on which we graft the Christian Gospel. Second, African theologians must be first-rate biblical scholars, competent in the biblical languages, as well as the social, political and cultural conditions of the biblical period. Unfortunately, if there are few African theologians, there are even fewer African biblical scholars who could provide the systematic and dogmatic theologians with the necessary source material, of sufficiently high quality so that African Christian theologies will rise above the level of the banal and peripheral.[19]

The second source which is being tapped for the development of African Christian theologies is African traditional religions and philosophies. African scholars are therefore urged to steep themselves in the religious traditions and patterns of thought of their people. Three points need to be emphasized here. First, what precisely is the value to be accorded to African religious beliefs and practices? Second, one is staggered by the fact that in the writings on African traditional religions, there is great diffidence in using the research of anthropologists, sociologists and even historians.[20] Much of the material for the study of African traditional religion is in oral form, particularly the myths and legends; there has, however, been a tendency to neglect the historical dimensions and developments of traditional religions, and to describe their beliefs and practices in a continuous present tense.[21] In this sphere, African theologians need the insights, and can gain from the methodology of historians of Africa who have patiently sifted and carefully pieced together the vast mass of oral tradition and converted them into coherent historical patterns.

The third source for the development of African Christian theologies is the theological heritage of the western churches, which was largely shaped by the trinity of African theologians: Tertullian, Cyprian and Augustine. At the outset of the quest for African Christian theologies, there was a sharp reaction against western theology and great fears were expressed that its sterility, represented by the Death of God movement, would infect the virile life of the African churches. Fortunately, this period of over-reaction is coming to an end and African theologians are beginning to see that there is theological pluralism in the western world, which makes it possible for us to select those insights of western theologies that are meaningful to, and significant for, African Christians, and to abandon those aspects which are culturally conditioned.[22] The theological heritage of the Eastern Orthodox churches has been largely neglected, especially the kind of theologies produced by Orthodox churchmen in exile. However, with more frequent visits by African theologians and churchmen to eastern Europe for the Prague Peace Conference, with the linking of the ancient Coptic Church of Egypt and Ethiopia with the All Africa Conference of Churches, there are good signs that more fruitful encounters will take place, and that these will enrich our own quest.

I think that, after the initial outbursts against missionaries and western theologies, African scholars are beginning to recognize three things. First, the universal faith of Christianity is always exhibited in local manifestations, and we must therefore theologize primarily for our own local communities. Secondly, Christianity is greater and richer than the totality of its cultural manifestations. Thirdly, our links with the Universal Church give us opportunities to have our theological ideas and reflections subjected to the critical scrutiny of Christian theologians from other parts of the world.

The fourth source for the production of African Christian theologies is the Independent African churches. These churches have innovatively adapted certain aspects of Christian faith and practice to their African milieux; but though their sermons, rituals, hymns, ethical rules, church structures and patterns of ministry abound in Africanisms, most of them lack a coherent and systematic theology. They therefore constitute part of the raw material for the building of African Christian theologies.

"The threshold of a new era. . . ."

I will now assume the role of chronicler. The year 1965 saw the discussion of various aspects of biblical revelation and African beliefs here at Ibadan.[23] In 1971 and 1972, two consultations were held in East Africa. The first one was in Tanzania, and amidst the sloganeering it was suggested that black awareness is a new upsurge against white spiritual, social and political domination. This situation calls for a relevant theology in action. The impact of Africans of the Diaspora was tremendous at that conference.[24] The second conference was held at Makerere University, Uganda, and probed more deeply into the question of producing a relevant theology for Africa today. The theme of the conference was "African theology and church life," and it underlined the point that theology arises from church life and genuine theology cannot be divorced from the life of the Christian community. It was stressed that unless content was put into the phrase "African theology," it may degenerate into an empty slogan. Several aspects of the Christian faith and African beliefs were considered, and John Gatu of Kenya made the staggering suggestion that African values and rituals should be resuscitated and incorporated into daily use in Christian worship. This led to the question of the possibility of African theologians taking a wrong point of departure, if they regarded the cultural concepts of Africa's rural past, which are meaningless to countless urban Africans, as the frame of reference for the creation of African Christian theologies. The Makerere consultation underlined the need to popularize African theology and help African Christians regain their lost identities; in this way, the atmosphere will be created for genuine evangelization which will result in indigenization.[25]

I would like to mention briefly two publications produced by the Africa region of the World Student Christian Federation. The first, entitled *A New Look at Christianity in Africa,* was put out after the AACC Assembly in Abidjan in 1969 and nine African theologians from East, West, Central and South Africa contributed papers on various aspects of the emerging African theology. The aim and scope of this little volume is admirably summed up by Aaron Tolen, who writes: "The various articles included in this book represent an attempt to present some viewpoints on Christian theology which are emerging in Black Africa today. No one should look here for a systematic presentation: on the contrary, we have tried to bring together opinions which can serve as points of departure for a systematic organization of what is already being called by some 'African theology.' Our aim has been to present to our readers the way in which Africans, and particularly Black Africans or 'Blacks of the Diaspora,' participate in the Christian faith and try to express it. This is only the beginning. . . . To be really African, to be adopted by African man in his wholeness, the Christian faith must encompass and arise out of the African vision of the world and the cultures of our peoples. The task of ensuring this is essentially the responsibility of Africans. It must be assumed in a painstaking, honest and comprehensive manner."[26]

Like all collections of essays written by a variety of scholars, the quality of the articles is uneven; but this volume focuses attention on some basic issues and provides signposts for future theologizing in Africa. My one regret is that there was no contribution from francophone Africa.

The second publication appeared in 1972, when the WSCF

magazine *Presence* devoted a whole issue to African theology. African scholars, and European scholars working in Africa, contributed and there is an intriguing interview with the Rev. A. Adegbola. The editorial summarizes the scope and nature of the task to which these scholars were called: "Africa is on the threshold of a new era. Expensive western structures of inherited institutionalized religion will not remain forever. As the old dies, the new must emerge. This is the point at which the churches in Africa need theoretical and practical help. Genuine African aspirations must come to the fore; imaginative and creative experiments should be carried out regardless of cost; innovation should be witnessed in all spheres of life, including services of worship. . . . Schools of theology should not be patterned after their European and American counterparts. Rather the teaching should be tuned to the demands of present day Africa in order to adequately respond to the beating pulse of these changing times."[27]

To sum up, the quest for African Christian theologies, which has been vigorously pursued in the last decade, amounts to attempting to make clear the fact that conversion to Christianity must be coupled with cultural continuity. Furthermore, if Christianity is to change its status from that of resident alien to that of citizen, then it must become incarnate in the life and thought of Africa and its theologies must bear the distinctive stamp of mature African thinking and reflection. What African theologians have been endeavouring to do is to draw together the various and disparate sources which make up the total religious experience of Christians in Africa into a coherent and meaningful pattern.

One further point needs to be considered before we start on the perilous task of defining the future agenda for the quest for African Christian theologies. In the Republic of South Africa, African theology is equated with Black theology and the emphasis on blackness indicates the ethnic implications of the task; considerable attention is given there to the exposition of the Gospel in terms of liberation from political, social and economic injustice, and the creation of a new sense of dignity and equality in the face of white oppression and discrimination.[28] It is surely at this critical point that African theologians are challenged by the

Gospel to raise African Christian theologies above the level of ethnic or racial categories and emphases, so that Christians everywhere will see that Christianity is greater and richer than any of its cultural manifestations, and that the Gospel of liberation is for the oppressed and the oppressor alike. To catch this vision and to overcome the temptations, African Christians need the sympathetic understanding of Christians from other parts of the world.

Paths to follow in the years to come

The future agenda for the quest for African Christian theologies flows from what has been achieved so far and the task is gargantuan. The first item on the agenda should be the interpretation of the Bible in the African context by competent and well-equipped biblical scholars. The second should be the question of the uniqueness of the Christian revelation and the value we assign to other religions, mainly traditional religions and Islam. Dialogue is a fashionable word in theological circles today and Pavey says: "In the 70s we need to discover a Christ who can make men at home in their own environment. The onus is on us to take part in such a discovery. The way is through dialogue."[29]

The third item is the critical study of African traditional beliefs, rituals and practices in the light of the research carried out by anthropologists, sociologists and historians. Attention should now be turned to regions or individual ethnic groups and particular topics, like God, the ancestors, witchcraft, rather than to general studies of African traditional religions.

The fourth item concerns the quest itself. We must now move from the peripheral to the details of the impact of Christianity on individual African ideas and practices. Fr Adrian Hastings has given us a great start on Christian marriage in Africa.[30] The Association of Theological Institutions in East Africa in 1974 considered "The ancestors and the communion of Saints" at their Conference in Nairobi.[31] The Department of Religious Studies of Ibadan University has held a seminar on man, the proceedings of which are published in *Orita*.[32] Mbiti rightly says that all theology is Christology, but there are no signs that Christological ideas are being wreslted with by African theologians. This aspect of African Christian theology needs to be given top priority.

The final item that I wish to suggest in the quest for African Christian theologies is twofold. First, we need to study the Independent churches more carefully and critically and to assess their value for the development of African theology. Second, the Christian experience in Africa is not confined to the Independent churches; though mission-founded churches have tended to be conservative and less innovative in their ideas, structures, discipline, hymnody, patterns of ministry and theological training than the Independent churches, they have become aware of the need for discovering an authentic African Christianity.

In conclusion, I would say that the quest for African Christian theologies must not be conceived as producing a theology for Africans *per se*: rather, it should be looked upon as a medium by which Africans and non-Africans can think together about the fundamental articles of the Christian faith in Africa. The quest must therefore be ecumenical and all inclusive. Suspicions about syncretism and powerful emotions have been aroused, but let us remember that good theology, like good poetry, is the recollection of powerful emotion in tranquillity.

NOTES

1. E. Bolaji Idowu, *Towards an Indigenous Church*, pp. 22ff. London: Oxford University Press, 1965.

2. See further in E. Ayandele, *Holy Johnson*, chapters 4, 8 and 9. Also E. W. Blyden, *Christianity, Islam and the Negro Race*. African Heritage Books I, chapter 3. Edinburgh: University Press, 1967.

3. D. B. Barrett thinks that the translation of the Bible into African languages was a major factor in the development of Independent African churches. D. B. Barrett, *Schism and Renewal in Africa*, pp. 15ff. Nairobi: Oxford University Press, 1968.

4. John Mbiti, "Some African Concepts of Christology." In *Christ and the Younger Churches*, ed. G. F. Vicedom, p. 51. London: SPCK, 1972.

5. Robin Horton, "African Conversion." *Africa*, Vol. XLI, pp. 85-108, 1971. Humphrey J. Fisher, "Conversion Reconsidered: Some His-

torical Aspects of Religious Conversion in Black Africa." *Africa*, Vol. XLIII, pp. 27-39, 1973.

6. E. Bolaji Idowu, *op. cit.* Harry Sawyerr: *Creative Evangelism*. London: Lutterworth Press, 1968. S. G. Williamson, *Akan Religion and the Christian Faith*. Accra, 1965.

7. John K. Agbeti, "African Theology: What It Is." *Presence*, Vol. V, No. 3, pp. 5-8, 1972.

8. Basil Moore (ed.), *Black Theology: the South African Voice*. London: Hurst & Co., 1973.

9. *Ibid.*, p. ix.

10. Harry Sawyerr, "What is African Christian Theology?" *Africa Theological Journal*, 4, pp. 1ff, 1971.

11. A. Shorter, *African Culture and the Christian Church*, p. 219. London: Geoffrey Chapman, 1973.

12. Trevor E. Beetham, *Christianity and the New Africa*, pp. 15ff. London: Pall Mall Press, 1967.

13. Sawyerr, *op. cit.*, p. 14.

14. *Ibid.*, p. 19.

15. E. B. Idowu, in Kwesi Dickson and Paul Ellingworth (eds.), *Biblical Revelation and African Beliefs*, p. 16. London: Lutterworth Press, 1969. More recently at the consultation of African theologians held at Makerere University, Uganda, John Mbiti said: "Theology is a universal treasure of the Christian faith. Ultimately it knows no designations. But when African theologians theologize as part of the universal Church responding to its situation in Africa, there we get a contribution to Christian theology which may rightly be termed African." The papers of this consultation are probably to be published.

16. M. E. Glasswell and E. W. Fashole-Luke, *New Testament Christianity for Africa and the World*, pp. 175ff. London: SPCK, 1974.

17. D. B. Barrett, *African Initiatives in Religion*. Nairobi: East African Publishing House, 1971.

18. Samuel G. Kibichu, "African Traditional Religion and Christianity." In *A New Look at Christianity in Africa*. Geneva: WSCF Books, Vol. II, No. 2, 1970. Dr Kibichu makes this point more forcefully and gives cogent arguments for his views in his doctoral thesis.

19. G. C. Oosthuizen, *Post Christianity in Africa: a Theological and Anthropological Study*. London: Hurst & Co., 1968. See particularly chapters 6 and 11.

20. For example, little mention is made of the significant writings of anthropologists like Evans-Pritchard, Banton and Meyer Fortes. I give examples of these writers' works which are of fundamental importance in the study of African traditional religions. E. E. Evans-Pritchard, *Theories of Primitive Religions*, Oxford, 1965; *Nuer Religion*, Oxford, 1970; *Witchcraft Oracles and Magic among the Azande*, Oxford, 1973. Meyer Fortes, *Oedipus and Job in West African Religion*. Monica Wilson, *Religion and the Transformation of Society: a Study in Social Change in Africa*, Cambridge, University Press, 1959. M. Banton (ed.),

Anthropological Approaches and Rituals: Readings in Religious Beliefs and Practices, New York, 1965. (This list is by no means exhaustive.) Two perceptive articles have appeared in *Africa* in recent years. Robin Horton, "African Conversion." Vol. XLI, pp. 85-108, 1971. H. J. Fisher, "Conversion Reconsidered: Some Historical Aspects of Religious Conversion in Black Africa." Vol. XLIII, pp. 27-40, 1973. I understand that Horton has sent in a reply to Fisher's article and this will soon be published. These two articles will repay patient study and careful scrutiny by those engaged in the quest for African Christian theologies.

21. T. O. Ranger and I. Kamambo, *The Historical Study of African Religion.* London, 1972.

22. Kwesi Dickson, "Towards a Theologia Africana." In *New Testament Christianity for Africa and the World, op. cit.*

23. Kwesi Dickson and Paul Ellingworth (eds.), *Biblical Revelation and African Beliefs, op. cit.*

24. White scholars were excluded from the Dar es Salaam Conference and Black Power representatives from the USA and Britain were very vocal. For a critical appraisal of this Conference, see Eliewaha E. Mshana, "The Challenge of Black Theology and African Theology." *Africa Theological Journal,* No. 5, pp. 18-30, 1972.

25. Discussions on black theology and African theology were continued in New York in 1973.

26. *A New Look at Christianity in Africa, op. cit.,* p. 2.

27. *Presence,* Vol. V, No. 3, p. 1, 1973.

28. Basil Moore (ed.), *op. cit.*

29. Quoted by D. B. Foss, "Evangelism or Dialogue." In *Evangelism in Modern Sierra Leone,* ed. E. W. Fashole-Luke, Freetown, 1974, p. 40. See further P. J. Pavey, "Proclamation or Dialogue." CMS *Bulletin,* January 1971.

30. Adrian Hastings, *Christian Marriage in Africa.* London: SPCK 1973. (Another useful volume by Adrian Hastings is: *Church and Mission in Modern Africa.* London: Burns & Oates, 1967.) Alyward Shorter, *African Culture and the Christian Church,* London, 1973, is a solid and useful piece of work. The Pastoral Institute, Gaba, Uganda, is doing some exciting work on African theology.

31. See E. W. Fashole-Luke, "The Ancestors and the Communion of Saints." In Glasswell and Fashole-Luke (eds.), *op. cit.*

32. *Orita: Ibadan Journal of Religious Studies.* Vol. VI, No. 2, December 1972.

Trinity and Community

Christopher Mwoleka

Bishop Christopher Mwoleka of Rulenge, Tanzania is committed to the "Ujamaa" way of life—the Tanzanian policy of socialism—and he explains it in terms of the Trinity as a life of sharing in community. The mystery of the Trinity, he says, teaches us that "life is not life at all unless it is shared . . . in all its aspects." The Bishop asks whether the common concern of Marxists and Christians for the transformation of society "from self-centered love to other-centered love might constitute a meeting point between us and them, or at least a point of dialogue." His article is reprinted from *AFER (African Ecclesiastical Review)*, July 1975 (XVII/4), published by the Pastoral Institute of Eastern Africa Gaba at Eldoret, Kenya.

I am dedicated to the ideal of Ujamaa because it invites everyone, in a down to earth practical way, to imitate the life of the Trinity which is a life of sharing.

The three Divine Persons share everything in such a way that they are not three gods but only One. And Christ's wish is: "That they (his followers) may be one as we are one. With me in them and you in me, may they be completely one . . ."

Have you ever considered why Christianity is different from all other religions? All great religions believe in one God. It is only Christianity which believes that this one God is three Persons (God is not just one person).

Why should God have revealed this Mystery to us? Christ referred to it very many times. It is a pity that many people find it very difficult to understand what this mystery is all about. Many Christians do not know what to do with it except that it must be believed. It is a dogma they cannot apply to their daily life. So they push it aside to look for interesting devotions elsewhere.

Not an intellectual puzzle

I think we have problems in understanding the Holy Trinity because we approach the mystery from the wrong side. The intellectual side is not the best side to start with. We try to get hold of the wrong end of the stick, and it never works. The right approach to the mystery is to *imitate* the Trinity. We keep repeating the mistake that Philip made by asking: "Rabbi, show us the Father!" Christ was dismayed by the question and rebuked Philip: "Philip, have I been with you so long and yet you don't know me? He who has seen me has seen the Father. How can you say: show us the Father? Do you not believe that I am in the Father and the Father in me?" Then Christ continued to say: "He who believes in me will also do the works that I do, and greater works than these will he do."

On believing in this mystery, the first thing we should have done was to imitate God, then we would ask no more questions, for we would understand. God does not reveal Himself to us for the sake of speculation. He is not giving us a riddle to solve. He is offering us life. He is telling us: "This is what it means to live, now begin to live as I do." What is the one and only reason why God revealed this mystery to us if it is not to stress that life is not life at all unless it is shared?

If we would once begin to share life in all its aspects, we would soon understand what the Trinity is all about and rejoice.

A way of life together

If in the Catholic Church there is something faulty with our methods of presenting the message of the Gospel, the Good

News, it is this: we have not presented religion as a sharing of life. All that people know about religion is the carrying out of commandments—ten of God and seven of the Church—reducing Christianity almost to the same category as the natural religions. We have behaved as though God had not revealed His inner intimate life to us. What we should do is to present the Trinity to people, not in abstract ideas, but in concrete facts of our human earthly life: present the life of the Trinity as shared and lived by us Christians here and now.

Why did God upon creating human beings not put us straight into heaven, but instead put us here on earth? The reason why we should first have to wait here for a number of years before going to heaven would seem to be that we should practice and acquire some competence in the art of sharing life. Without this practice we are apt to mess up things in heaven. So we are here for practice. And for this practice, God has given us toys with which to practice as children do. Before children grow up and build real houses, own real farms, rear cows or drive cars, they first pass through a period of practicing with toys those things which they see their parents doing. For toys, God has given us material things. Material things, therefore, are not accidental. They are necessary for our condition here on earth. We cannot do without them. Material things must not be despised or ignored, but must be used as training equipment for the job that we have to do eternally. All I want to say is this: it is by sharing the earthly goods that we come to have an idea of what it will be like to share the life of God.

As long as we do not know how to share earthly goods, as God would have us do, it is an illusion to imagine that we know what it is to share the life of the Trinity which is our destiny. If you cannot manage with toys, nobody is going to entrust you with the real thing.

Do we reveal the true face of God?

The question is: Have we imitated the Holy Trinity in sharing earthly goods? Have Christians tried to do this in all earnest?

Could I truthfully say: "All mine are thine, and thine are mine", to each and all? This is what we are supposed to imitate (John 17, 10). Then in what sense can we be said to be practicing to live the life of God? How can we dare to profess the religion of the Trinity? The Fathers of the Vatican II Council rightly made a confession: "We Christians have concealed the true face of God and of religion more than we have revealed it." (Church in the Modern World. No. 19.)

You know how those who deny God and religion define life. Let us quote the extremists—the Marxists. They try to figure out what life should be at its best and dream of a society in which "each will give according to his capacity and receive according to his needs." We know that they have made fantastic efforts and that they have not succeeded. They have used methods that we do not and cannot approve. But their vision and their dream could be said to aim at a transformation from *"cupiditas"* to *"caritas"* (from self-centered love to other-centered love). It could be a Trinitarian life expressed in human and material terms. If the Marxists fail to achieve their goal, the main reason would seem to be that they try to impose the ideal from the outside upon people without the necessary corresponding interior dispositions. If we Christians claim to possess these interior dispositions of charity by the grace of Christ, then we should be able to express them in a concrete material way in a manner that would make the Marxists wonder at our success. Would this not constitute a meeting point between us and them, or at least a point of dialogue?

Tanzanians are not Marxists, nor do they deny God. Ujamaa is aimed at sharing life in as many of its aspects as possible. The Government is trying to set up social structures that are viable for this kind of life. I think it is the duty of Church members to supply the interior dispositions needed for this kind of life, as Vatican II exhorted us: "The Church admonishes her own sons to give internal strength to human associations which are just" (G.S. 42).

So in Tanzania, Providence has already provided a new horizon for the apostolate that would bring all persons under the rule of Christ.

This is why I shall not let this chance slip out of our hands.

DISCUSSION QUESTIONS

1. "We approach the mystery (of the Blessed Trinity) from the wrong side." How does the author justify this statement?

2. Does the Blessed Trinity mean more in your life than would be the case if you simply believed in a One-Person God?

3. Why does the author see the mystery of the Trinity as the heart of the Christian idea that religion is a "sharing of life"?

4. Can you think of any reasons for initiating a dialogue with Marxists? Would such a dialogue not be dangerous to faith?

5. Do you agree that socialism gives a better basis for Christian living than does capitalism?—or is this question too political?

The Lord's Prayer—
In The Ghetto

Canaan Banana

A Methodist leader of the black Nationalist Movement in Zimbabwe (the nationalist name for Rhodesia), the Rev. Canaan Banana, studied at Wesley Theological Seminary in Washington. D.C. during 1973-75. While at Wesley some of his writings were published under the title *The Gospel According to the Ghetto,* from which this adaptation of "The Lord's Prayer" is taken. In an introduction, Mr. Banana explained his writing "as an attempt to interpret the Christian message within the context of the experience of those who are victims of a hostile society. . . . It affirms the need for the ghetto masses to become co-partners with God in His divine mission of moral, economic, political and social revolution." Upon arrival back in Rhodesia, Banana was arrested and imprisoned by the government, but has since been released.

OUR FATHER WHO ART IN THE GHETTO,
DEGRADED IS YOUR NAME,
THY SERVITUDE ABOUNDS,
THY WILL IS MOCKED,
AS PIE IN THE SKY.

TEACH US TO DEMAND,
OUR SHARE OF GOLD,
FORGIVE US OUR DOCILITY,
AS WE DEMAND OUR SHARE OF JUSTICE.

LEAD US NOT INTO COMPLICITY,
DELIVER US FROM OUR FEARS.

FOR OURS IS THY SOVEREIGNTY,
THE POWER AND THE LIBERATION,
FOR EVER AND EVER. AMEN

The Relation of
Union to Mission

Burgess Carr

"Liberation, growth, sharing and prophesying"—this is how
churches in Africa see their mission for the remainder of this
century, according to Dr. Burgess Carr. Mission and unity, however, are interdependent in the church (Jn. 17:21), and there are
factors causing the churches in Africa to seek organic union for
the sake of mission. The development of African theology and
the call for a moratorium on missionaries—issues of self-hood
and self-reliance—are "linked," he says, "in a relationship of
identity to mission" and are pointing to the need for organic
union of the churches. Dr. Carr, an Anglican from Liberia, is
general secretary of the All Africa Conference of Churches, with
headquarters in Nairobi, Kenya. His article is reprinted from
Mid-Stream: An Ecumenical Journal for October 1975 (XIV/4),
published by the Council on Christian Unity of the Christian
Churches (Disciples of Christ) in Indianapolis, Indiana.

Introduction

This subject has been a central preoccupation of the "ecumenical" discussion ever since the World Missionary Conference
in Edinburgh, 1910. The representatives from the "mission
fields" of Africa and Asia are reported to have contributed significantly to the "Edinburgh vision" by *pleading that denominationalism be transcended in the interest of Christian unity*. Hence
the ecumenical movement has been called a child of the missionary movement. This is both true and complex.

It is true in a double sense. First, through the missionary movement, the Christian message is no longer regarded only as having *validity* for the entire human race; it has now become the *valid possession* of peoples on all six continents. It has become "ecumenical" in the classical and correct sense, i.e. "worldwide." Secondly, the missionary movement has provided the ferment and dynamism which have given rise to a more precise and specialized definition of the word "ecumenical," i.e. "that which concerns the unity and renewal of the Church."

However, the complexities of denominational rivalry, political and economic colonialism, lack of courage and clearsightedness on the part of Western missionary societies and churches in relating to the "modern world," and perhaps most significant of all, the fact that both the missionary movement of the eighteenth century and onwards and the ecumenical movement of the twentieth century were essentially movements of inspired individuals (Oldham, Brent, Azariah, Baëta, Visser 't Hooft—to mention but a few) continues to raise this question of *the relation of union to mission* as an agenda item for the *churches*.

An assessment of the nature and content of African Christianity

In the volume on *History's Lessons for Tomorrow's Mission* published by the World Student Christian Federation in preparation for the World Teaching Conference on the Life and Mission of the Church held in Strassbourg, July 1960, Hendrik Kraemer wrote

The astounding consequence of the sudden collapse of colonialism and the resurrection of a host of Asian and African countries from colonial subjection to national sovereignty, has appeared to be *a striking metamorphosis* in their position in world politics, accomplished with the same rapidity as their transition from colonial status to independence . . . "the end of Western colonialism" is indeed a colossal event that must necessarily have revolutionary consequences for all movements, institutions, interests and agencies which operated in pre-independence days . . . and continue to exist today. (pp. 195-96.)

He was writing in 1960, the year of African Independence, and he lamented the fact that "the 'older churches' and Western missions are in the slow, too slow process of digesting the 'great change.' . . ." In spite of the optimistic and zealous call to *expectant and worldwide evangelism* enunciated at Whitby (1947), pessimists in the missionary movements in the late forties and fifties were saying that "If things continue as they are now tending, Africa may become a Mohammedan continent." The belief was generally held that the churches in Africa would have to pay a heavy price for the fact that they had originated mainly in the time of modern missions under colonial aegis. Barrett[1] quotes an English theologian and an African historian as predicting that "any realistic appreciation of the situation must suggest that, by the end of the century, Africa will be overtly less Christian than today" (p. 42).

But it is Barrett himself whose "empirical" research has demonstrated that these pessimistic predictions were wrong. In mid 1972 out of a total African population of 367,380,000 the total number of professing Christians was 149,300,000 (40.6%). This latter figure is growing at a rate of 5.0% per year—2.8% by demographic increase and 2.2% through conversion.[2] Barrett attributes this rapid and phenomenal growth of Christianity in Africa "to the labours of a vast army of catechists, evangelists and laymen," and goes on to predict that by the year 2000 there would be a grand total of over 351 million Christians (46% of the population) in Africa.

The question has been raised whether this numerical upsurge in African Christianity represents "A new pulsation in Christian history" or whether this is nothing more than a "mass expansion of nominal Christianity." In the volume on *The Gospel and Frontier Peoples,*[3] Professor John Mbiti describes

these African converts as beggars of Christian spirituality, ideas, cash and personnel from their "superior" overseas missionaries, Church boards and centers of Church organizations. Even if it is not stated in so many words today, basically African Christians still regard the missionary or his home Church overseas, to be the "omniscient" in all matters pertaining to the Christian faith; as the "omnipotent" in money and wealth. . . . This attitude has pushed African Christians to the opposite corners where they play the roles of being "omni-ignorant," "omniweak" and "omnipoor."

He attributes this situation to the fact that

Evangelism has been carried out under a false cultural superiority and the Church in Africa has developed in the context of a false cultural inferiority. . . . Missionary culture told Africa in effect that "unless you were (culturally) circumcised, you cannot inherit the Kingdom of God." So unless they mutilated a large portion of their cultural foreskins, unless they became culturally Westernized, and then Lutheranized, Methodistized, Anglicanized, Roman Catholicized, Presbyterianized, Africans could not inherit one centimeter of the Christian faith. We were told that if we wanted Christianity (and this we had been persuaded passionately to want) we had to pay the price: we had to lay down our cultures, despise them as the missionaries did, condemn them as the missionaries did, and run away from them since missionaries had declared them to be dangerously demonic.

This critique suggests that the spiritual climate in which many of these conversions were made was devoid of any appreciation for the theology of African culture; consequently the missionary-controlled and -led groups of Christians that have become autonomous churches in Africa have been and still are lacking any truly theological conception of the Church. The change from "mission" to "Church" came about mainly as a result of a political accommodation on the part of missionaries to the nationalist sentiments of Africans. In the post-World War II years, Africans' pressure to rid themselves of every form of alien control and to *take over power* reached its peak. This power struggle still continues, as evidenced by the moratorium debate, and weighs heavily upon the search for the organic union of the churches.

To complete the picture, however, it is important to mention two other aspects of the Christian presence in Africa that are of a more positive character. The first is the search for a distinctive interpretation of the Gospel in theological terms deriving out of and utilizing African traditional values and beliefs which constitute a vital aspect of the African reality, inform and shape our world view, and endow our existence with meaning and worth. This is what we call *African theology*. Essentially it involves liberating the Gospel from its Western wrappings in order that the truths which Jesus of Nazareth reveals about God may encounter the spiritual, cultural and intellectual worlds of the African personality: the contours and contents of his mind, his cosmology and eschatology, his institutions and values, his history, politics, philosophy and ideology.

The second positive aspect relates to the African Independent Churches. It is here where Africans find themselves able to celebrate unashamedly and gloriously the longed-for freedom— from many forms of slavery—that they have experienced through conversion to Jesus Christ. Here African theology comes to life in music and song, prayers and sacramental acts of healing and exorcism, art forms and architecture, liturgy and dress, Church structures and community life.

Clearly therefore any assessment of the African response to the Gospel message certainly must take account of the phenomenal growth in numbers, but even more important is our response in word and actions. In *word* we are attempting a systematic reformulation of theology to reflect those insights of *corporateness* and *communality* which guarantee harmony in the cosmos; and in *actions* we are discovering that the Christian faith is essentially one of *joy* that must be lived *celebrationally*.

At the Church Union consultation held in Accra, Ghana last July, Pere Mpila, a Roman Catholic from Zaire, suggested that "only as the churches succeed in developing a genuinely African response to the Gospel will they be able to overcome their differences. As they free themselves from the Western confessional heritage and re-articulate the mystery of Christ's revelation in African terms, they will find that their differences can be overcome . . . *African theology and the unity of the Church are interdependent,"* because by subjecting the various Christian confessions to "critical evaluation . . . it will uncover the true 'catholic' content inherent in each confession."

I contend that in order to develop a *catholic* theology capable of uniting the African churches in "ecclesial communion," greater attention must be given to this traditional trinity of *corporateness, communality and celebration,* so essential to our religious heritage, in formulating the theological basis for the organic union of the churches.

Illustrations of the relation of union to mission

In spite of everything that has been said concerning the theological and biblical imperatives for the organic union of the churches, history shows that it has always been certain secular pressures which have driven the churches to seek ways of overcoming the scandal of their divisions. The opposite is also true. In the search for union, the churches have found it far easier to reach theological consensus than to resolve matters relating to administrative power and prestige, property, finances, etc.

At the present time, the moratorium debate, given new urgency by the Third Assembly of the All Africa Conference of Churches in Lusaka in 1974, has brought a new dimension to the search for unity among the African churches. The moratorium issue centers upon *selfhood* (a theological concept) and *self-reliance* (an economic-political concept). I do not need to repeat here what I have said above about the search for our authentic African Christian selfhood. This is what African theology is all about. But let it be clearly understood that selfhood and self-reliance are linked in a relationship of identity to mission. In a word, the real measure of our capacity to contribute significantly to the humanization of the world is directly dependent upon a rediscovery and perhaps even a re-defining of our identity as African Christians.

In this process methodology is important. Until now the classical approach of those social anthropologists whose studies have provided the orientation for evangelization, Bible translations, etc. in Africa, has been fiercely particularistic. Every single ethnic group has been studied as though it existed as an isolated static population entity. As a result one hears doubts expressed concerning the legitimacy of speaking at all about an African identity or African theology.

We can now begin to correct the over-stress that has been placed on ethnic chauvinism (tribalism)—by the Church no less than by other modernizing forces in Africa. While it is true that traditionally ethnic groups in Africa enjoyed political autonomy, and that their economies were mainly self-sufficient, other cultural aspects, especially in the sphere of religious beliefs and practice, were very often widely shared. Thus to comprehend the African personality, serious consideration must be given to our historic totality as well as to our geographic or ethnic globality. Hence the rejoinder to the call for a moratorium that charges the African churches with advocating isolationism and denying the catholicity of the Church is ill-conceived and superficial. Universality is at the very heart of traditional African culture. It expresses itself religiously in the corporateness through which men and women relate to the cosmos, and socially in the communality with which they relate to one another in time and eternity. The unique contribution of the African Independent Churches to the ecumenical movement lay in their articulation of this genuine African search for a profoundly universal ecumenism that can be celebrated and not suppressed by the imperialistic structures of finance and personnel policies that perpetuate dependency.

As I visit churches throughout Africa in an attempt to interpret the moratorium so that they may comprehend its fullest meaning for their life and witness, I discover that the discussion inevitably points towards the need for the organic union of the churches. There are many reasons for this. First of all, the churches are becoming aware that in our time history is passing through another great metamorphosis. One aspect of this process has to do with the shift in power from those countries which until now, have had a monopoly over the world's wealth, technology, etc. to those newly emergent nations, euphemistically called the Third World, but which nevertheless are the proud owners of the primary resources that produce wealth and power.

Some of the implications for this shift in power for the present structures of dependency in African Churches were highlighted by the General Secretary of the Christian Council of Nigeria in his report of March, 1975 to his Standing Committee. Extracts from this report have been published in the *Nigerian Christian* under the caption "Overseas Aid Will Stop." I will quote the concluding paragraph.

One final remark on overseas aid: it will stop anytime from now. The amber light was given last year when our annual asking of 25,000 U.S. dollars was slashed to 12,000 U.S. dollars. Nowadays, the unlimited wealth of Nigeria is published with so much frequency and gusto that our overseas friends have a feeling that the Church should be able, in such a country flowing with milk and honey, to generate enough funds for its operations. The donor agencies' attitude to aid being given to the Third World, particularly Nigeria, (incidentally, a donor agency now ranks Nigeria with the First World!) is undergoing a good deal of metamorphosis. In the not distant future the amber light which was given last year will be followed by a red light which may never give way to green again. Overseas aid will then stop for ever.

A month ago, at a consultation on the "Internationalization of Missions" called by the Lutheran Church in Liberia, I listened to the United Methodist Bishop in my country say exactly the same thing as the General Secretary of the CCN, even if he was using a different figure of speech. "I am telling the people in my Church," he said, "that the handwriting is on the wall; and it is not written in Hebrew or Latin or Greek. No! It is written in English if you read English, Kpelle, if you read Kpelle, Bassa, if you read Bassa, Kru, if you read Kru,[4] etc. It says, *'The time has come for the Methodist Church in Liberia to stand on its own feet.' "* Before that session had finished, during which the moratorium was hotly debated, the United Methodist Bishop announced that he and the Lutheran Bishop had agreed that at their next annual Conventions early in 1976, they intend to nominate a joint committee to initiate union negotiations between their two churches.

But the impetus for union is not generated only by financial pressures. This year I spent Holy Week making pastoral visits to the churches in Lesotho, Swaziland and Mozambique. In each place I found the churches struggling with a particular aspect of their mission that has given the highest priority to unity and eventual organic union. In Lesotho it was the prophetic witness of the churches in defense of human rights and in the promotion of justice, reconciliation and peace in their country. The political crises which have tormented the Basotho people since pre-independence politics began, but especially since 1970, are now seen to be the direct result of antagonisms spread by Protestants and Catholics among their converts, on the one hand, and alliances between the churches *as churches* and political parties, on the other. Now they are crying out for help in disengaging themselves from their unholy alliances and in forging new links of unity between Catholics and Protestants through the Christian Council of Lesotho and its commitment to justice, human rights and the relief of the enormous human suffering which is the direct result of the denial of justice and human rights to the children of Moshoshoe.

In Swaziland, where I ate the Last Supper with the churches, the pressures towards unity have as much to do with a rediscovery of Swazi identity (a process which is also taking place in the political sphere) as it does with the obvious need for union imposed by the rural organization of Swazi society. In Swaziland there is no room for comity agreements, since the "kraal" or tribal homestead and not the towns or villages is the organizational pattern of traditional society. The churches are small, and among Lutherans, Anglicans, Roman Catholics and some of the Independent Churches I sensed a strong conviction that genuine ecumenism was the only rational basis upon which the churches could fulfill their mission. Among the Lutherans and Anglicans there is even a disposition to form an organic union arising mainly out of the need to combine manpower and other local resources in order to effectively carry out their evangelistic and social tasks. "We only confuse the people, when today someone calling himself a Methodist comes to my kraal and says to me 'you have to pray with your eyes closed.' The next day another comes as a Roman Catholic and tells us we haven't got to close our eyes when we pray. Whom are we to follow?" was the question put to me by a man of 77 years.

I spent Good Friday and Easter in Mozambique. Here the churches are urgently aware of the necessity to recast their identity and to unite in order to take full advantage of the opportunities independence has brought to spread the Gospel throughout their country. Moreover, it is generally accepted that the needs of the churches for leadership development, literature and the facing of the challenges of various forms of frontier ministries (e.g. to students, to the masses who will now rush into the cities from the rural areas, to women and to repatriated refugees, etc.) are so massive that only through unity, indeed some believe through organic union, can the Church fulfill its mission in the New Mozambique.

A Conciliar Consensus on the Relation of Union to Mission

The Lusaka Assembly of the All Africa Conference of Churches reached a very clear consensus concerning the mission of the churches in Africa for the remainder of this century. The consensus is defined in terms of liberation, growth, sharing and prophesying: liberation from structures of dependency towards authentic selfhood; growth through evangelization, communication, education and identification with Africa—its problems and its promise; sharing what we have, what we experience and what we discover for the total enrichment of the whole people of God in Africa, and prophesying against the demonic principalities and powers that impede the advancement of God's reign of love, righteousness and reconciliation, justice and peace in our nations and societies. As we discover ways to deepen and strengthen commitment to this consensus, I am convinced that we shall re-enforce the "unifying drive of the churches in Africa." Liberation and unity, the twin theme of our First Assembly ("Freedom and Unity in Christ") held in Kampala twelve years ago, and now the theme of the Fifth Assembly of the World Council of Churches—the first to be held in Africa—in 1975 provides the context in which we situate our missionary calling as African Christians who are "part of the world community and must also share in the redeeming work of Christ."

NOTES

1. David B. Barrett, "A.D. 2000: 350 Million Christians in Africa" in *International Review of Mission,* Vol. LIX, No. 233 (January 1970) pp. 39-54.

2. *Ibid,* p. 45 ff.

3. *The Gospel and Frontier Peoples,* ed. R. Pierce Beaver. South Pasadena, Calif.: Wm. Carey Library, 1973, p. 81.

4. Kpelle, Bassa, Kru: languages in Liberia.

The Challenge of our Stewardship in Africa

Kenneth D. Kaunda

The president of Zambia, Kenneth D. Kaunda, is the son of African missionaries who left their native Nyasaland (now Malawi) and went to work among the Bemba people to the north. Therefore in delivering the keynote address at the Third Assembly of the All Africa Conference of Churches at Lusaka in 1974 he spoke not only as president of the host country but as a committed member "of the household of faith" (Gal. 6:10). Dr. Kaunda urged the delegates and their churches to "translate into practice Christ's message. . . . His message is very clear. It is universal and all-embracing. . . . Our challenge is to give practical interpretation of this important universal message so that we can lead Christ's life." He commended the Church for its help in fighting "injustice and terrorism against the masses by minority regimes" in southern Africa, and challenged the Church to take the lead "in advocating socio-economic and political systems that guarantee a fair distribution of wealth and opportunities." He also explained that "when we in Zambia talk about Zambianisation in the Church we are not referring to the mere replacement of expatriates with Zambians. We mean something much deeper—namely that Zambianisation must reflect our values so that it has real meaning to the lives of all our people." President Kaunda's address is reprinted from the published proceedings of the Lusaka assembly, *The Struggle Continues* (Nairobi: AACC, 1975).

The Third Assembly of the All Africa Conference of Churches is being held at a very crucial time in the history of the continent and indeed in the history of the world. Africa has undergone dramatic political changes since the end of the 1950s. Decolonisation and the emergence of independent African nations have had a far-reaching impact on the social, economic and cultural structures. The traumatic political changes and the consequent readjustment of the relations between people and institutions have in many cases led to stresses and strains within and between institutions. Some institutions have tended to be conservative while others have spearheaded the great revolutionary changes. Readjustment in the relations between institutions has been necessary but the ties of many African institutions to the external world have always promoted unnecessary conflict. Sometimes the conflict has been based on matters of ideology or principles; sometimes on policy and so forth.

However, two institutions on which African success must be founded remain those which are the source of moral authority and justice. These are Government and the Church. The Church is the custodian of moral supremacy in the State while Government is the custodian of justice. Indeed, a good Government cannot do without morality just as the Church must depend on the strength of justice in the State in order to make moral supremacy a practical reality.

This is why we welcome this assembly of church leaders at this time in the history of this country and Africa. The epoch-making changes that are taking place on our continent require a very strong and indestructible moral base which naturally must be founded in the Church. Morality and justice must be twin sisters of freedom and independence based on the principles of human equality—equality before God and before the law of the land. Africa's quest for socio-economic and political order which is in accord with African values and aspirations, cannot, in the circumstances of our commitment to the building of a moral and just society, involve politicians alone. Leaders in all walks of life, including the Church, cannot be passive observers of the process of change, and in the creation of an inter-dependent society. We all are active participants in building a new Africa which fulfils our aspirations. We all must enjoy the benefits of this fellowship which this great movement in history has brought in its train.

If there is anything which we the people of Zambia feel we have achieved so far in this respect, it is that the Church can no longer live apart. The Church in Zambia is not a passive observer in the great task of building a humanist society. It cannot afford to be. The Church is in the forefront of the movement towards the establishment of a genuine humanist society.

Indeed this is not strange. We believe that a good church under good leadership can never be in conflict with a good government under good leadership guided by a well organised party with firm principles founded on justice. Where the quality of goodness characterises the leadership of local or national institutions, there will always be harmony based on love, understanding and genuine feeling of fellowship nourished by morality and justice. The goals of the Church are the goals of the State. The cause of the Church is the cause of the people and Government. Government values the moral principles on which the Church is based. The unfulfilled moral challenges of today become political problems of tomorrow.

The Church, therefore, has tremendous tasks in building African nations and African unity. The responsibilities of our stewardship lie beyond the frontiers of conventional Christian practice. Our stewardship is basically the acceptance from God of our personal and collective responsibilities for the lives of our fellowmen and the affairs which make life worthwhile for every human being.

—Creating conditions for genuine peace is our responsibility.
—Creating conditions of freedom and justice is our responsibility.
—Creating conditions of equality among all men without discrimination as to race, colour, ethnic grouping or station in life is our responsibility.

Equality is not a passive principle, it is a condition which must be created by everyone working together in the spirit of love and understanding in accordance with Christian principles.

In this connection the principles upon which Christianity is based are very clear, yet contradictions in practice abound. In the western world, which is regarded as the home of Christianity, these principles are honored more in breach than in observance.

Inequality is virtually glorified as a condition which must be accepted by humanity. The capitalist system has as its dominant feature the exploitation of one person by another, accompanied in Southern Africa by unbridled suppression and denial of civil liberties. We have had people prophesying to be Christians—holding the Bible in one hand and a gun in the other. These are people who have been responsible for the human suffering which this continent has experienced since the days of slave trade.

But we must not look to the past with all the grim human suffering which the continent witnessed. We must look to the future and face the unfolding grave responsibility we have for our fellow human beings. Let us translate into practice Christ's message. According to my understanding of Christianity, Christ was born into this life so that he should be a model of human life on earth—rejecting, fighting and conquering sin. He imparted to us the values of modesty and self-sacrifice. He showed us how to discharge the obligations of our stewardship. He belonged to all, worked for all, suffered for all, so that all may be saved. His message is very clear. It is universal and all-embracing. Christ's work is unifying. The substance of the message is the unity of the human race, harmony and inter-dependence among all persons on earth based on love and understanding. For this is the only way people can live in community. Christ's work and Christ's message cut across the barriers of ideology, race, color and ethnic grouping. This is why Christian service must be blind to race or color; this is why when we in Zambia talk about Zambianisation in the Church we are not referring to the mere replacement of expatriates with Zambians. We mean something much deeper —namely that Zambianisation must reflect our values so that it has real meaning to the lives of all our people.

Christ's life is in conformity with the theme: *"Living no longer for ourselves."* Indeed Christ is, in our context, a leading humanist. His political, economic and social philosophy speaks louder than one can elaborate in such a short space of time. Our challenge is to give practical interpretation of this important universal message so that we can lead Christ's life. It is not enough to imitate him. We should genuinely lead his life.

Peace under conditions of inequality and exploitation is not genuine. Genuine peace must be based on equality of opportunity and a fair distribution of wealth. This is one of the greatest challenges of the Church in practice. Our political, economic and social system must have a framework that ensures built-in conditions of equality. The greatest danger to Christian principles is materialism and greed that has characterised the so-called modern society. I believe that Christianity today in many countries of the world is too commercialised; yet it is very clear that if materialism should be the dominant feature in life, the competition nourished by greed will make service and personal sacrifices less important in Christian life. Greed leads to exploitation of man by man. Greed leads to dishonesty. Greed leads to jealousies and conflict. It destroys the basis of justice and morality. The Church must not glorify greed or social systems that promote greed. The Church must lead in advocating socio-economic and political systems that guarantee a fair distribution of wealth and opportunities. The Gospel is very clear on the dangers of wealth to the building of Christian life. The Gospel declares: "It is easier for a camel to go through a needle's eye than it is for a rich man to enter the Kingdom of Heaven."

I urge the Church in Africa, clergymen and laymen alike, to work out a correct approach to the practice of Christianity.

Therefore, Church leaders must be in the forefront in guiding the African nations and African leaders to move away from economic and social systems that glorify inequality. Let the Church help put the new nations firmly on the road to prosperity which is based on human equality.

For us in Zambia, humanism is our guide. Humanism does not advocate poverty. Humanism advocates the fullest improvement of the human condition based on fair distribution of national wealth and equality of opportunity.

We the leaders in Africa have a great task of discharging the responsibility of our stewardship. We are not living for ourselves. We are responsible for the lives of our fellow beings. We are responsible for creating economic, social and political conditions which make a full life possible, enjoyable and worthwhile for all.

We have another responsibility in Africa. We must restructure conditions of almost five centuries of history which started to unfold after the first white man set foot on this continent. For years, inequality and oppression have been accepted as the mode of life in Southern Africa. Now the course of history has been turned. We must move in the direction of more equality among all human beings. The majority must have the right to participate in shaping their own destiny. This imposes a very heavy responsibility on the African leadership. African leaders whether free or still oppressed must be united more than ever before in developing the spirit of forgiveness. This spirit must be promoted and nourished even under the most tempting conditions like those existing now in this part of the world. We still have to discharge the obligations of our stewardship to each and every human being entrusted to our care.

We in Zambia feel the concern for each and every human being in this part of the world. History and geography have for all these years bound us together into a new community with a common destiny. We all have responsibilities towards one another. African leaders have time and again declared their intention and have accepted their responsibility to build non-racial societies. Liberation Movements have from time to time re-affirmed their commitment to non-racialism. They have always said that their armed struggle is not against the white man. It is against injustice, oppression, exploitation and colonialism which it has been their misfortune to endure for years. In many ways the Liberation Movements are helping to create conditions in which the aspirations expressed in the Christian Gospel can be fulfilled.

The minority regimes in Southern Africa suffer from moral bankruptcy, and justice is not in their vocabulary. They need a saviour. We need to help them to be more enlightened and to understand that the great forces of history cannot be turned back from the goal of independence based on majority rule, and greater human integration which seems to be the order which God has ordained. A few reactionary elements may try to place obstacles in the way of change. In our view, they can only slow down the dramatic developments towards majority rule but they will never stop them.

The Church has made a tremendous contribution in carrying the banner of human rights very high. The Church has helped to fight injustice and terrorism against the masses by minority regimes. This has greatly shaken the foundation of the oppressors and has opened new prospects for peace and co-operation.

We African leaders have a great responsibility. We cannot discharge this responsibility alone. We shall need the assistance of those we are required to serve. There is a lot of sacrifice we must make. In these moments of trial, no time is our own time. No life is our own life. We, like Christ, belong to all and our work is in the service of all. We must, therefore, discharge this service with honor and dignity. But we can only succeed if there is a willingness among the racists in Southern Africa to help create conditions for peace based on love and not exploitation, equality, not racial superiority.

Our Christian way of life must be genuine and the Church must be a model which people must be proud to emulate in their daily life. We cannot nourish the spirit of Christian fellowship unless there is commitment to live a genuinely Christian life.

For our part, through humanism, we will continue to endeavor to make Christian principles our way of life. But we require the assistance of each and every leader in the Church to uphold moral supremacy so that with justice to which our Party and Government are committed, we can genuinely build a society of free people, a prosperous society, a member of the African family, a member of the human family. This is why we have made many sacrifices since our independence to help others fulfill their aspirations in the spirit of internationalism.

Finally, this is an important Assembly and I sincerely hope that out of your meeting will come a new out-look towards the work of the Church on our continent. I, therefore, pray that your deliberations may be successful. And now I have the greatest pleasure to declare the Conference open.

Thank you and may God bless you.

Daring to Live for Christ

Manas Buthelezi

What is to account theologically for the identification of much of the Church in South Africa with the racist policies of that government in oppressing the black majority population? Dr. Manas Buthelezi, in his third contribution to the *Mission Trends* series, says that "the greater part of the Christian Church in South Africa has been held captive by a theology that abstracts Christian life from human life"—the result of "a false unbiblical dichotomy." This is theologically untenable, as Buthelezi points out, for "if Christian life is other than human life, the incarnation of Christ is then of no significance." For Christians to live for Christ means that "acts of Christian motivation become incarnate in the social, economic and political structures." And the suffering experienced under oppression by those who dare to live for Christ should be endured, not with resignation or as an end in itself, but "as a step towards liberation." This, he says, "is redemptive suffering." Dr. Buthelezi, formerly director of the Christian Institute in Pietermaritzburg, is now general secretary of the Evangelical Lutheran Church in South Africa. His article is reprinted from the July 1975 *Journal of Theology for Southern Africa,* published quarterly by the South African Council of Churches, Braamfontein, Transvaal.

To live for Christ means in the first place to live like Christ. It is axiomatic to say that Christ is the exemplar of the life after and through him. The Bible tells us that in order to save humanity the divine Christ became man, and in order to be a truly sav-

ing man the human Christ suffered. Therefore for Christians to
dare to live for Christ means to be truly human even to the point
of suffering in the interests of others.

When I say to live for Christ means to be truly human,
some may understand this as an undisguised blasphemous hu-
manisation of the Christian life. For this reason, before discussing the question of suffering it is necessary that I should first say
a few words on the concepts "human" and "Christian."

By Being Human

To be human and to be Christian sound contradictory to
many Christian ears. Over the centuries a false unbiblical dichotomy has been made between human life and Christian life. This
explains the present anomalous situation in which sometimes
those who profess to be concerned with spiritual regeneration
often harbor blind spots in their consciences when it comes to
questions of human rights and racial justice. In the United States
the Southern "Bible Belt" has for many years been at the same
time a haven for the Ku Klux Klan and other professing racial
bigots. In our own country the national Christian zeal to keep
the Sabbath holy is not deemed contradictory to the parliamen-
tary knack for creating discriminatory legislation that subjects
black human beings to indignity. The ironical thing is that it is
mostly those of the Jewish faith who, out of proportion to their
numbers, have courageously championed the course of the un-
derdog and the victim of human injustice in this country.

Is the Jewish faith proving itself more dynamic and relevant
to the political and moral problems of South Africa? Under
these circumstances is it a desirable thing to encourage the prose-
lytic Christian mission to the Jews in South Africa? Should it not
be the other way round?

Be this as it may, the fact of the matter is that the greater
part of the Christian Church in South Africa has been held captive by a theology that abstracts Christian life from human life.
One of the basic maxims of this theology seems to be "the more

sanctified your life becomes the more irrelevant human and earthly things become." In other words, here Christian growth is a matter of the eclipse of human life by the Christian life. This eclipse accounts for the blind spots in many a Christian conscience. While professing brotherhood of all in Christ, Christian people have made laws and regulations which ban fellowship in restaurant and toilet facilities, to cite one example of the universal aspect of human life.

Some remind us that all Christians "meet at the foot of the cross of Calvary mountain"; they overlook the fact that if this is true Christians must also meet as human beings at the foot of Table Mountain in Cape Town in order to make laws and vote on matters that relate to the welfare of the body which is the temple of the Holy Spirit.

Christian life is in fact life through, under and after Christ. If Christian life is other than human life, the incarnation of Christ is then of no significance. The identity of the Christian life is not something abstract; it is a concrete reality which is embedded in our social, economic and political relations. Through the Bible we know Christ only as incarnate; hence it follows that we can identify Christian life only as it enshrines itself in our politics, economics, and social policy. It is either here or nowhere. It is false to think that we are Christians only as we go to Church and pray to God. These are only essential moments of inspiration and refueling and should not be confused with the full thrust and ramifications of Christian life itself.

Just as God does not wave a wand—to use Luther's phrase —in bringing children to the world, but uses man and woman, Christ gave us new life not by just remaining God but by becoming man. We cannot bypass what is around us and what is already given in human life in order to give concrete expression to the impetus of Christian motivation in life. It is as acts of Christian motivation become incarnate in the social, economic and political structures that we speak of Christian life as an everyday phenomenon. To dare to live for Christ means to have a Christian impact on these structures. It is a daring act because it involves the risk of suffering just as Christ suffered as he made concrete his love for humanity.

By Suffering for Others

There is a danger in indiscriminate drawing of parallels between forms of suffering and the redemptive suffering of Christ. It is a dangerous type of soul care which, as it were, attempts to domesticate the sufferer to suffering. Suffering is in the first place an evil and no one should be trained to regard as normal the state of being a victim of evil. As such it is there to be removed or alleviated.

Having made these general remarks, I will then go further and make a distinction between two forms of suffering.

1. *Oppressive Suffering:* This is the more common and universal form of suffering. It is oppressive because it exposes the victim to other forms of suffering and cripples initiative and resolve. The victim resigns himself to it without making any effort to rise above it. Suffering becomes a way of life; a form of god over the victim.

Endurance of such suffering thus becomes a cult, a form of idolatory and a sabotage of the design of God for the victim. Let me illustrate this by a few examples.

Lack of adequate education facilities breeds a culture of ignorance which envelops the victims in its oppressive power. This remains imperceptible to the victims because "he who knows not knows not that he knows not."

The victims then fail to cope with the demands of their environment and are further exposed to disease and hunger. They either die or live by simply hanging on the barest thread of existence.

In South Africa the bulk of the victims of the sufferings described above are black. Their lot is not just due to the fateful cruelty of nature, but largely due to a highly sophisticated discriminatory system of legislation. This system breeds exploitation of black labor and an unfair distribution of wealth, power and life opportunities.

To liken the suffering of the black people to that of Christ is not just theologically mischievous but a gross manifestation of a callous Christian conscience. This is a suffering that oppresses.

2. *Redemptive Suffering:* Redemptive Suffering can be characterised as follows:

(a) It is suffering after the model of Christ's suffering. Christ became man and suffered in order to save human beings from the bondage of sin.

(b) It is suffering which is not an end in itself but which is endured in the course of a struggle to realize the well-being of fellow human beings.

(c) As such it flows out of love for the other. It is power-over-oneself suffering so that others may be free. The power to endure suffering comes from the intensity of the resolve to realize the objective that lies beyond suffering.

(d) The redemptive power of suffering equips you to set aside your own security and interest in order to serve the interest and security of others.

(e) The articulation of suffering of oneself as well as that of others is the beginning of the redemptive phase of suffering. Personal suffering at this phase is a window through which one becomes aware of the suffering of others in a more experiential way.

At this moment in South African history the suffering of the black people is becoming redemptive. The black people are now regarding their suffering as a step towards liberation instead of a pool of fate and self-pity. Right in the midst of the experience of suffering the black people have made themselves believe that they can do something about their own liberation. Black consciousness is an instance of how the black people have transmuted their present suffering into the medium of liberation towards self-esteem. This is redemptive suffering.

African Proverbs Related to Christianity

Frances Randall, S.N.D.

When a team of African Christian undergraduates and teachers at colleges in Kenya collected unwritten Kenyan traditional proverbs and studied them beside the Christian Scriptures they discovered, "It's all here, Christianity is all here." Reporting on the project, Sister Frances Randall, S.N.D.—a missionary lecturer at Kenyatta University College in Nairobi—says that as they became aware that "the most expressive proverbs had myriad correlations in the message of Christ . . . the realization dawned that the Christian faith had to assert both a fulfillment of the past and must emerge as something entirely new." Such proverb/scripture correlation—"Even an ant can hurt an elephant"/"Let anyone who thinks he stands take heed lest he fall" (1 Cor. 10:12)—is being used now in religious education to incorporate African experience into Christian tradition with greater meaning and appreciation for both. Sister Randall wrote her report for the February 1976 issue of *AFER (African Ecclesiastical Review)*, published by the Pastoral Institute of Eastern Africa Gaba at Eldoret, Kenya.

This is an attempt to summarize the intentions, process and results of team efforts in exploring Kenyan traditional proverbs, a venture embarked upon during this last year. The objective of the research was to study the African experience as it has come out of the past, as it relates to Christian Scripture, and its projections for being a redemptive force in the future; to reflect on

this experience and affirm it within the truth of the gospel, in accordance with Jesus' words, "If you live according to my teaching, you are truly my disciples; then you will know the truth and
the truth will set you free" (Jn. 8:31).

This research is about life, about religion, about education.
About life—about families, about teachers, farmers, students
and other workers—work and leisure and birth and marriage
and the traumas of social conflict. It is a query into the integrity
of human existence.

Specifically, I have examined the proverbs of a people—
profound truths, couched in obscurity. Proverbs from a people
who chose to respond to life, to take their powerlessness as a cue
to create new forms of power, within and around them, confront-
ing their own humanness and that of others, people who chose to
enter the *silva obscura,* a womb from which life, hope and de-
cency might issue. And so near are these contemporaries to my
own soul, that to reject them is to reject myself. And finally to
know these is inevitably a summons to act on their behalf, as a
resulting imperative of conscience. I have also examined the effectiveness of religious education in an effort to discover whether
the aptitudes and capacities it creates in the young adult help to
further his or her maturity, and whether it fosters a genuine
Christian understanding of life.

Theology and Tribal Experience

This project was conducted over a ten month period and involved undergraduates from Kenyatta University College and
teachers from primary teacher colleges throughout Kenya. Since
the focus was a correlation of culture with the Christian ethic,
the initial step was to gain a clearer concept of God's revelation.

With this in mind, we began to take a closer look at the scrip-
tural account of the Exodus-event. We chose parallelisms between the situation of the Israelites in Egypt and that of the
tribes in Kenya. We related this parallelism between slavery of
the Israelites and the slavery oppression of the Africans under
European "pharaohs." In much the same way as the Israelites

came to know Yahweh as God of the oppressed, the team concluded that Africans have come and must continue to come to a growing awareness of God as the God of the oppressed. In a very real sense the people, places and events which are operative in a project of this nature are in theological reflections, the revelations of God's power and love for His black people. We, through reflection and sharing came to affirm that the Israelites came to know God through what he did for them and He revealed His name in connection with this activity and saving power.

"Who *is* your God?

Yahweh who brought us out of the land of Egypt!"

Through the medium of "Go down Moses," the team was inspired to struggle with the truth of the past and present tension between Egypt and the promised land, then through an internalization of the symbols for good and evil come to a deeper awareness of the African experience immersed in oppression, exploitation and colonialization.

The intention, as well as the hope, was to move toward that point of intensity where deep internalization of the symbols could generate an atmosphere rich with the remembrance of the mighty deeds of Yahweh and His fidelity expressed in liberating the oppressed, and then in this mystery, make a response to the Righteous One.

In accordance to the original outline, attention and time were devoted to the New Testament Gospels, particularly to the Gospels of Matthew and Mark. Deeper theologizing was carried out within the scope of the Lucan account. The attention given to Luke's Gospel was centred in the following passage:

> The Spirit of the Lord has been given to me
>> for He has anointed me,
>> He has sent me to bring the good news to the poor,
>> to proclaim liberty to captives
>> and to the blind new sight,
>> to set the downtrodden free,
>> to proclaim the Lord's year of favor.

The experience of the black oppressed people was seen and repeatedly referred to against the background of this passage quoted above, in which the poor, captives, blind and downtrodden are understood as the oppressed masses. The search revealed that any ongoing quest for an African theology had to be rooted in the basic idea of Jesus as anointed for the "Church." Otherwise the theology would fall short of personal identification with the life-experience of Kenyans.

Finally, we focused on the section in Luke's Gospel, known as the "Great Intercalation" by using the parables of the Prodigal Son and the Good Samaritan. In focus, the Word became sharply "judgmental" and aroused some discomfort among the group who could see that in many ways the church had really failed to administer as father and minister of hope for the oppressed.

Concretising Our Aim

Within this phase it seemed most appropriate to concretise our aim, that of capturing the feelings of the Kenyan through the collecting of his feelings about life through his proverbs. Teachers from teacher training colleges throughout the country were contacted and invited to participate in this research. During the holiday months, the team and co-opted members collected unwritten proverbs.

During the following months these proverbs were sorted into categories and classified according to similarities of thought and interpretation. Excitement was high during this phase. "It's all here, Christianity is all here," was the statement repeatedly heard. Fulfillment was great as these Christians found that the most expressive proverbs had myriad correlations in the message of Christ. This was such a startling new idea, that even as they explored these concepts the realization dawned that the Christian faith had to assert both a fulfillment of the past and must emerge as something entirely new. Christianity had burst forth from the womb of its birth.

Proverbs are not created, but born to life. They do not come into being like signs as a result of the creative faculty of the human imagination. The proverbs of darkness, light and water, for example, were given to man with his existence in the world. It is significant to note that of the hundreds of proverbs collected, the team chose proverbs connected with these themes, familiar, comfortable and concrete psychological and sociological conditions where humans respond to their heritage. From this flowed the multitude of personal-level proverbs such as father, teacher, lover, guide. These are proverbs which can only be constituted if human beings are seen as partners in the relationship they indicate even though the role may be a passive or subordinate one.

"Water tastes sweeter from a gourd."

"He who wants papyrus ash, burns papyrus."

"The eyes of a frog cannot prevent a zebra from drinking."

"The father and son are one thing."

"She who cannot dance blames the drum."

Matching Proverbs and Scripture

The task of matching Christian Scripture thought with the thought contained in the proverb was the next focus. After a consensus was reached concerning accuracy of interpretation, Scripture scholars were contacted and requested to examine the correctness of the correlation of the two.

For this phase the considerations focused upon the use of the Proverb/Scripture thought within the corpus of the Church and school. It was decided to illustrate this material in the form of posters, with simple, culturally focused, line drawings.

This it was believed may encourage an affective response which can translate knowledge into action and enrich human response to God. The team believed that this illustrated-type approach was vital as the present emphasis in the nation on art and culture, should from its inception be presented simultaneously with religion in order to assure a balanced educational emphasis.

Final Selection of Texts

To select twenty five pictures, illustrated in a literal manner rather than in an interpretive way, thirty posters were placed on public display.

The following was the final selection:

UNIT ONE

1. He who gossips is like a granary full of holes.
   What comes out of a man's mouth proceeds from the heart, and this defiles a man (Mt. 15:1).
2. Find a path or make one.
   I say to you, if you have faith as the grain of mustard seed, you will say to the mountain, "Move to yonder place," and it will move (Mt. 17:21).
3. He who wants papyrus ash burns papyrus.
   Where your treasure is, there will your heart be also (Mt. 6:21).
4. The foolish bird builds a nest in a dead tree and does not know it will be cut down.
   No one puts new wine into old wine skins; if he does, the new wine will burst the skins and it will be spilled (Lk. 5:37).
5. The father and the son are one thing.
   The glory that is his as the only son of the Father (Jn. 1:14).

UNIT TWO

1. Young sugar cane gives no beer.
   Brethren, do not be children in your thinking, be mature (1 Cor. 14:20).
2. Even an ant can hurt an elephant.
   Let anyone who thinks he stands take heed lest he fall (1 Cor. 10:12).
3. The family members are those who know what happens in the family.
   To you has been given the secret of the kingdom of God (Mk. 4:11).
4. Where a strange tree grows another will follow.
   Temptations to sin are sure to come but woe to him by whom they come (Lk. 17:1).

5. A pot cooks the food but does not eat it.
   One man sows, another reaps (1 Cor. 3:8).

UNIT THREE

1. Water tastes sweeter from a gourd.
   If anyone thirsts, let him come to me; let him drink (Jn. 7:37).
2. There are some things like earthen pots which if broken cannot be repaired.
   What does it profit a man if he gains the whole world and suffers the loss of his soul (Lk. 9:25).
3. Cows must graze where they are brought.
   There is nothing I cannot master with the help of the One who gives me strength (Phil. 4:13).
4. Unless you call out who will answer?
   Ask and it will be given unto you (Mt. 7:7).
5. You are the one who eats of your father's labor.
   You received without pay—give without pay (Mt. 10:8).

UNIT FOUR

1. Good seed is known at the harvest.
   As you sow, so shall you reap (Gal. 6:7).
2. One camel does not make fun of another camel's neck.
   There are many parts, yet one body (1 Cor. 12:30).
3. He who runs alone thinks he is the fastest.
   Let him who boasts, boast of the Lord (1 Cor. 10:12).
4. One does not send a child to collect honey.
   Be wise as serpents and simple as doves (Mt. 10:16).
5. A bell needs its tongue.
   Cut off from me you can do nothing (Jn. 15.5).

Conclusions

After months of exploring the subject of religious education by means of response to culture/scripture correlation, thus observing reactions to the Africans' experience within the mystery of the Incarnation, we were able to formulate a few opinions and convictions, and refine a sense of direction for further development of our research.

1. We recognize the limits of this research, since it is based on a population of twenty six schools in a limited area, and touches only a scattered sampling of proverbs and the religion syllabus. Thus, we were careful not to interpret our data in terms of generalities. However we feel that this sampling does give reliable insight into the value of teaching religious education as a trustworthy tool for developing in youth the capacity to further his or her maturity and a genuine Christian understanding of life. Also a re-enforcement by way of cultural media is an effective approach.

2. We consider this project as one segment of a whole response to God's revelation, and see its value as a beginning for the youth of Africa, providing them with a body of knowledge, understanding and appreciation of traditional values. As a help to see its richness and relevancy to the revelation of God, and the necessity of preserving this basic African value, we exhort Christian leaders to incorporate the African tradition into a meaningful Christianity for the indigenous people by the use of such posters referred to in this study as a basis for instruction; and educators to use this art form as a supplement especially in the area of African traditional religion.

3. We maintain that education in Kenya must represent not only an authentic reflection on the experience of Kenyans, but must be a prophetic voice speaking to this present situation, as lived by Christians in this present decade. Education must, if it intends to remain credible to Africa, make it possible for Africans to choose life. For this to come about the educator must hear and appreciate the continuation of God's saving mystery as it is enacted in the African experience.

4. African theology will keep on developing as long as it can speak about the art of loving and living in its own context. Such reflections must artistically describe African history and life style in such a way that the descriptions will inevitably lead to esthetic, educational and liturgical celebration just as the activity of Yahweh in the Old and New Testaments was described in a definite cultural art-form and was celebrated in community.

5. Finally, our concluding aspiration was to delve deeper and deeper into the subject of African education and explore the

area in more detail historically, culturally, scripturally, with the hope of formulating an authentic interdisciplinary approach to penetrating the wealth of the African experience.

In short, we concluded on a positive note. We hope that our proverbs will influence an enrichment of education in such a way that education will become for Africans their creative way for participating in a life fully lived.

Discussion Questions

1. "It's all there—Christianity is all there." What do you think is meant by this statement concerning traditional wisdom? If Christianity is "already there," what is new about the Gospel?

2. Is sufficient attention given to the context from which the various proverbs emerged? Why is the context so important in all literary forms, including both proverbs and the biblical writings?

3. Do you agree that proverbs are really an expression of wisdom, or do you think that they are mere observations based on experience, but without integrating it, in view of the fact that so many contradictory proverbs exist?

4. What is the value of finding sentences in scripture that correspond to proverbs? Is there any criterion for deciding which are the more important sentences, or is it simply random choice?

5. In what ways can proverbs be effectively used in religious and artistic education?

IV: Asian Perspectives

Let My People Go

Harvey Perkins, Harry Daniel
and Asal Simandjuntak

Asking "What are the basic missionary concerns and strategies in Asia today?"—three executives of the Christian Conference of Asia (CCA; formerly the East Asia Christian Conference) discuss the issues in terms of liberation—"Let my people go"—as "the central theme of God's redeeming work." The issues are complex: cultural identity and theological integrity—evangelism and social justice—poverty and dependence—sending and receiving relationships—denominationalism and Christian unity—nation building and political oppression—to name a few. On the controversial question of a moratorium on foreign missionaries, the CCA—they point out—has *not* adopted the position of the All Africa Conference of Churches in favor of a moratorium. "Amid the diversity of Asia and of its Christian churches, such a stance would have little validity or significance. . . . There are alternatives to the total strategy of moratorium." They conclude: "Only a deeper identification with the responsibilities and priorities of mission will give clarity and freedom of judgement as to what the selfhood and mission of the Asian church requires." The CCA—an organ of continuing fellowship and cooperation among 16 member councils and 78 churches in 17 countries bounded by the Karachi-Sydney-Tokyo triangle—operates as a regional agency within the wider ecumenical movement. Its first assembly was at Prapat, Indonesia in 1957; the seventh assembly at Manila in 1977. On the CCA executive staff with headquarters in Singapore, Harvey Perkins (Australia) is Development and Service Secretary, Harry Daniel (India) is Associate General Secretary, and Asal Simandjuntak (Indonesia) is Mission and Evangelism Secretary. Though not an official CCA statement, the study document—issued in December 1974—has been widely circulated and discussed within the CCA membership.

A. In God's Mission in Asia, "Let My People Go"

1) This is a message and an invitation to share in a program in mission. We offer it to all those who work in committees of the CCA and to persons in positions of leadership in the member councils and churches throughout Asia.

   We write with the conviction that the CCA should be seeking to enhance in the churches of Asia a sharp consciousness of mission. What are the basic missionary concerns and strategies in Asia today?

2) Mission belongs to God. His is the word. He is the word. His word is His action in creation and in redemption to restore His creation. God is a missionary God.

   Because God is missionary, His Son Jesus Christ is His "sent one" or "anointed one"—His missionary. His people are called to be co-workers with Christ as the Son pursues the mission of the Father.

3) Our participation in mission is a humble one. The mission is not ours. To participate in His mission is our total calling. That calling is to discern God at work in the signs of our time. That is what shapes our missionary strategies. That calling is also to understand the situation of men and women and their societies—their need of God. That is what shapes our missionary concerns.

4) We have given our message the title "Let my people go." Let us explain why. With this cry, Moses demanded that his people be released from slavery. "Let go" is a call for libera-

tion. From that time on, liberation has been the central theme of God's redeeming work.

The cry was also God's. Moses was His servant through whom He was calling a "people of God" into being. "I will be your God if you will be my people." From that time on, His people, His community have been called to be a liberated and a liberating community.

The creation story expresses how deep is that call. It is both a story of God's creative action and a story of the brokenness of His creation in the relationships of human beings with God and with each other. Then comes the Exodus story. God's redeeming action is toward the victims of His broken creation. He calls the victims to be His people. Through that people, He moves in mission to restore the wholeness of His creation.

5) In the missionary movement of the Father's Word, Jesus came. To people at the mercy of others, he offered the mercy of God, and called them into His community of mercy. For this he was anointed. To the broken and bruised, to the captive and those who could no longer see the way, he came with healing and liberty, deliverance and sight (Luke 4:18-19). Christians are those who know and confess His name, who bear it and proclaim Him. That is evangelism.

6) Our Asian consciousness begins in the awareness of being victims. The centuries of exploitation in the colonial days before our political independence, and today the continuing economic exploitation of our people and our resources, determine our present history. The Gospel is to us. We are called into the forefront of the missionary responsibility of the Christian church because it is of peoples such as ourselves that God's cry is made, "Let my people go." Liberation is the good news we receive from Christ. Liberation is the good news we are called to share with our fellows. The words of Moses and the declaration of Jesus' ministry at

Nazareth declare both the situation within which the Asian mission is set and our Asian calling to that mission.

7) We hear the call to mission as part of the call of God to His people everywhere and also as His particular call to us who know Christ as the Redeemer in our particular Asian setting. God is one, the world is one and His call to mission is one. We give our obedience to that call in the context of our Asian setting and as Asian mission.

B. *To Asian Responsibility in Mission, "Let My People Go"*

8) Our Asian history, as part of the people of God called in Christ, makes it difficult for us to express our responsibility in mission. We have been "receiving" churches, and in many ways we still are. The word "mission" denotes to us something foreign, something which came to us in western missionaries and resources, something we received and responded to, rather than our calling which requires of us both response and responsibility. The missionary movement has come to us as something western, something which brings in its company the values of western society as if these values are the values of the Christian faith. With it, our ways of life have become western and our cultural roots have been loosened. Because it has been western, the missionary movement has been carried out with tremendous material resources, leaving unexamined the question whether those resources are really necessary for our participation in the mission of God. We often feel dependent in consequence, and act in a dependence which inhibits our imagination to see ways in which mission can proceed with our given scarcity of such resources. Even missionaries are mainly western because western resources are necessary for missionaries to be sent. Our poverty becomes what disqualifies us from participating in mission. "Let my people go."

9) From these facts arises the cry to "indigenize." The call to

indigenization is not a primitive cry to revert to an earlier cultural state. Culture is itself dynamic and it is impossible to go back to a past that does not exist. But there are values and perspectives in our dynamic cultures which the word of God in Jesus Christ must meet, encounter and renew.

—To find expressions of faith and ways of life in which the word of God meets our culture, corrects and transforms it and produces the Christian style which belongs to us as the people we really are!
—To make that possible, claim some freedom with whatever sacrifice by relying less or not at all on western personnel and resources!
—To enter deeply into dialogue with people or other faiths in our midst!
—To read the Bible through our own cultural eyes and the eyes of our poverty rather than through the eyes of western culture and affluence!
—To engage ourselves in the struggle of the poor and the search for justice (righteousness) in our own societies, and challenge the structures of exploitation which oppress, both from the affluent world and within our own societies!
—To let "third world" theologies emerge!
—To seek a style of life in Christian community which is appropriate to our situations, which will be seen by others to whom we witness as a style which belongs and can be theirs.
—To build that style of life on our deeper sense of community and enrich it rather than feed upon the individualism of the western world!
—To find the dynamic of our life in sharing each other's burdens rather than in relying on western resources to relieve them or to make us privileged in the eyes of our fellows!

The call to indigenize is not inconsistent with the universality of the faith in God or of His call to mission. How western should our churches be? How important are our own cultural identities and expressions of faith and life? What does it mean to be indigenous in our societies which are being superimposed rather than transformed by western culture all the time?

10) Responsibility for mission lies primarily with the Christian community in each place. It is not a western missionary responsibility to evangelize the world. Our responsibility is set in the context of our situations, and that context is something with which we live and in which we can move as no foreigner whose life and faith is set in another context.

—The rise of national selfhood and the newly-found sense of national dignity is something to be recognised in the proclamation of the Gospel and to be addressed by it.

—The social and economic instability of our lives in our various national situations gives a depth of meaning to Jesus' proclamation of good news to the poor, which must be our proclamation too, and central to the context of mission in our hands.

—As there are tensions in our countries between the pressures for national unity and the demand for freedom, so in many situations within the churches there are tensions between the pressures for Christian unity in the national scene and the self-contained life of ethnic churches. In the struggle with these tensions, let us claim the new understandings and point to forms of community for our nations which western denominational divisions can never do.

—The ideological conflicts and political pressures in which our lives are set challenge us to seek in our context the meaning of liberation which the Gospel in its fulness offers.

—We also live, usually as small Christian minorities in the midst of a plurality of religious allegiances. This fact requires us to recognise the deeply religious character of our peoples and to proclaim Jesus Christ, not as the leader of another religion, but as the Liberator of everyone. For this proclamation, "Let my people go."

C. For Asian Priorities in Mission, "Let My People Go"

11) This is the context of mission in which the CCA Executive Committee has suggested it is important that national consultations on the concerns of mission take place in Asian countries. It is important for us to define our priorities in mission. In these days, when there is talk about "moratorium," meaning temporary suspension of relationships with western mission boards which send personnel and resources, it is necessary to face, anew and radically, questions of priorities in mission. A moratorium on the past as a mental approach can release us to look into the future of mission and the priorities of mission in the future. Into new priorities "let my people go."

12) A few questions may stimulate us. We all recognise how much of our time, energy and resources are spent in running our church administrations and institutions. Within them, we can close ourselves from what is going on around us and make decisions with the institutions primarily in mind—rather than the people, their lives and their struggles. If we all try to put the interest of the institutions behind for a while, what are our real priorities in mission?

We claim one faith, but our ideas, even our ideologies and certainly our practices, differ. What provides us with our stance? That is often left unexamined. Jesus came to proclaim good news to the poor and release to the captives. What does it mean to be the community of the poor? What are the priorities in mission which follow?

We are facing heavy political pressures in many places. Such external pressures upon us often produce in us self-questioning and re-appraisal of our work. How do our contemporary situations make us think anew about the priorities of our missionary engagement?

13) CCA cannot determine priorities for the churches. What it

can do and has done is to establish the priorities which will guide it as it facilitates the movements of people in mission between Asian countries. We share these again with you, because they may be suggestive and stimulating in your own considerations.

Evangelism—to encourage new understandings, strategy and experiment in evangelism.

Mobilization of local congregations—to build up congregations in new understanding of what it means to be the people of God, and how to participate in God's mission in a world of social change, living faiths and ideologies.

Social justice programmes—to develop a new understanding of and commitment to justice and liberation.

Migration of people—to care for people as they move into new situations in search of work and livelihood, and to help them as minority communities to participate more fully in the societies into which they move.

Understanding our neighbours—to understand the histories and cultures of Asian countries and the life of churches in those contexts.

14) Listing areas of priority is comparatively easy. Making decisions about new priorities is much more difficult. We have traditional priorities which we have inherited from western missions, such as church growth, education and healing ministries. These priorities need to be reshaped for the sake of growth in quality; for more indigenous styles, content and objectives of education; for more community-oriented rather than institution-centered approaches to healing. But they are entrenched in institutional approaches around churches, schools and hospitals and are difficult to change. It is also difficult to implement new priorities when so much of energy and resources are expended on these traditional and institu-

tional priorities. Perhaps some examples will help to bring
the CCA listing to life.

—There are a few situations in which the goal of evangelism
has been the conversion of total village communities rather
than of individuals within them. These programs reflect understanding of the communal character of village people,
and express a strategy of seeking community allegiance to
Christ. There are other situations where programs of village
development have opened the way to very effective village
evangelism.

—There are places where congregations have been renewed
and mobilized as they have become involved in work with
trade unions and industrial management, helping the poor
to define their needs and methods of attaining their goals,
and as they have supported the social service programs of
groups adhering to other faiths in their midst as well as their
own.

—In situations of political repression, there are churches
which have found new life and understanding of the liberating Gospel they profess as they have become involved in vig-
ilant action in defense of human rights and civil liberties.

—The recent conference on minorities has led to major
changes of policy in one industrial firm in relation to employment of ethnic minorities in its midst.

—Those who have worked in Asian countries other than their
own can testify to the understanding they have gained and
which they have been able to share with their churches.

D. With Asian Resources for Mission, "Let My People Go"

15) When we look into these examples, we find that more limited resources from outside Asia have been required. One
problem with our traditional priorities is that they have been
determined by others and have been developed in styles
which are inherently dependent on personnel and resources
from outside the Asian region. Today, they consume the
limited resources of our own. Our action on new priorities

must spring from our initiatives, reflect our agendas, implement our decisions. As we seek to review our understanding of the priorities of mission in the future, we need to relate our review to the question of greater reliance on our own resources, and greater use of external resources for our priorities.

16) One contributor to our discussion has recalled how Isaac first built his altar, then pitched his tent, and finally dug his well. All were necessary to his life and selfhood (Gen. 26:25). He compares the history of Asian churches and draws attention to how we have built our churches and developed our national church organizations but have done these things in foreign style and in heavy reliance on foreign resources. He suggests that is why we have not dug our wells very well, why we have not tapped our resources through the commitment of those who have joined the people of God. Isaac had to draw water in his own place. Our Asian churches need to dig our wells and draw our water in the life and the commitment of our local congregations. As we do so, we will find new strength as some of our churches have already found, for witness.

17) The question of resources arises in relation to both personnel and funds.
   —How much do we rely on western personnel in our churches?
   —How much do they affect our style and give us a foreign image which inhibits our identity, delays our indigenization, and impedes our proclamation?
   —Do western workers help us to be, or hinder us from being, churches of the people?
   —How much do they contribute to the gap between the urban and village styles of our churches?
   —How acceptable to us is the gap between expatriate and local stipends in equivalent positions?
   —Do we have clear views as to how we can use western workers effectively for our chosen priorities?

18) There are also questions about how our people serve our priorities in mission.

—Does the gap between the urban and the village pastor divide the fellowship of our ministries?
—Do the modernized styles of our central and institutional church work produce false aspirations, jealousies, resentments and power struggles in our churches?
—As there is a question of what is the acceptable gap between expatriate and local stipends, have we faced the internal question of what is the acceptable gap between the highest and lowest levels of stipend in our ministries?

19) For years, the CCA has tried to encourage movements of persons in mission between Asian countries with the help of financial contributions of western mission boards to the Asian Missionary Support Fund. We help with only a few. It seems that more of our people in Asia go to the west than exchange with one another. We acknowledge that our missionary responsibility reaches to the western world and seek further opportunity to fulfil it. We acknowledge too that to work in other churches in any part of the world broadens experience and understanding. But we still have to ask why so few between Asian countries?

—Is it that there is more money and other factors in the west? If so, what does that say about our commitment in mission and our identification with the poor?
—Do we hesitate to replace western workers with our own people or with Christians from other Asian countries? If so, how important is it to us that the western worker is paid for by others?

20) So let us face questions too about financial resources.

—Does the extent to which we use foreign funds hinder us from developing our own stewardship?
—Peoples' commitment is related to how we give ourselves, what we put into the cause, what it costs us to do it. Do

foreign funds affect adversely the depth of commitment to the Christian cause among our people?

—Do they create a style of church life which is not ours and inappropriate to our situation?

—Do they create structures which we cannot maintain ourselves?

—Should we be more self-reliant and live more on the basis of our scarcity of resources?

—What are the guidelines which help us to be selective about how much of such resources we are ready to use and how we use them?

21) Many Asian churches are looking hopefully for capital investments in property and endowment funds to enable us to continue to live and work in the style which foreign resources have set for us. How does this enable us to be identified with the poor and to proclaim good news to the poor who have no such financial maneuverability? We already have wide gaps between the central and urban church style and the village style. But it is the village people who have strong cultural roots. How can we claim the cultural rootage of the poor for the identity of the whole church if church establishments continue along the rich man's way with the devices of property income and endowment funds?

22) Does our reliance upon foreign funds hinder us from sharing our own resources between our own churches, between richer and poorer congregations? The news that one mission board would need to reduce its grant to a national church recently led to a conversation in that church on how to develop its inter-regional sharing. Have we developed our own inter-church sharing programs within our own churches? Can we move the richer congregations to share more with poorer congregations in the fellowship?

23) In the CCA, we acknowledge that we too are heavily dependent on foreign funds. The question of our life-style is always with us. How can we, as well as, say, some national

denominational offices be closer in style to the normal life-style of our churches insofar as that is possible in an international setting?

If dependence on foreign resources is what stops us from developing our own resources or another style more appropriate to our own resources, how serious do we regard that dependence to be? How radical must be our answer?

E. In Our Relationships with Others in Asian Mission, "Let My People Go"

24) Historically, many of our churches in Asia have been related over a long period of time with churches in North America, in the United Kingdom, Holland, Germany and other countries of Western Europe. Within our own fellowship in the CCA, the relationship between "sending missions" and "receiving churches" is represented through the involvements of mission boards in Australia and New Zealand. Styles of relationship vary within the basic "sending and receiving" relationship. Some relationships began with pioneering missionary movements and have continued as relationships with autonomous churches in Asia. Other relationships developed later as church relationships through which smaller supplementary assistance is received. Some sending agencies rely on appeal methods and require a close identification of particular projects for their appeal purposes. Others secure their financial resources through a church budget system and so are able to use more general methods of funding. What styles of relationships do we really want to have, if any, with these agencies in the future? In what particular ways do we want them to change?

25) One mission board has recently changed its style of relating with churches overseas. It offers people in response to requests, and the requesting churches have the right to accept or decline the offer and are exercising that right. Per-

sons so engaged are employed by the receiving churches rather than the sending mission board and the employing churches have the right to terminate as well as to engage and are exercising that right too. The employing churches have the right to set the field stipends for those whom it employs. In this way the employing church decides what is the acceptable gap between payments to local and expatriate workers. The employing church is responsible to pay those whom it employs. The mission board makes an annual block grant to the budget of the receiving church and the church decides the use of its budget—how many expatriate workers will it employ, where it will seek them and what it will pay them. In this way the requesting church makes all the decisions about its strategies and priorities. How it uses expatriate personnel is one among the many questions of priority which the church has to decide.

26) This example leads to several questions which we may ask and which may suggest possible future patterns of relationship.

—Do we feel that sending mission boards and service agencies have too determinative a role in relationships with us, either by making unilateral decisions which affect us or influencing our own decisions too much?

—Do we want expatriate workers in our churches to be in our employment to the extent that we engage and terminate them, set their field payments at a level we consider appropriate in our national conditions and pay them?

—Do we wish to receive open grants as contributions to our Church budgets so that we have freedom to decide how all resources available to us are used according to our priorities?

—Do we operate on declining annual grants according to a schedule planned with our supporting bodies so that we are planning our growth in self-support?

—Have we developed personnel plans over some years ahead so that planned replacement of expatriate workers is possi-

ble and training programs to that end are also planned?
—Is it helpful for our freedom to seek the services of expatriate personnel through ecumenical rather than denominational channels?

27) We should also note the initiatives within Asia. There are indigenous missionary societies within our countries which serve in other areas of their own country or beyond it without using external resources. Some churches have missions departments which seek resources from their own congregations and through which bilateral movements are arranged with other churches.

Although the Asian Missionary Support Fund of the CCA operates with resources received from western mission boards, it facilitates movements by supporting the international costs of movements between Asian countries while the churches involved in each movement support at local salary levels and to meet family needs. Do not these examples point to styles of movement in mission toward which Asian churches should move as deliberate policy and in increasing measure?

F. Is Moratorium Necessary to "Let My People Go"?

28) Four years ago, the General Secretary of a church in Africa urged a moratorium on all western personnel and funds into the church of his country. It meant that all western personnel should leave, and none take their place. It also meant that no more funds should be received to support church work or its service in the community. He claimed that this was necessary for a time in order that the African church might find its real cultural identity, might change its style and determine its priorities freely. Moratorium does not mean moratorium on mission, a temporary suspension of mission. It means moratorium for mission, a temporary suspension of the flow of resources, so that the church may find

how to obey its missionary calling in its own country and cultural reality and decide its own priorities and style of mission. The proposal envisages that relationships may be renewed after a reasonable period, but on the terms and for the purposes of the church within the priorities and style of mission which the African church has set in the meantime.

29) Since then, a debate on moratorium has developed in many parts of the world. The Ecumenical Sharing of Personnel (ESP) Committee of the World Council of Churches has become a focal point of debate. The argument for moratorium is that "True partnership and interdependence among churches, in obedience to the Gospel, might better be achieved by pressing for independence through a period of search for selfhood rather than by modifying existing patterns of relationships in a more gradual way" (ESP 1972). Both sending and receiving churches need liberation from past patterns of domination and dependence if the response of each to God's mission is to be renewed.

30) In May 1974, the Assembly of the All Africa Conference of Churches (AACC) recommended to member churches a moratorium in Africa. It described the option as "the only potent means of coming to grips with being ourselves" and so sharing as an African church "in the redeeming work of Christ in our world." It recognised the tremendous effects such an option would exercise on the structures and programs of African churches, but saw also out of that option a new freedom in evangelism and a new drive for Christian unity in Africa. "To be truly redeemed," the report said, "one must die and be reborn"—African and viably African.

31) The Christian Conference of Asia has not taken such a stance. Amid the diversity of Asia and of its Christian churches, such a stance would have little validity or significance. In this paper, intended as message both to the committees and the member churches of CCA and to the ESP

Committee of the WCC, we who write it have taken the position that we should engage each other in a process. The issues raised by the African call for moratorium are real. We have raised them as we share our concerns with you in this paper. But moratorium is a matter for each or any Asian church in its relationships with western churches and ecumenical agencies. Our task is to draw attention to the context which makes the option for moratorium important. Our task is also to stimulate an important process in which our churches need to engage—a process of reconsidering.

—What is the mission of God and what is our calling to participate in that mission as co-workers with Jesus Christ?
—What is the context of our missionary calling in Asia today and what are our priorities of mission in that context?
—How should resources of personnel and funds (Asian and external, if any) be used in serving those priorities? It is to stimulate that process that we have written to a large extent in a self-questioning way. It is for that process that we seek earnest cooperation, and issue our invitation. Through that process, and in their own contexts, churches may find their own answers.

32) There are alternatives to the total strategy of moratorium. It is commonly agreed amongst us already that the first area for a "selective moratorium" is the salaries of local pastors. These should be the whole responsibility of the local congregation and the national church. In comments received from within national situations in Asia, one contributor who supports moratorium makes an exception in the case of service to the needy and destitute. Another would seek a moratorium on personnel only. Still another selective moratorium style would be to change our relationships with western boards and agencies so that we are free to seek the participation of expatriates from places we choose while maintaining an unearmarked financial resource flow on a declining basis. The Lausanne Covenant says that "a reduction of foreign missionaries and money in an evangelized country

may sometimes be necessary to facilitate the national church's growth in self-reliance and to release resources for unevangelized areas." These are examples of partial or gradual approaches to moratorium such as AACC has declined to opt for.

33) We should take note of the fact that in the history of some of our churches in Asia, moratorium has been forced upon them. Some of our member churches experienced forced moratorium during the years of World War II. One contributor testifies to the renewal and new life of evangelism which was released in a church in his country as a result of this experience. National member churches in one country have been experiencing forced moratorium regarding personnel for many years and the values and problems of that experience need to be shared with us all.

One contributor has written in anticipation of a forced moratorium in the future in his country as a result of Government policy. He speaks of the need for staged moratorium regarding personnel; of the cooperation of government to enable local people to be trained for positions held by expatriate personnel within a defined period; of policies of declining financial resource adopted in consultation with missionary societies; and of movements toward Church Union, encouraged by the pressure of political events regarded as inevitable.

34) Contributors from two other countries oppose the proposal totally. "The churches are interdependent. The question should be viewed from the point of view of growing togetherness and having common responsibility in mission and service." There lies the issue. Are the churches genuinely interdependent or is the prevailing situation one of dependence, one way? Does not interdependence involve a mutual responsibility toward each other, in which the doors of western churches are as open to our participation as are the doors of our churches to their participation? These are days in which

we recognise that mission is in six continents, not three. The western world is passing through a deep crisis in faith. It is also involved in economic crisis and social sickness—the result of its acquisitive individualism and rapacious use of resources—ours as well as theirs—for their own profit. All the sickness of the affluent which Jesus described is apparent in western life. There are urgent missionary needs today in the countries from which the modern missionary enterprise originated.

35) Therefore there is another important question about moratorium. Would moratorium release the western church for new roles and new priorities in mission? Would it liberate a western church to see its mission among its exploited migrant communities and ethnic minorities or in a struggle in the seats of world power for a more just economic order in the world or in caring evangelism that people who have lost their way may find Him who is the way? We have been receivers for so long that we see our western brothers and sisters in Christ as "givers" rather than as churches with their own responsibility for mission in their places and with as many problems of missionary engagement as we have. Do we seek to understand their sense of mission? Do we acknowledge that they too have an option for moratorium as much as we have? In so far as moratorium for mission is on the past and for the future of mission, do we seek to share in their future tasks of mission? Will we offer to them in their life what we have received in faith and grace from God in Jesus Christ?

36) The immediate advantages of what we receive can benumb our judgements so that we are hardly capable of seeing the good that could come out of choosing a radical alternative to our present relationships. Only a deeper identification with the responsibilities and priorities of mission will give clarity and freedom of judgement as to what the selfhood and mission of the Asian church requires. Into that freedom, "let my people go."

From Israel to Asia—
A Theological Leap

Choan-Seng Song

Does God deal directly with "the nations" or is his redemptive activity mediated only through the Church? Choan-Seng Song from Taiwan complains that western theologians "obstinately persist in reflecting on Asian or African cultures and histories from the vantage-point of that messianic hope which is believed to be lodged in the history of the Christian Church . . . and redemption loses its intrinsic meaning for cultures and histories outside the history of Christianity." Song believes this is "a distortion of the message of the Bible" and he is "convinced that a very big theological blunder has been committed by those theologians who have forced God's redemption into the history of a nation [Israel] and of the Christian Church, and have consequently institutionalized it." Contrary to the traditional western understanding of "salvation history," Song argues that the Old Testament "prophetic tradition consists in a refusal to recognize the history of Israel as identifiable with the totality of God's acts in the redemption of his creation." Israel was *not* to be "the nation through which God's redeeming love would be mediated, *but* to be a symbol of how God would also deal redemptively with other nations." Therefore, says Song, other nations can learn from the experience of Israel "how their histories can be interpreted redemptively. . . . An Asian nation will thus be enabled to find its place side by side with Israel in God's salvation." This "theological leap" from the experience of Israel—"symbolically transported out of its original context to a foreign one"—to the cultures and histories of Asian peoples and nations is consistent, according to Song, with the radical interruption in history of

211

"the Word become flesh" and with "the dialectic of salvation revealed to us through the witness in the Bible." Formerly professor of theology and principal of Tainan Theological College in Taiwan, Dr. Song is now associate director of the Commission on Faith and Order of the World Council of Churches in Geneva. His book, *Christian Mission in Reconstruction: An Asian Attempt* (Orbis Books, 1977), enlarges on some of the concerns expressed in this essay which first appeared in the March 1976 issue of *Theology,* published bi-monthly in London by the Society for Promoting Christian Knowledge. It is reprinted by permission, with revisions by the author.

1

The usual premise on which history is based is that of continuity. This applies to almost any kind of history, from the geological history of the earth to the history of ideas. It is no less true of personal history: that of a person from cradle to grave. Every object such as a pebble or a tree, every idea such as logos or matter, every race from the bushmen in Australia to the Finns in Scandinavia, has its own history to tell as to how it came into existence; how it happens to be where it is and not somewhere else; what function it has played, and still plays, in the whole complex of changes which has occurred in the entire physical world, or in the world dominated by the human race. The story has to be inherently connected. Once it becomes disjointed, the story-teller becomes incoherent and consequently, unintelligible. The audience has to guess how the story may be continued. The sequence is broken. One is left in suspense until the thread of the story is picked up again and joined together.

History, in plain language, is story. The historian is a story-teller. His task is to put into an intelligent continuity things and events which at first sight seem disjointed and without inner relationship. His task is to trace continuity in discontinuity, to make every effort to fill gaps whenever and wherever they are found. In short, he is responsible for finding a meaning in material of many and varied kinds, thrown together with no apparent connections. In a sense, history can be compared to painting. The picture on the canvas takes shape, conveys meaning, and inspires human aspiration, from different colors on the palette. Objects which the artist seeks to capture on his canvas, ideas and visions in his mind become related to each other in a coherent way.

History, therefore, does not consist solely of chronological data—facts or statistics. These are of course important, but they have a meaning higher than themselves, namely, the meaning of life, and I must add, of death. Ultimately, our historical activity is directed to the search for such meaning. It is a human determination not to let absurdity have the final word about human existence. But the role of historical activity is not merely negative. It does not exhaust its effort by struggling against the force of absurdity. It seeks to liberate the human mind from bondage to the past and to fulfil the meaning of the present through the vision of the future. It is in this sense that the Bible speaks of salvation in history.

But a strange thing happens. Meaning, which is supposed to give continuity to history, often disrupts that continuity. It stops the flow of history, diverts its course, and introduces new elements into it. The dynamics of history, therefore, do not consist primarily in continuity. Rather it is interruptions that make history an exciting experience. The kind of history that can be predicted, although it is still in the future, belongs already to the past. History then becomes an experience of death in advance. Tyranny gives rise to exactly this kind of history. The power seized and consolidated by a dictatorship steers the history of a people along a carefully marked course towards a predetermined destiny. The historical continuity of a nation under dictatorship can only be broken by a revolution. Revolution assumes the role of introducing new meaning into the life of the people, and of creating a new beginning for the nation. It interrupts history, sometimes peacefully but more often violently. History then gains a new lease of life and resumes its uncertain course.

History in the Bible derives its meaning from God's redemptive acts. Events and experiences taken into the orbit of redemption interrupt the normal course of history. They become the bearers of a meaning which anticipates fulfilment in future. Redemption is the power which enables us to leap into the future and frees us from slavery to the sinful past and from an absurd fate.

Without exaggeration, therefore, God's redemption can be compared to revolution. It *is* God's revolution. How violent it can be is illustrated by many an example in the Bible. The event of the exodus is God's revolution in history *par excellence*. It began violently. It cost all the first-born sons in the Egyptian families. It threw the pursuing Egyptian soldiers into the Red Sea. But it continued with the people of Israel. Again and again the violence of God broke in to turn their history upside down. For the people of Israel God's redemption was anything but a peaceful affair. It was more than a nation, any nation, could bear. And so they sought escape in the institutions of religion and monarchy and attempted to contain it in them. But they had to pay dearly for all these attempts. Prophets warned that God's redemption could not be contained in a human establishment. Israel could not institutionalize itself into a history of salvation. The warning was not well heeded. The prophets often found themselves engaged in a war of attrition with their own people.

The most drastic revolutionary act of God's redemption takes place in the person of Jesus Christ on the cross. His execution was carried out by a political institution which had yielded to the pressures of a religious one. This latter clung tenaciously to a historical and ideological continuity. It sought to arrest God's revolution in Christ in order to maintain its continuity. By crucifying Christ, it responded to revolution with human violence. And for a time they seemed to have succeeded. Jesus' cry on the cross seemed to have sealed their victory over God's revolution: "My God, my God, why have you forsaken me?" But there was a fatal miscalculation. The historical continuity they deemed sacred was nevertheless disrupted, God's revolution of redemption was carried forward, beginning "in Jerusalem and in all Judea and Samaria and to the end of the earth" (Acts 1.8).

2

The Christian Church, which has inherited God's salvation in Christ, has not altogether succeeded in avoiding the mistake of attempting to institutionalize God's revolution. In the course of its development it has tended to regard itself as the institutional heir to the messianic hope of the kingdom of God. This tendency is strongly reflected in ecclesiastical structures, in the crystallization of its faith in creeds and confessions, and in theological formulation of it. Above all, the history which the Christian Church has carved out for itself within world history has come to be identified with the meaning and purpose from which it derived the reason for its existence. The classical example of this is the famous dictum of Cyprian: outside the Church there is no salvation. The Church becomes the custodian of God's redemption. The fact that the Christian Church has played an enormously important role in the formation of western civilization reinforces the identification of the history of the Christian Church with the so-called "history of salvation." The Christian Church in its historical existence becomes the *fons et origo* of God's truth and salvation. It is in this way that western Christian mission was conceived and carried out. People in histories and cultures outside western Christendom were redeemable, in so far as they were salvaged and incorporated into the salvation history represented by the history of Christianity.

Although disillusion with western Christendom has greatly changed people's minds about the identification of its history with the history of salvation, it is true to say that western theology continues to find it difficult to dissociate itself from what may be called the ideologization of faith. Nowadays, it is almost impossible even for western theologians to do theology without taking into account the realities represented by histories and cultures outside the western milieu. But they obstinately persist in reflecting on Asian or African cultures and histories from the vantage-point of that messianic hope which is believed to be lodged in the history of the Christian Church, so that the relations of these cultures and histories to God's redemption become intermediate, and redemption loses its intrinsic meaning for cultures and histories outside the history of Christianity. The universal nature of God's dealing with his creation forfeits its particular and direct application, except within the cultures and histories affected and fostered by Christianity. I cannot but believe that this is a distortion of the message of the Bible.

This habit of doing theology always through the history of the western Christian Church must be called into question. It must be possible above all now, for Asian Christians to engage in theological reflection on the direct relationship of Asia to God's redemption.

First of all, the communities of faith we find in the Bible have a symbolic function derived from their relation to God's purpose of redemption. I have hinted earlier that the great merit of the prophetic tradition consists in a refusal to recognize the history of Israel as identifiable with the totality of God's acts in the redemption of his creation. True, God works within the history of the people of Israel. This is how they read the meaning of the exodus, and of the tumultuous vicissitudes they had to go through. They experienced God's redemption through personal and national crises. But their prophets began to see the hand of God working also outside their limited historical and geographical domains. The people of Israel were singled out, under a divine providence inexplicable to us and even to them, not to present themselves to the rest of the world as the nation through which God's redeeming love would be mediated, *but* to be a symbol of how God would also deal redemptively with other nations. In the light of the experiences unique to Israel, other nations should learn how their histories can be interpreted redemptively. An Asian nation would have its own experiences of exodus, captivity, rebellion against Heaven, the golden calf. It would have its own long trek in the desert of poverty or dehumanization. What a nation goes through begins to take on redemptive meaning against the background of the history of Israel, symbolically transported out of its original context to a foreign one. An Asian nation will thus be enabled to find its place side by side with Israel in God's salvation. The Old Testament has shown how the history of a nation can be experienced and interpreted redemptively. If this is so, the theology which regards Israel and the Christian Church as the only bearers and dispensers of God's saving love must be called into question.

Perhaps it is difficult for theologians steeped in the tradition of what is called "salvation history" to be convinced that this theological leap, or the leap of faith, from Israel to Asia can be justified biblically. What to me is an existential necessity may seem to be a theological blunder to them. But I am becoming more and more convinced that a very big theological blunder has been committed by those theologians who have forced God's redemption into the history of a nation and of the Christian Church, and have consequently institutionalized it. It is of paramount importance to know how other people can see and experience redemption and hope in the sufferings which descend on them with cruel consistency. They want to know how the chains of sufferings can be broken, and to experience salvation in the present and the future. It is to these people that Asian Christians must address themselves, sharing their longing for liberation. Surely there must be a direct relation between their sufferings and God's saving love manifested in the people of Israel and in Jesus Christ.

Unless we, like the second Isaiah (see Isaiah 44.28 and 45.1-4 about Cyrus), the writer of the Melchizedek legend (Genesis 14.17-20) and Ezekiel (29.19-20), begin to see those alien to our faith as making a contribution to the development of human community, as agents of God, our reading of history will be one-sided and, for that reason, poor and inaccurate. An important corollary is surely this: Christian interpretation of history is not complete unless it is tested and corrected by non-Christian, or even anti-Christian, interpretations of history.

What enables us to look at events and happenings within history from a perspective other than that of the historical continuity represented by the Christian Church? The answer must be found in "the Word become flesh," the Johannine formulation of God's redeeming love in history. If the Word had remained transcendent, if it had not embodied itself in flesh in human history, no interruption of a radical kind would have taken place in the history of Jewish religion. The Word become flesh was a stumbling block to the preservation of continuity in history. And, since it could not be ignored, it had to be done away with. The continuity of the Jewish nation, of Jewish religiosity, could be maintained, in the shrewd calculation of Caiaphas, the high priest, by having Christ executed to placate the Romans, who constituted a political threat to that cherished continuity. The

conversation between the members of the Sanhedrin and Caiaphas thus stands out as an ominous human conspiracy against
the divine intervention in human history. "What are we to do?
For this man performs many signs." This was the expression of
consternation followed immediately by the discovery of a political dilemma. "If we let him go on thus, every one will believe in
him and the Romans will come and destroy both our holy place
and our nation." Caiaphas gave cunning counsel: "You know
nothing at all; you do not understand that it is expedient for you
that one man should die for the people, and that the whole nation should not perish" (John 11.46-50). The stage was thus set
for Golgotha. And there it was a gentile Roman soldier who
released the blood and water of life. The flesh which the Word
had assumed was broken by that Roman soldier's spear.

Paul was freed from the historical continuity of his own nation and its institutional pietism to carry the gospel of the resurrected Christ to the gentiles (Philippians 3.5-7). But he did not
stop here. He had to bring the blessings of God's salvation back
to Israel from the gentiles. In Romans he labored at this dialectic of God's redemption or, as he calls it, mystery (11.25), expressing it in highly emotive language: "Now I am speaking to
you Gentiles: inasmuch then as I am an apostle to the Gentiles, I
magnify my ministry, in order to make my fellow Jews jealous,
and thus save some of them" (v. 13). His own response to this
mystery of God's salvation is doxology—who could help but be
doxological when given a glimpse of it? "O the depth of the
riches and wisdom and the knowledge of God! . . . For from
him and through him and to him are all things. To him be glory
for ever. Amen" (vv. 33-36).

It is this saving mystery, to which we can only respond
doxologically, that holds history together and constitutes the continuity of meaning and value in what we all have to go through
as individuals or community. We all have to scrutinize histories
and cultures, that is, movements of peoples and nations, in the
light of the dialectic of salvation revealed to us through the
witness in the Bible. Human history seen in this light would no
longer be a linear movement, borne and sustained by the history
of Israel and the history of the Christian church, understood as

the agents through which God's saving grace is mediated to the rest of human history. The disarray of the western churches in this post Christian era is enough to affirm the untenability of such a simplistic design.

3

In light of the above discussion, present-day Asia poses a momentous challenge to Christian theology. Several factors have contributed to the change of attitude in Asia towards Christianity. First, the tide of secularization which has engulfed the West since the Second World War has greatly weakened the spiritual role of the churches in western society to the point of panic and confusion, and this has had negative repercussions in Asia as in Africa. Related to this are various attempts in the West to find in Asian spirituality answers to the spiritual vacuum created by secular culture in western consumer society. Not all these attempts can be considered as serious or conducive to the recovery of western spirituality. However, this recent phenomenon of seeking in Asian faiths and ideologies for the rejuvenation of western spirituality should cause Christian theologians in both East and West to take more seriously the faiths and ideologies which have developed independently of Christianity. Any Christian understanding of revelation and salvation which fails to give adequate account of the ways in which God has worked positively through the indigenous faiths and ideologies in Asia, is woefully inadequate.

Another significant factor—contributing to the irreversible change of attitude in Asia towards western Christianity—came with the resolute rejection of Christianity by China as it became a Communist state. The colossal efforts of western churches for more than a century to incorporate the masses of humanity on the Asian continent into "salvation history" faltered and consequently were shaken to the roots in that event. The fact that more than a quarter of humanity has officially rejected the Christian faith from the West should continue to be a matter of profound soul-searching and discussion. A Christian theology which goes about its business as if the ideological challenge of China makes little difference is defective and useless. An understanding of Christian mission in terms of evangelizing and converting the pagans and bringing them into the fold of the church is irrelevant in the context of modern China. We are faced with the agonizing question: What does it mean to speak of "the hand of God" at work in China today?

A question such as this causes me to realize that the concepts and standards which have a time-honored place in the traditions of western theology have very limited usefulness in Asia today. One cannot assume the church as the base of theology—as western theology does—when one is doing theology in a multi-religious context or in the context of a political ideology which offers an alternative way of salvation. These conditions alone force theologians in Asia to do theology differently. The question is not what God is doing through the church but what he is doing in the world where the church as we normally understand it is non-existent or too weak to have a significant impact. What does it mean when atheistic Communist regimes continue to expand their frontiers and act as liberators from poverty, starvation, social injustices and human indignity?

One thing is certain: the historical continuity of God's salvation which the churches in the West and their offshoots have sought to represent is interrupted and broken in Asia. It was a violent break with great human sacrifice and cost. But—as I indicated earlier—the God experienced by the people of Israel was often a God of violence. And the cross on which Jesus was crucified is a symbol of violence. Also we recall that the vision of a new heaven and a new earth in the Bible is preceded by violence of cosmic magnitude. Theology has to be done in the midst of violence—both human violence and divine violence. The important difference is that God's violence leads to life and hope, whereas human violence usually leads to despair and death. Be that as it may—theology is born out of violence. Its task is to discern the seed of divine violence in the midst of human violence. Its mission is to enable Christians to turn human violence of despair and death into divine violence of hope and life. It is from this point of departure that Asian theologians must reflect on the mission of God in Asia today—what he is to the Asian masses, and what he is doing with the poverty and suffering which constantly has Asia in its grip.

Thus a conceptual and propositional theology—which has been characteristic of western theology—can barely touch the heart of Asian humanity. Western theologians must first address themselves to their own situations, and wrestle with the question of how Israel can be existentially related to suffering and hope in the West today. Israel must become their existential experience. The danger of propositional theology lies in its hidden claim to universal validity. Black theology in the United States has forcefully rejected such a claim. The God of a white theologian who has no experience of what it means to be black in a society captivated by white supremacy is not the God of black people. God for black people must be black. Jesus too must be black. In other words, black people look for a black messiah. Let us recognize that one cannot do theology for those who live, suffer and die in a society with different cultural, socio-political demands and responsibilities. The most one can do is give mutual support and encouragement through sharing of theological experiences and interpretations of human suffering and hope in given situations. Theology of essence—which western theology has tended to be—must be replaced by theology of existence. Theology cannot deal with the question of what God *is*. Its task is to come to grips with what God *does*—and we cannot know what God does apart from events and realities in which we are involved existentially.

Black theology is a theology of existence, as is liberation theology in Latin America. Black theology in the United States cannot be transferred to Europe. It cannot even be exported to Africa. Black theologians in the United States cannot do theology for their black brothers and sisters in Africa, because what the latter have to face is qualitatively different from the former. Likewise, the liberation theology of Latin America cannot be imported by others who live in different socio-political situations. Similarly, the theological task in which Asian Christians are engaged, in the face of aggressive Communist ideology, desperate poverty, suffering, and the continuous religious search of the resurgent religions in Asia, should not seek relevance beyond Asia. Freedom from external theological interference, the conscious effort to become true to a particular situation, and liberation from the claim to universal validity—these make theology become alive, useful, dynamic and, above all, authentic. An ecumenical theological community must be built on the foundation of situational authenticity. The great missionary principle propounded and practiced by St. Paul applies equally to the doing of theology. He said:

> I am a free man and own no master; but I have made myself every man's servant, to win over as many as possible. To Jews I became like a Jew, to win Jews; as they are subject to the Law of Moses, I put myself under that law to win them although I am not myself subject to it. To win Gentiles, who are outside the Law, I made myself like one of them, although I am not in truth outside God's law, being under the law of Christ. To the weak I became weak, to win the weak. Indeed, I have become everything in turn to men of every sort, so that in one way or another I may save some (1 Cor. 9:19-22).

If this great Pauline principle had been taken more seriously by theologians as well as missionaries, the impact of the saving love of God in Jesus Christ on Asian peoples and Asian cultures would have been far more profound and decisive.

In the final analysis, the Word has to assume Asian flesh and plunge into the agony and conflict of the mission of salvation in Asia. This flesh will be broken as it was broken on the cross. But when this Asian flesh assumed by the Word is broken, the saving and healing power of God will be released into the struggle of men and women for meaning, hope and life. And Christians outside Asia—especially those under the long history of the church in the West—will be enriched by it. This is the mystery of God's salvation which works both ways between Israel and the nations. We must be open to this divine mystery and make it the alpha and the omega of our Christian commitment and theological reflection.

Pilgrim or Tourist?

Kosuke Koyama

The massive impact of technology on traditional Asian societies "is shaking our basic self-identity because it is disturbing our spiritual relationship with the holy," says Kosuke Koyama, a Japanese theologian on the faculty of Otago University in New Zealand. Making his third appearance in the *Mission Trends* series, Koyama illustrates this with his experience of riding in an elevator barefooted, holding his shoes in his hand, on a visit to the Pagoda of the Sacred Eight Hairs in Rangoon. The "elevator" approach to a "slow" God, says Koyama, symbolizes the problem of relating technology to the holy—it causes a "temporary loss of self-identity," and makes one "neither pilgrim nor tourist." He offers no solutions, only a question—"Can technology be made a creative servant of the person who lives by the grace of the searching God?" A former missionary in Thailand and executive director of the Association of Theological Schools in Southeast Asia, Koyama's latest book is *No Handle on the Cross* (Orbis Books, 1977). This piece is taken from his book *Pilgrim or Tourist?*—a collection of fifty short theological meditations, published in 1974 in Singapore by the Christian Conference of Asia.

In Rangoon, Burma, the famous Shwe Dagon Pagoda stands on Singuttara Hill. It is an impressive monument. Its perimeter at the base is 1476 feet. Its height is 344 feet. The octagonal base of the Pagoda is surrounded by 64 small pagodas. I have been there a few times. It was built, tradition says, to enshrine the Eight Sacred Hairs of the Buddha which the Buddha himself personally gave to faithful visitors from Rangoon. The gold gilded Pagoda is a marvel to view from nearby as well as from a distance. Visitors are required to remove their shoes and socks at the foot of the hill. (". . . put off your shoes from your feet, for the place on which you are standing is holy ground." Exodus 3:5) The approach itself is already in the sacred territory of the Sacred Eight Hairs. Every barefoot step prepares one to come into the presence of the holy.

This becoming barefoot is not for getting ready to run. It shows respect and humility to the holy object which the devotee is approaching. There is an interesting story in the Hindu tradition. Krishna, an incarnation of Vishnu, stole the clothing of the shepherdesses while they were bathing. The maidens, realizing what happened and where their clothes were, cried for their clothes. Krishna told them that they must come and get them. The maidens, seeing no other way possible, came to Krishna wholly naked to retrieve their clothes. In this seemingly erotic story is hidden the rather impressive religious insight that one must not come to god "covered up." He must come to god "naked."

When I took off my shoes I felt that I was exposed. My modernized and well protected feet found it hard to walk bare over gravel, stones and heated pavement. The acceptance of all this inconvenience, and in particular of the feeling of being exposed, forms the religious sense of humility and respect. Under the hot Rangoon sun I began to trudge up to the hill where the Pagoda stands. It was a slow climb. Every step was a ceremonially slow step. The sweat on my forehead was, as it were, religious sweat. The time I spent walking up to the Pagoda was a holy time. When I arrived at the foot of the Pagoda itself, my mind was prepared to see it right in front of me. I recalled how in Japan the Meiji Emperor Shrine in Tokyo, Ise Imperial Grand Shrine in Mie Prefecture, and a host of others have long approaches to the main shrine, some as long as a mile or more. No bicycles and no automobiles are allowed. Even the emperor himself must walk from a certain point. The holy must be approached slowly and carefully with respect and humility. The holy must not be approached by motorcycle or helicopter. It must be approached by walking.

Walking is the proper speed and the proper posture that can prepare a person to meditate. Thus the universal use of the automobile is, I am afraid, producing a less-meditative mankind! The un-holy (everyday things) may be approached by running or on motorcycle (even if the muffler is broken). But that which is holy must be approached slowly. Such thoughts came to me as I walked up to the Pagoda.

The God that the Bible proclaims reveals himself to be the holy God. He revealed himself to be holy by becoming *slow* for us. The central affirmation of the Bible is that God does not forsake man.

Can a woman forget her sucking child, that she should have no compassion on the son of her womb? Even these may forget, yet I will not forget you.   Isaiah 49:15

For a brief moment I forsook you, but with great compassion I will gather you. In overflowing wrath for a moment I hid my face from you, but with everlasting love I will have compassion on you.   Isaiah 54:7, 8

The whole Bible is a commentary on that one passage in the Book of Genesis: "Where are you?" (3:9)—*God in search of man!*

What man of you, having a hundred sheep, if he has lost one of them, does not leave the ninety-nine in the wilderness, and go after the one which is lost, until he finds it?
     Luke 15:3, 4

This search is the *holy* search. In his holy search the holy God did not go "on a motorcycle" or by "supersonic" jet. He became *slow,* very slow. The crucifixion of Jesus Christ, the son of God, means that God went so slow that he became "nailed down" in his search of man. What speed can be slower than the dead stop of being "nailed down"? If God revealed in such a way his holy character, people must approach him in the same manner.

On my second trip to Rangoon I found that meantime they

had built an elevator to the top of the hill where the Pagoda stands! Invasion of technology and speed! No longer a slow approach is necessary. Electric energy will put you instantly in front of the Pagoda of the Sacred Eight Hairs in a matter of 15 seconds or so. No steps. No sweat.

At the entrance of the elevator on the ground level, however, there is a sign which says that shoes must be removed before entering the elevator. For the first time in my life I rode an elevator barefooted. My shoes in my hands shouted at me that they must be worn on my feet. While I was feeling the strange sensation of suspension between becoming a pilgrim and becoming a tourist I reached the top. If I had walked up the hill barefoot, I would have been a pilgrim, and if I had kept my shoes on in the elevator I would have been a tourist. But now I was neither pilgrim nor tourist! A strange sensation of temporary loss of self-identity swept over me.

The traditional way of *slow* approach has been disturbed by the massive impact of technology. The whole of Asia is disturbed and disrupted in this way today and perhaps so is the whole world. Technology is shaking our basic self-identity because it is disturbing our spiritual relationship with the holy. Today all kinds of "elevators" are being built in front of the "holy pagodas." Singapore hotel elevators do not give me this problem. A Hong Kong shopping center elevator does not give me this problem. But the Shwe Dagon Pagoda elevator does! The number of "Shwe Dagon Pagoda elevator" situations is increasing today all over the world.

Should we prepare to come into the presence of the holy "on a motorcycle"? Should we train ourselves in a new style of relating ourselves with the holy? Am I old fashioned in speaking of "the *slow* God"? What should be the relationship between technology and our relationship with the holy? Can technology be made a creative servant of the person who lives by the grace of the searching God?

Theological Declaration
by Christian Ministers
in the Republic of Korea, 1973

Since the declaration of martial law in South Korea on October 17, 1972, Christians—clergy, laity, missionaries—have taken a leading role in the protest against the "absolutization of dictatorship and ruthless political oppression" by President Park Chung Hee. As a result of their prophetic witness, missionaries have been deported, clergy and laity have been arrested, tortured and imprisoned, and students and professors have been dismissed from their universities (any criticism of the government is illegal). To set forth the faith that undergirds their struggle for democracy, and to chart the course of that struggle, a group of Christian ministers in South Korea issued this underground declaration on May 20, 1973. The call for solidarity with their struggle to the churches throughout the world should have particular significance for churches in the U.S.A. since the South Korean government of President Park is supported substantially by United States financial and military aid. The declaration was brought out of Korea secretly and has been circulated widely through various religious news services. It is reprinted here from *Documentation on the Struggle for Democracy in Korea*, edited by the Emergency Christian Conference on Korean Problems, and published through the National Christian Council of Japan in 1975.

We make this declaration in the name of the Christian community in South Korea. However, under the present circumstances, in which one man controls all the powers of the three branches of government and uses military arms and the intelligence network to oppress the people, we hesitate to reveal those who signed this document. We must fight and struggle in the underground until our victory is achieved.

The historical situation of the Korean people has been very grave since last October. President Park's consolidation of power has had certain demonic consequences for the life of the Korean nation and people.

The Christian community, as an integral part of the Korean people, now stands up and speaks out on the present situation, compelled by the divine mandates of the Messianic Kingdom.

Since World War II, our people have gone through trials and sufferings, of social chaos, economic deprivation, and especially the tragic Korean War and the resulting political dictatorships. It has been an ardent aspiration of our people that a new and humane community might be restored to their lives. However, the hopes of the people for such a restoration of humane community have been cruelly crushed by President Park in his absolutization of dictatorship and ruthless political repression. This is done in the name of the so-called October Revitalization, a set of false promises which is only the sinister plan of some evil men.

We Christians are compelled to speak out and take accompanying actions on the following grounds:

1) We are under God's command that we should be faithful to his Word in concrete historical situations. It is not a sense of triumphant victory that moves us today; rather it is a sense of confession of our sins before God; and yet we are commanded by God to speak the truth and act in the present situation in Korea.

2) The people in Korea are looking up to Christians and urging us to take action in the present grim situation. It is not because we deserve to represent them. We have often fallen short of their deeper expectations, and yet we are urged and encouraged to move on this course of action, not because we envision ourselves as the representatives of our people, but because we are moved by their agony to call upon God for their deliverance from evil days.

3) We stand in a historical tradition of such struggles for liberation as the independence movement by Christians

against Japanese colonialism. We realize that our Christian community has often lacked the courage to take a decisive stand, and that the theological outlook of the official bodies of our Christian churches has been too pietistic to take up revolutionary roles. However, we do not feel disheartened by the weakness of some of our brothers; rather we are determined to seek our theological convictions from the historical traditions of our church.

The firm foundation of our words and deeds is our faith in God the Lord of history, in Jesus the proclaimer of the Messianic Kingdom, and in the Spirit who moves vigorously among the people. We believe that God is the ultimate vindicator of the oppressed, the weak, and the poor; he judges the evil forces in history. We believe that Jesus the Messiah proclaimed the coming of the Messianic Kingdom, to be subversive to the evil powers, and that his Messianic Kingdom will be the haven of the dispossessed, the rejected, and the downtrodden. We also believe that the Spirit is working for the new creation of history and cosmos, as well as for the regeneration and sanctification of individual man.

In this grave historical situation, we as a Christian community believe:

1) that we are commanded by God to be representatives before God the Judge and Lord of History, to pray that the suffering and oppressed people may be set free.

2) that we are commanded by our Lord Jesus Christ to live among the oppressed, the poor, and the despised as he did in Judea; and that we are summoned to stand up and speak the truth to the powers that be, as he did before Pontius Pilate of the Roman Empire.

3) that we are compelled by the Spirit to participate in his transforming power and movement for the creation of a new society and history, as well as for the transformation of our character; and that this Spirit is the Spirit of Messianic Kingdom who commands us to struggle for sociopolitical transformation in this world.

Therefore, we express our theological convictions on the following issues:

1) The present dictatorship in Korea is destroying rule by

law and persuasion; it now rules by force and threat alone. Community is being turned into jungle. Our position is that no one is above the law except God; worldly power is entrusted by God to civil authority to keep justice and order in human society. If anyone poses himself above the law and betrays the divine mandate for justice, he is in rebellion against God. Oriental tradition, too, understands that good rule is carried out through the moral persuasion and virtue of the ruler. One may conquer people by the sword; but they cannot be ruled by the sword.

2) The present regime in the Republic of Korea is destroying freedom of conscience and freedom of religious belief. There is freedom neither of expression nor of silence. There is interference by the regime in Christian churches' worship, prayer, gatherings, content of sermons, and teaching of the Bible.

The Christian Church and other religious bodies must be the defenders of conscience for the people; for destruction of conscience is a most demonic act. In defending the freedom of religious belief against interference by the regime in Korea, Christian churches are also defending freedom of conscience for all people.

3) The dictatorship in Korea is using systematic deception, manipulation, and indoctrination to control the people. The mass media have been turned into the regime's propaganda machine to tell the people half-truths and outright lies, and to control and manipulate information to deceive the people.

We believe that Christians are witnesses to truth, always struggling to break any system of deception and manipulation, for to tell the truth is the ultimate power that sets men free for God's Messianic Kingdom.

4) The dictatorship in Korea uses sinister and inhuman and at the same time ruthlessly efficient means to destroy political opponents, intellectual critics, and innocent people. The use of the Korean Central Intelligence Agency (CIA) for this purpose is somewhat similar to the evil ways of the Nazi Gestapo or the KGB of the Stalin era.

People are physically and mentally tortured, intimidated and threatened, and sometimes even disappear completely. Such treatments are indeed diabolical acts against humanity.

We believe that God has created humans in body and soul. Body as well as soul will be resurrected at the day of judgment of the Messianic Kingdom. We believe especially in the sanctity of the human body; therefore any violation of it is equal to killing a man. It is a murderous act.

5) The present dictatorship is responsible for the economic system in Korea, in which the powerful dominate the poor. The people, poor urban workers and rural peasants, are victims of severe exploitation and social and economic injustice. So-called "economic development" in Korea turned out to be the conspiracy of a few rulers against the poor people, and a curse to our environment.

We as Christians must struggle to destroy this system of extreme dehumanization and injustice; for we are witnesses to the ongoing movement of the Messianic Kingdom in history, in which the poor will be enriched, the oppressed will be vindicated, and peace will be enjoyed by the people.

6) The present regimes in the South and North are using the unification talks only to preserve their own power; and they are betraying the true aspirations of the people for the unification of their land. We believe as Christians that the people deeply yearn for authentic community on the basis of true reconciliation. Without transcendence beyond the past experiences of bitter conflict and differences in ideological and politico-economic systems, and without transformation of our historical conditions of oppression, true unification cannot be realized.

A Call for Action and Support

1) *To the people in Korea:* Withdraw any form of recogni-

tion of the laws, orders, policies, and other political processes of dictatorship that have been wrought since October 17, 1972. Build various forms of solidarity among the people to struggle for the restoration of democracy in South Korea.

2) *To the Christians in Korea:* As preparation for the above struggle, we Christians should renew our churches by deepening our theological thinking, by our clear stance and solidarity with the oppressed and poor, by the relevant proclamation of the gospel of the Messianic Kingdom, and by praying for our nation; and we should prepare ourselves for martyrdom, if necessary, as our forefathers did.

3) *To the Christians of the world:* Most of all we need your prayers and solidarity, and we ask you to express our common bond through actions of encouragement and support.

Conclusion

Jesus the Messiah, our Lord, lived and dwelt among the oppressed, poverty-stricken, and sick in Judea. He boldly stood in confrontation with Pontius Pilate, a representative of the Roman Empire, and he was crucified in the course of his witness to the truth. He has risen from the dead to release the power of transformation which sets the people free.

We resolve that we will follow the footsteps of our Lord, living among our oppressed and poor people, standing against political oppression, and participating in the transformation of history, for this is the only way to the Messianic Kingdom.

May 20, 1973

Mission and Movements
of Innovation

Stanley J. Samartha

"How can we be committed Christians . . . and, at the same time, be open to movements of innovation, of renewal, and of unfamiliar creativity among people of other faiths and ideologies? Can we be committed to the mission of the Church without being closed, and can we be open to insights from others without being shallow?" In response to these questions, Dr. Stanley J. Samartha from India—in the keynote address at the 1974 meeting of the International Association for Mission Studies in Frankfurt, Germany—said that while "there cannot be an indiscriminate acceptance of all movements" of innovation, Christians should be willing to take "certain risks" and "move out of the security of old positions to the more adventurous grounds of unknown relationships." The problem is one of "discerning the points where God is at work and of participating in his continuing mission," and this requires "certain criteria . . . both for discernment and for cooperation." The central criterion, of course, is Jesus Christ, but Samartha argues that "the name 'Christ' biblically and theologically cannot be restricted to the historical figure of Jesus of Nazareth." Instead, he maintains, "Christ is at work wherever people are struggling for freedom and renewal, seeking for fulness of life, peace and joy," and Christians should relate to these efforts "even though we do not know where we are being led." Dr. Samartha is director of the Program for Dialogue with Persons of Other Faiths and Ideologies in the World Council of Churches, and *Courage for Dialogue* (Orbis Books, 1977) is a collection of his recent essays. *Mission Trends No. 1* included his article "Dialogue as a Continuing Christian

Concern." This essay is reprinted from the April 1975 issue of
Missiology: An International Review, the quarterly journal of
the American Society of Missiology.

I

In seeking to understand renascent movements within various religions and new developments in certain ideologies,
attention should be given to the resources of power that are
manifest in them, the spiritual sustenance they give to their
followers and the "missionary" thrusts inherent in their activities.
Further, the implications of this study for a fresh understanding
of the Church's mission today is part of our continuing quest.

What does it mean to participate in God's continuing mission
in the world today as we live together with our neighbors who
belong to various faiths, cultures and ideologies? How can we be
commited Christians who firmly believe that "if any one is in
Christ he is a new creation" (II Cor 5:17) and, at the same time,
be open to movements of innovation, of renewal, and of unfamiliar creativity among people of other faiths and ideologies?
Can we be committed to the mission of the Church without being
closed, and can we be open to insights from others without being
shallow? Can the word "mission"—and all that means to us in
Christian obedience throughout the history of the Church—be so
easily connected with the words "movements of innovation" with
a simple conjunction "and" without any qualifications whatsoever? The observations made in this brief address are based on
my own cultural background, my involvement in the life and
work of the Church of South India, and my present work in an
ecumenical context which brings me into personal contact with
people of various faiths, cultures and ideologies. This obviously
imposes certain limitations, but at the same time personal involvement helps to make theological questions to become spiritually
vital, existentially concrete and practically urgent in human relationships.

So much has been written about "mission" and the "crisis
in mission," and so often have documents emerging from world
conferences on mission been reflected upon, analyzed and cri-

ticized, that it is hardly possible to say anything new on the subject. The smoke of old battlegrounds still clouds our vision. All that can be done here is to put a few points about a Christian understanding of mission in a framework which may be helpful while discussing movements of innovation.

The mission of the Church stems from the activity of God for the salvation of all mankind. Christians understand this to be an activity of the love of God which they see particularly embodied in Jesus Christ. The Cross of Jesus Christ and its vindication in the resurrection have a central place in the Christian understanding of salvation. The Church's mission is a response to, and participation in, God's continuing mission in the world. Certain characteristics of this mission are obvious: first, its *comprehensiveness,* the totality of its sweep. Nothing is excluded from the all-embracing love of God and the activities of the Holy Spirit. Through Him who is before all things and in whom all things hold together, God will reconcile to Himself things in heaven and things on earth (Col 1:15-20; Eph 1:9-10). Second, its *wholeness*: it touches the whole of human life in all its concerns. Therefore, the debate in mission as to where the emphasis should be—on the sacred or the secular, the spiritual or the material, the vertical or the horizontal—is really not helpful because it separates what God has joined together. The content of mission, the message of salvation in Jesus Christ concerns the whole person (Lk 4:16-21). Third, its *historical* character, in the sense that while the comprehensiveness of God's mission cannot be limited by temporal factors, and while the mysterious action of the Holy Spirit cannot be bound by visible communal walls, Christian mission has a beginning in the Incarnation of God in Jesus Christ, in his life, death and resurrection and the coming of the Holy Spirit. "Then Jesus said to them again, 'Peace be with you. As the Father has sent me even so I send you' " (Jn 20:21). Fourth, its *congregational* nature. It is not what an individual says or does about Jesus Christ that constitutes mission. Individuals are not called upon to defend mission but to be obedient to God in His continuing saving activity and to be in fellowship with His people. "And he called the twelve together and gave them power and authority over all demons and to cure diseases, and he sent them out to preach the Kingdom of God and to heal" (Lk 9:1-2). The Church, as the body of Christ and as the community of the Holy Spirit, seeks to serve God in the world through its worship, its service and its witness. The implications of these related characteristics of Christian mission can, of course, be elaborated.

The Fifth Assembly of the Christian Conference of Asia (Singapore, June 1973) drew attention to the variety of understandings of mission. Some emphasize mission as primarily preaching the gospel for conversion. Some stress Christ's offer of the truly human. Some point to Christian presence through service. Others understand mission in terms of Christ's identification with the poor and the oppressed. But the Conference rightly states, "This diversity of understanding is to be embraced and held together within a common commitment to Jesus Christ as our Lord so that each can inform and enrich the other" (Extract from *Minutes*).

But our specific purpose is to see how the content and practice of Christian mission today can be stated without betraying our commitment, on the one hand, and without denying the reality of renewal movements on the other. In attempting to do so— a task which is only in its preliminary stages—we must take into account not only the witness of the Scriptures, but also of the tradition and experience of the Church and the ways in which the Holy Spirit is leading the Church in contemporary history. If we are really serious in affirming that we believe in the *living* God, the Lord of history, then the activity of His Spirit *now* and our sensitivity to discern His work, even in areas unfamiliar to most of us, becomes significant. This emphasis on the *now* is important because it affirms that God deals with people directly and not necessarily through an extension or expansion of the *Heilsgeschichte* conceived in western theological terms. C.S. Song points out that one must not be misled into a situation in which the heritage of people other than Western-Judaeo-Christian becomes subservient to the main stream of salvation history (1974). Movements of innovation and the commitment to mission which they draw from their respective resources must be seen as part of the pluralistic context in which we live with our neighbors today and as belonging to the comprehensiveness of God's continuing saving work.

II

The plurality of cultures, religions and social systems is not new in the history of mankind. Within the Church—recognizing that it is Catholic and not monolithic—the plurality of customs, ecclesiastical structures, theological formulations and ethical attitudes has been generally accepted. But the critical fact in our situation today is not so much the phenomenon of plurality as the living fact of pluralism. The Church can neither ignore nor conquer nor absorb the *fact* of pluralism—i.e., the promise and the threat of religious and ideological pluralism. It is this fact which makes it difficult to put theological content into the conjunction "and" in the formulation of our theme. In what way or ways is "mission" related to "movements of innovation"? Is it over against them or in cooperation with them or in some ways which we cannot precisely formulate now? "Pluralism", says Raymond Panikkar, "is a modern word standing for the old, perhaps abused term of *mysterion*." He goes on to observe,

> Pluralism means the existential acceptance of the other as the other, i.e., without being able to understand or to co-opt him. Pluralism is humble, only knows that I or we may not possess the whole truth and does not pass judgment as to whether the other may also be right or, as it may turn out, wrong (1972:11).

The movements of innovation must be seen in this living context as our neighbors in an inter-dependent world struggle for renewal. We have to recognize and make room for them, even though we may not fully know or understand them and most of the time may be perplexed by their belief and conduct.

A recent consultation on primal world views of Africa sought to understand the significance of some new movements as they seek "wholeness of life" drawing on their own spiritual and cultural resources (*Study Encounter* 1973). Some of the more recent movements in Hinduism, particularly those which go beyond the boundaries of its motherland and which attract younger people abroad, need critical study. Recently the *Illustrated Weekly of India* presented a series of articles on "The Godmen of India," referring to the movements of yoga, transcendental meditation and Krishna consciousness which seem to attract quite a few followers in the West. Are these merely attempts "to convert Hinduism into a consumer religion" (*Quest* 1973), or a sign of the spiritual vitality of Hinduism to meet modern human needs or an aggressive symptom of its new missionary thrusts? Buddhism has been a missionary religion earlier than Christianity in far gentler ways. Some of the new movements within it, such as *Rissho Kosei-kai* in Japan, with their emphasis on lay people and on practical guidance to meet the problems of daily life, but with no less stress on the teachings of the Buddha, put a big question mark before the prophets of secularization who, not too long ago, confidently predicted that religion was being swept away from the high roads of modern life.

The Islamic Summit Meeting held at Lahore in February 1974, may have far-reaching consequences for Muslims and their relationships to people in other faiths. Should Christians be scared by talks about the combination of oil money and Muslim missionary expansion? Should there not be some recognition on the part of Christians that certain Christian leaders—Metropolitan Khodr of Mount Lebanon, the Greek Orthodox Patriarch, Elias IV of Damascus, and Ghassan Tueni, head of one of the most important Arabic newspapers in Beirut—were invited to the Islamic Summit? The Patriarch made a speech in the plenary in which he referred to Christians and Muslims working together to common goals, and to the new man in the coming civilization. Is this a sign of fanaticism or of some openness on the part of Muslims? The variations of Marxism, particularly movements in China, need special attention because they have been ignored so long. A recent writer draws attention to the quality of "spiritual" energy released by the Chinese revolution that has empowered a whole people to recover their freedom, self-respect and dignity (see Douglass and Terrill 1970:174ff.). It is difficult for me to make any observations about "the Post-Christian West," partly because I am not emotionally in tune with the situation and partly because I am not quite sure whether the description "*Post*-Christian" is sufficiently precise and accurate. Even while ecclesiastical structures are disintegrating, old theological formulations becoming obsolete and traditional channels of missionary movements clogged with shipwrecks, there is still the vital core of the Christian faith which surely has not disintegrated. To think otherwise would be a symptom of despair, not a sign of hope. It would amount to a betrayal of the Gospel.

Certain features of the new movements—religious or ideological—may now be noted.

1. The Gospel itself, directly or indirectly, has been one of the factors in generating new movements. The Gospel does produce a ferment even while it is being opposed or attacked or rejected—or received with joy.

2. One particular emphasis in all new movements is on a fuller, more satisfying *human* life here now. Whether it is in the revolution in China, or group counselling through the *Hoza* in Japan, or the medical program of the Ramakrishna mission or in *yoga*—human life has become important. This has been unnecessarily misunderstood in the debate about "humanization". But surely the good news of the Gospel is not about the being of God, but about the action of God in Jesus Christ to love and to save human beings.

3. The movements of innovation also represent the search for new forms of *community,* partly as a protest against traditional, petrified forms of community that stifled freedom, and partly because of the pressures of modern life that demand new groupings and new relationships.

4. Life in the community cannot be sustained if the individual *person* is not taken seriously. Therefore, many new movements go back to their original resources to discover a framework of *meaning* in which the person has a vocation and to discover the community goal. The relation between the provisional goals in history and the ultimate goal of history (the *vyāvahārika* and the *pāramārthika*) is a question with which many are struggling.

5. In seeking renewal, religious movements of innovation go back to the *spiritual core* of their respective faiths. There is considerable evidence that in spite of "new interpretations" this "spiritual core" has become hardened. Therefore, it is very unlikely that pluralism will give way or lead to syncretism.

6. The significance of *China* must somehow enter into the discussion on new movements. New China, says Song, has emerged

. . . as a formidable spiritual force and institution contesting for supremacy against other spiritual forces. . . . What we have in New China is a secularized version of salvation history. It is no less salvation history even though its basic ideological thrust is that of atheistic materialism (1974).

What is the implication of attitudes like this for our understanding of mission today?

7. In the global context, and also in particular countries, the *inter-relation* between religious movements of innovation and ideological movements is by no means clear. This is partly because the traditional boundaries between religions are becoming blurred, and partly because, in the demand to meet human needs, there is considerable traffic across the borders.

III

If we acknowledge the comprehensiveness of God's mission in the world and the activities of the Holy Spirit in history, including contemporary history, then surely the new movements we are talking about cannot be outside God's all-embracing work. The question, therefore, would be one of discerning the points where God is at work and of participating in his continuing mission. This might mean not only cooperating with our neighbors but also being in critical engagement with them in the total search for renewal. But certain criteria are necessary both for discernment and for cooperation. In seeking these, two points must be kept in mind. First, our lives are already inextricably bound up with those of our neighbors. We are already interdependent and involved together with them in the struggle for renewal. Therefore, we cannot examine the movements "objectively" from "neutral" ground, define criteria in the isolation of our theological fortresses and *then* seek cooperation. Fresh ways of understanding and practising mission must come as we live and work together in the world. Second, any attempt to relate "mission" to "movements of innovation" at the present stage can only be what Paul Löffler describes as "a preliminary exercise," an "interim orientation," "a search for clues" (1968:34). Therefore certain risks must be taken. One must move out of the security of old positions to the more adventurous grounds of unknown relationships. It is, therefore, in this light that a few observations are made here.

There are some who relate God's saving activity in Jesus Christ to the activities of His Spirit outside the visible boundaries of the Church by ways of what may be described as *inclusivism*. The other is already in the stream of God's healing and redeeming work, even though he may not know it or acknowledge it. This "inclusion without consent," putting the Christian label on the other without his leave, can be as patronizing as excluding him or her from the household of God. A different way of looking at this would be to say that, not only the Christian, but all those involved in movements of innovation also *participate* in the same mission of God in the world which we Christians distinctively understand as manifest in Jesus Christ. This would provide a starting point for cooperation with our neighbors, but would also raise the question of criteria in an acute way because there cannot be an indiscriminate acceptance of all movements. Some movements, including those within Christianity, can bring disintegration and new forms of bondage in the name of newness.

Another way would be—and this brings to the forefront certain criteria—to acknowledge as from the Holy Spirit all those activities, wherever they are to be found, which bear the marks of the ministry of Jesus Christ. Very early in his worship ministry (Lk 4:16-21), Jesus spells out the inter-related activities of his ministry. Where there is a certain "parallel" or a "convergence", is there any valid reason to ignore the parallelism or to reject co-operation? One may also refer to Jesus' answer to John the Baptist's inquiry: "Are you the Christ or do we look for another?" (Lk 8:19; Mt 11:3). Without answering the question directly, Christ points to a concrete set of facts: Look around and see for yourselves what is happening. "The *who* of Christ cannot be individualized by pinning him down to a 'here' or a 'there' or pinpointing his localized presence" (Panikkar 1972:16ff.). What is demanded of us is to open our eyes and ears and to be on the lookout for the One who is constantly "the coming One."

This leads us to the question, who is Jesus Christ? It is not necessary here to go into the familiar discussion on "the larger Christ" or "the cosmic Christ." In relation to people of other faiths and ideologies, and in particular with reference to the movements of innovation, we are concerned with questions like: is Jesus Christ the *only* one or is he one among the *many*, which are less than helpful. The crucial question is *who* is he in whose name there is salvation, healing and renewal? And here it may be emphasized that the name "Christ" biblically and theologically cannot be restricted to the historical figure of Jesus of Nazareth. He who was before Abraham (Jn 8:58), he who is the same yesterday, today and tomorrow (Heb 13:8), he who is the Logos and who became flesh (Jn 1:14), is also the One who is continuing his work today. He is the One who makes all things new and calls us to participate in his work everywhere. If we take seriously the implications of our faith, viz., that we believe in the *living* God, in Christ who is the Lord of *history*, including contemporary history, and in the promise that the Spirit will guide us into all truth, then can we deny that Christ is at work wherever people are struggling for freedom and renewal, seeking for fulness of life, peace and joy. The fact that we may be perplexed in our discernment and disturbed in our traditional ways of thinking and obedience does not mean that we can deny his activity. The struggle between newness of life and petrified tradition, between truth and distortions of truth, between God and the idols is going on everywhere. It will be a mistake to regard it as a contest between Christianity and "non-Christian religions" or between Christ and atheistic ideologies.

And lastly, there is a more basic question which we must face openly because it cannot be avoided. In what ways do we understand the "truth claims" and messages of "salvation" on which the spiritual life of millions of our neighbors have been sustained over the centuries? Can we continue along the lines we are so used to in the colonial era, treating other religions as false, ordinary, discontinuous, distorted, partial, incomplete, preparatory, etc., in their various polite and impolite combinations? To what extent have certain ideological assumptions distorted, not only our understanding of the Gospel, but also our attitude to people of other faiths? If, in an interdependent world, the search for renewal is a common quest, a shared search for all people, what is it that separates us and what is it that unites us at the deepest level? Let us not give negative answers too quickly. We may say we do not yet know, but we must find out as we continue to live in dialogue with our neighbors.

As we struggle to understand the meaning of mission in relation to new movements, we must venture to move into new relationships with people, even though we do not know where we are being led. Nothing in the Christian life or in the history of the Christian Church suggests that there can be creativity without taking risks, or newness without suffering. Our hope lies in the continuing work of the Holy Spirit in judgment, mercy and new creation.

REFERENCES CITED

Douglass, Bruce and Ross Terrill (eds.)
  1970 *China and Ourselves: Explorations & Revisions by a New Generation* Boston: Beacon Press
Hunter, Neale
  1970 "The Good Earth and the Good Society" *China and Ourselves: Explorations & Revisions by a New Generation* Douglass and Terrill, eds. Boston: Beacon Press 174ff.

Illustrated Weekly of India
  1973 "The Godmen of India" March 16
Löffler, Paul (ed.)
  1968 *Secular Man and Christian Mission* Geneva: World Council of Churches
Panikkar, Raymond
  1972 "Salvation in Christ: Concreteness and Universality—the Supreme" Paper presented at Santa Barbara, California

Quest
  1973 "The Incarnation Explosion" 82:65, 66
Song, Choan-Seng
  1974 "New China and Salvation History—A Methodological Enquiry" Paper presented to LWF/PMV Seminar in Bastad

Study Encounter
  1973 "The Wholeness of Human Life: Christian Involvement in Mankind's Inner Dialogue with Primal World Views: a Consultation" IX, 4

An Asian's Reflections after Vietnam

Tissa Balasuriya

A Catholic priest in Sri Lanka maintains that in the postwar period "the way in which Vietnamese Christians act, and the way in which their country's leaders will react towards them, will no doubt be greatly influenced by the attitudes and reactions of Christians of other countries, especially those of the West." He advocates that Vietnamese Christians—who are predominantly Roman Catholic—and their government "will be greatly helped in their attempts to understand one another if the Christians of other countries do not consider the coming to power of the new regimes as a tragedy, but instead see in this a sign of possible liberation." The people of Indochina, with their deep religious traditions, face the challenge "to humanize communism," and Father Balasuriya hopes that as the Catholic communities participate in this task "Rome will not encourage them to oppose all change, and that the new regimes will not force them to a schism based on a nationalistic ideology." The lesson of Indochina, he argues, should be a warning that the Church must "rediscover the profound radicality of the Gospel, and to try to live it, before we are forced to do so by a revolution of an Asia half-starved." Father Balasuriya is director of the Center for Religion and Society in Colombo, Sri Lanka, and his article is reprinted from the January 15, 1976 issue of *CCA News,* published by the Christian Conference of Asia in Singapore.

The end of the war in Vietnam has greatly changed the situation of the Church in that country. Practically up to the end, many Vietnamese Catholics—and by no means the minority—supported the now-defeated government. Their Church was, to a large extent, materially dependent on foreign funds and personnel. Their ideological orientation was to the right.

It is a pity that during the sixties and seventies, not enough attention was paid to the Vietnamese situation in its entirety; those who did speak during that time, belonged to fringe groups. For most of the churchmen, the demons of capitalism seemed much less dangerous than the dangers posed by communism.

A Dilemma for the Churches

Today, the upheavals of March and April 1975 have put the Christians of Indochina in a situation reminiscent of China in 1949.

Admittedly, the 2 million Catholics of South Vietnam—who represent 10% of the population—are proportionately more numerous than were the Chinese Catholics. Their leaders are native-born. There are approximately 2000 Vietnamese priests and 5000 religious. Catholics were among the leaders of the country. Furthermore, the Marxist attitude towards religion has changed greatly since 1917 and 1949. The problem of the Vietnamese Christians now is to know whether or not they can, without after-thought, collaborate in the building of a socialist Vietnam under the direction of a Marxist government. It is not apparent whether in their minds this attitude is reconcilable with that which they consider to be the good of the nation, and above all, with their understanding of the Christian faith. On the other side, the new communist government could hold suspect the loyalty of people who were the most adamant adversaries of the North.

The Christians of South Vietnam are therefore faced with the same problems which confronted the Christians of the USSR in 1917, Eastern Europe and China after 1949, North Korea since 1950, North Vietnam since 1954, and Cuba since 1960. All these Christians could not count on help from the Churches of other countries. At the most, they were encouraged to resist, or even to face martyrdom. Furthermore, the leaders of these Christians were not prepared to cooperate with the new regimes,